William Blake

D1194855

Portrait of
Mrs Blake   1820   J. T. S^{t}

MARTIN BUTLIN

William Blake

TATE GALLERY

BARRON'S
WOODBURY, NEW YORK

Exhibition organised in association with the William Blake Trust

Exclusively distributed in France and Italy by Idea Books
46–8 rue de Montreuil, 75011 Paris and Via Cappuccio 21, 20123 Milan

ISBN 0 905005 11 2 paper 0 905005 16 3 cased
Published by order of the Trustees 1978
for the exhibition of 9 March – 21 May 1978
2nd impression, with corrections, 1978
Copyright © 1978 The Tate Gallery

Published by the Tate Gallery Publications Department,
Millbank, London SW1P 4RG
Designed by Pauline Key
Origination by Adroit Photo Litho Ltd, Birmingham
Printed in Great Britain by Balding & Mansell Ltd, Wisbech, Cambs.

Contents

Cover/jacket
Elohim Creating Adam, 1795 (detail)
No.85, entry on p.59

Frontispiece
John Linnell, *Portrait of William Blake*, 1820
No.281, entry on p.134

Colour Plates

Foreword

Although the Tate is fortunate in possessing a substantial collection of William Blake's work, there have been very few opportunities recently for seeing a really wide range of his work at its best. It is, therefore, with great pleasure that we now present this exhibition, comprising paintings, drawings and prints as well as separate pages from some of Blake's books.

The exhibition has been selected and the catalogue written by Martin Butlin, Keeper of the Tate Gallery Historic British Collection, who is the compiler of a catalogue raisonné of Blake's work due to be published later this year by the Blake Trust.

Response to our requests for loans was enthusiastic and collectors, both public and private whether in this country, the United States or Australia, have been most generous in lending the finest work from their collections. We are most grateful to them all.

We should also like to thank the Blake Trust very much for its assistance. The Blake Trust's services to Blake have been enormous both through publications and facsimiles and through exhibitions that it has organised. A brief description is given on page 8.

After the exhibition closes at the Tate, a selection will be shown at the Whitworth Art Gallery, Manchester, from 10 June to 15 July under the auspices of the Arts Council.

Norman Reid *Director*

The William Blake Trust

The Blake Trust is an unusual organisation. With only voluntary staff and the comparatively small endowment of £10,000, it has, through the publications and the exhibitions it has arranged, helped to make Blake a household name and to bring his work and philosophic message before the widest possible public. What is not so well known is that, in addition to these activities, the Trust has been instrumental in making gifts to the Tate Gallery and to other galleries and museums in this country of some of Blake's finest works. Throughout its career it has been guided by its Chairman, Sir Geoffrey Keynes, whose Blake work spans the present century and who has provided the introductions and texts for all but one of the Trust's publications. It did not seem possible for someone not intimately concerned with the Trust's work to prepare an adequate summary of its achievements; therefore it seemed fitting to reprint, and, where necessary, to bring up to date Sir Geoffrey's own reports taken principally from previous exhibition catalogues:

The William Blake Trust was founded in 1948. I had long been made uneasy by the thought that the Stirling copy of *Jerusalem* in colour was an unique book, so that a very great work of art and imagination would be lost if any misfortune should befall it. Moreover, Blake never himself published any of his major poems or epics in ordinary typography. He preferred that they should be read only in the form of the Illuminated Printing invented by himself; this combined script with coloured illustrations, derived in some degree from the example of mediaeval manuscripts. I had accordingly initiated early in 1948 an attempt to produce a true *facsimile*, not merely a reproduction, of *Jerusalem* and in order to do this had persuaded the owner of the book, Colonel William Stirling of Keir, to allow his book to be taken to Paris where it could be copied by the Trianon Press. This was to be done by their special process of colouring by hand through stencils over a collotype base.

I had intended to pay for this rather expensive process by enlisting the help of a number of guarantors of £500 each, and the work had begun with the support of five of these generous persons. This was a most rash undertaking on my part, but it was an act of faith which was soon to find its justification. Walford Graham Robertson, for many years the leading owner of Blake's works, died after a long illness in September 1948, leaving a large fortune to be applied to charitable purposes at the discretion of the executors. The senior executor, Mr. Kerrison Preston, was himself deeply interested in Blake and his work, so that it was not difficult to gain his approval of the idea that a Trust should be formed with the help of a Graham Robertson bequest. This would have the specific purpose of making a facsimile of *Jerusalem*. With the advice of Mr. George Goyder, an admirer of Blake and an experienced man of business, a scheme was drawn up for the formation of a legally constituted non-profit-making educational charity with an adequate endowment provided by the Graham Robertson executors. A board of eight Trustees was appointed to administer the Trust with myself as Chairman, and all financial worries in forwarding our project were at an end. The original Trustees were Sir Anthony Blunt, The Earl of Crawford and Balcarres, George Goyder, Sir Geoffrey Keynes, Edward Croft-Murray, A. E. Popham, Kerrison Preston, and Francis Wormald. To this number have been added over the years Lord Cunliffe, Peter du Sautoy and Graham Reynolds, and, as American Associate Trustees, F. J. Adams, Philip Hofer, Paul Mellon, Haven O'More, Lessing J. Rosenwald and Charles Ryskamp.

At its inception, as already stated, the William Blake Trust had as its object the production of a true facsimile of *Jerusalem*. When in due course the book was published it became obvious that the Trust would in a few years succeed in disposing of 500 copies at a reasonable price, and that we should therefore be able to recover the outlay and to apply the proceeds to making a facsimile of another Illuminated Book. The same principle has made it possible to produce a succession of books until, after twenty-three years, the Trust is within sight of accomplishing the objective it had set itself: 'to make Blake better known by publishing the finest possible reproductions of his Illuminated Books and other works'. Any time-lag in recovering our outlay on a completed book has been covered by generous help from Mr. Lessing J. Rosenwald, Mr. Paul Mellon and Mr. Haven O'More. The Trustees are also indebted to these and other owners for the loan of the original books which have been copied.

With the recent publication of *The Book of Los* the entire corpus of Blake's Illuminated Books, in all sixteen volumes, has now been reproduced by the Trianon Press and published by them for the Blake Trust.

The constitution of the Trust was framed in such a way that we have not been tied down to too rigid a programme. Thus we have been able to include among our productions a large illustrated catalogue of Blake's *Illustrations to the Bible* (1957), *Samuel Palmer's Sketch-book* (1962), *The Gates of Paradise* (1968), *Blake's Water-colour Designs for Gray's Poems* (1972), *William Blake's Laocoön: A Last Testament* (1976) and *The Complete Portraiture of William and Catherine Blake* (1977). In addition to the unique copy of the *Jerusalem*, consisting of 100 illuminated pages, we have published facsimiles of two variant copies, a fine monochrome copy lent by Mrs. Rinder, and Chapter 1 consisting of twenty-five pages illuminated in delicate watercolours in a different manner from the unique complete copy. This was lent by Lord Cunliffe.

Throughout its career the administrators of the Blake Trust have depended entirely on the skill and devotion of Mr. Arnold Fawcus, Director of the Trianon Press, and of his craftsmen in Paris for the consistently high quality of the books we have sponsored.

The Trust has been able to arrange three exhibitions in connection with its publications: *William Blake, Poet, Printer, Prophet*; *Blake's Illustrations for the Poems of Thomas Gray*; and *William Blake's Illustrations for the Book of Job: The Making of a Facsimile*. The first two were shown at the Tate Gallery in 1964 and 1971 respectively, and the latter at the Victoria and Albert Museum in the winter of 1976–77. In these exhibitions, originals were necessarily supplemented by facsimiles, the technical process being shown in a series of showcases and through photographic montages. This has emphasized our debt to Mr. Fawcus by demonstrating the difficulties that have to be overcome if a true facsimile of Blake's work is to be achieved. These exhibitions have since been sent throughout the world by the British Council and the Smithsonian Institution. That they are still in circulation is a measure of the public's interest in Blake's work.

The ranks of Blake Trustees have been depleted by the death of Kerrison Preston, of Francis Wormald, and of Lord Crawford. Lord Cunliffe and Graham Reynolds have been elected in recent years. Before entirely ceasing its activities, the Trust will publish *William Blake's Illustrations for the Book of Job* in three volumes (including the only set coloured by Blake's hand), *William Blake's Engravings for Dante's Divine Comedy*, and *The Complete Etchings of Samuel Palmer, with the Related Sketches and Illustrations for Virgil and Milton*, and finally, the *Complete Catalogue of Blake's Works* by Martin Butlin. In connection with the Samuel Palmer volume, the Trust has arranged an exhibition to be held at the Victoria and Albert Museum in November and December, 1978.

I am indebted to my co-Trustees, to our Associate Trustees, and, among many others, to the individuals and organisations mentioned above for making the achievement of the Blake Trust possible.

To Sir Geoffrey's report should be added an anonymous encomium by a *Times Literary Supplement* reviewer to a band of disinterested, but determined Blake admirers: 'Books as Blake conceived them, poetry, painting and craftsmanship combined in a way unattempted since the Middle Ages . . . The reproduction is beyond praise . . . A degree of skill, knowledge and devotion has been brought to bear on the production of this series that it would be idle to look for again . . .'

The Art of William Blake

William Blake is one of the greatest of British artists. However, unlike his near contemporaries Turner and Constable, his claim to this rank has often been disputed, particularly outside the English-speaking world. As an artist his claim to greatness rests in particular on the quality of his visual images. That his thought is profound and valid for today, that he created his own philosophy and his own mythology cannot be denied, but profound thoughts, like good intentions, are not enough to create great art. Neither does the fact that Blake is a great poet justify in itself his claim to be a great artist. It is therefore the purpose of this exhibition to demonstrate Blake's achievement first and foremost as an artist.

Blake's excellence as an artist is of a very special kind. His images are the direct result of his thought and, when they reflect it with full benefit of his technique and sense of visual form, gain extra force from this foundation. On the other hand, because technique was not of the first importance to him, because he was as much interested in his thoughts or visions and in his poetry as in his work in the visual arts, his images can be weak, ill-expressed, even ludicrous. But one must judge an artist by his best work, not by his worst, nor even by some impossible-to-define average. It was therefore the intention when making the choice for this exhibition to pick his best works with only the minimum number of 'interesting' or 'historically important' works, or of those especially intended to make a point in the catalogue (one watercolour has indeed been deliberately chosen to illustrate, by comparison with another, the variable quality of Blake's work and his lack of self-criticism; see Nos.166 and 167).

The best works even of Blake's immaturity, those of the mid-1780s when he was in his early thirties, are already, in their rather impersonal manner, works of considerable force. These were followed, about ten years later, by the large colour prints of 1795, completely personal in style, technique and content and, in the best examples, with an impact unparalleled in Blake's work. This particular peak was not scaled again, but masterpieces continued to appear, either singly or in the series of more or less closely associated works which are a distinguishing mark of Blake's output: certain of his illustrations to the Bible (both the small tempera paintings and the watercolours); the sets of illustrations to the Book of Job; the illustrations to the poems of Milton and the *Divine Comedy* of Dante; the intricate compositions of 'The Last Judgment' and the 'Spiritual States' of Pitt and Nelson; the idyllic Madonnas and the deliberate bestiality of 'The

Ghost of a Flea', the climax of his extraordinary Visionary Heads; and also, from among his book illustrations, those to Young's *Night Thoughts* and Gray's *Poems* with their unique format, and the miraculous tiny woodcuts for Thornton's *Virgil*.

Above all, Blake's illuminated books were a unique achievement, for text and illustrations were not only, in part at least, executed simultaneously in one process, but were also by the same artist. Not even the mediaeval illuminated book achieved this degree of unity. These books, too, contain many of Blake's most striking images, whether of horror as in *Urizen* (see No.80) or of an extraordinary fantasy as in *Jerusalem* (see Nos.259, 261, etc.).

The visionary quality of Blake's art has sometimes been claimed as something different in kind from that of other artists, not just in degree. Indeed, in part because of the intensity of his visual experience combined with a vocabulary coloured by the great religious writings of English literature, Blake often expressed himself in terms that implied specific visionary experiences, and these were seized upon by his early biographers. According to Gilchrist, Blake, 'as he will in after years relate', had his first vision on Peckham Rye at the age of eight or ten; it was of 'a tree filled with angels'. Gilchrist also relates how, while working as an apprentice in Westminster Abbey, Blake saw a vision of Christ and the Apostles. It was Blake himself, in a now untraced letter to his friend and patron Thomas Butts, who described how he had seen a great procession of monks, priests, choristers and incense bearers, accompanied by organ music. According to J. T. Smith, Blake saw a vision of 'The Ancient of Days' at the top of his staircase at Hercules Buildings, Lambeth, though the composition it allegedly inspired has been shown to derive from visual and verbal prototypes (see No.66); indeed, he used preliminary drawings and underdrawing just like any other artist. Blake clearly believed his inspiration to be a form of vision; after his creative difficulties at Felpham he would say 'the visions were angry with me at Felpham'. When sitting for his portrait by Thomas Phillips they got into a discussion about the relative merits of Raphael and Michelangelo. When Phillips correctly challenged Blake's claim to have actually seen a work by Michelangelo he quoted the authority of the Archangel Gabriel. He claimed that Joseph, the sacred carpenter, had told him the secret of Italian tempera painting, and that his dead brother Robert had revealed to him the technique of stereotype printing.

However, a clue to the actual nature of Blake's visions is given in a letter he wrote to Hayley on 6 May 1800 about his brother. 'Thirteen years ago I lost a brother & with his spirit I converse daily & hourly in the Spirit & See him in my remembrance in the regions of my Imagination.' When asked by Mrs Aders where he had seen a vision of a field full of lambs which turned into sculpture he replied '*here*, madam', touching his forehead. As Frederick Tatham said, 'these visions of Blake seem to have been more like peopled imaginations, & personified thoughts'. The Visionary Heads, Blake's drawings of historical or imaginary personages purportedly conjured up in vision, are a special case. Produced for the credulous John Varley, they seem to be different in kind from Blake's other visionary experiences, and to have been to a considerable extent the result of Blake's determination to oblige his friend. This is supported by the fact that this particular form of image only seems to have appeared to Blake over a limited period, largely confined to the autumn of 1819.

Both types of vision have been explained as possibly a result of the physiological phenomena known as eidetic images, which are characterised by sharpness of definition, optical reality and involuntary appearance, often under conditions of nervous excitement producing a form of auto-suggestion. This ties in with Blake's own insistence that visions are not 'a cloudy vapour or a nothing; they are organized and minutely articulated beyond all that the mortal and perishing nature can produce' (see No.207). However, a particularly strongly-developed creative imagination coupled with an exceptional visual memory may well be sufficient explanation.

It is no discredit to Blake's achievement to treat it as a normal if exceptionally developed example of artistic creativity, nor to place it in its historical context. His images, despite his claims to visionary inspiration, were firmly based on a long tradition of figurative art, in which the human figure was used for emotional and moral effect. The tradition of figure painting was relatively unestablished in Britain; landscape seems to have been a more natural mode of expression, in which Blake's two rather younger contemporaries Turner and Constable achieved their greatness. Figure painting was mainly confined to portraiture. What native figurative tradition there was stemmed largely from Hogarth, small-scale figures used to point a moral rather than to elevate the spirit, illustrations to novels or plays such as Highmore's *Pamela* series or Hayman's Shakespearian subjects, and genre paintings, leading on to the great flood of nineteenth-century genre painting; all this shaded into the small-scale portrait group or conversation picture.

But Blake, both through inclination and through the luck of the particular artistic circumstances of his time, partook of the mainstream of European, or more specifically Italian, figurative art, in which subjects of high import were treated in a suitably elevated style. This style had characterised the art of Antiquity, the High Renaissance and much of seventeenth-century art, and was revived again in the mid eighteenth century by theorists such as Winckelmann and by a group of artists working in Rome in the 1760s, and in particular by the Scot Gavin Hamilton and the American-born Benjamin West. This development coincided with the creation of exhibiting institutions in Britain, first the Society of Artists in 1760, then (and pre-eminently) the Royal Academy which held its first annual exhibition in 1769. Blake's earliest exhibits (see Nos.20, 28–30) must be seen in the light of this Neo-Classical style based on antique reliefs and the compositions of Raphael and Poussin. It was a style based on figures inter-related by gesture, deployed across the surface of the picture and confined to a relatively narrow stage in the foreground, any landscape or architectural setting acting merely as a foil to the main action.

A slightly later manifestation of the style, also associated with Rome but with a group of artists who worked there mainly in the 1770s, was the strangely imaginative, almost mannerist development associated at its most extreme with Fuseli but also practised in England by Mortimer, Barry and Romney. These artists added an emotional *frisson* to the style and, while seeking inspiration in the same basic schools of art in the past, concentrated on rather different works, the Laocoön rather than the Apollo Belvedere, the works of Michelangelo rather than those of Raphael.

More important than individual sources of motifs or poses, though these have been amply demonstrated in Blake's work, was the common vocabulary established by this long tradition of figurative art, a vocabulary that the connoisseur could recognise intellectually and even the non-expert would perceive emotionally and sensuously because of the expressive effect of the forms. The Apollo Belvedere evoked, for the cognoscenti, the whole intellectual significance of this god of light, the epitome of reason, the arts and intellectual achievement; and for those who did not understand the significance of the subject's background, the classical poise, elegant form and smooth modelling would express the same general idea. Equally, the agony of the Laocoön was sufficiently expressive even if one did not know the story of the protagonist's tragic fate at the hands of the ancient gods. The vocabulary established by these models was as much a question of 'pathos formulae' conveyed by the entire body as of facial expression. Today, it is difficult to appreciate this vocabulary to the full, largely because the discipline of classical academic art collapsed in the nineteenth century; whatever this may have meant in the increased freedom of art to express a wider and stronger scale of emotion, it destroyed the assumptions on which all artists, whether conformist or rebel, could rely in the late eighteenth century. Blake came from the last generation that could assume a knowledge of this vocabulary. A number of artists of the time, although their roots were in the academic tradition, were in fact instrumental in breaking it down, including Stubbs, Blake himself, and Turner.

Blake's achievement as an artist is enlarged, not diminished, by this context. Using this common vocabulary, his revolt was all the greater and the uses to which he put it all the more revolutionary. But, in part to achieve his particular aims, he limited an already limited style still further. Partly through his training as an engraver, partly through his inclinations which led him to reject much of the discipline of the Royal Academy Schools, particularly as regards copying from life or sculptural casts, Blake minimised the three-dimensional elements of the style both in the figure itself and in its spatial setting. His figure compositions moved away from the narrative to the emblematic.

In some ways this development paralleled the increasing abstraction of much Neo-Classical art, but Blake's simplifications were never at the expense of the concrete, the specific. By the time he reached the age of about fifty he was able to equate this development with his role as visionary prophet. Visionary experience, far from being most suitably expressed in vague, suggestive forms, necessitated the sharpest clarity, avoiding the 'obscuring demons' of three-dimensional modelling through light and shade and all complex spatial connotations. In his later works, though he returned to a more three-dimensional modelling of the individual figure, this in no way represented a return to everyday reality.

Neither Blake's aesthetic theories nor his style were fully formed from the beginning. His theories were formulated only gradually, just as he only gradually achieved a truly personal independence from the formulae of contemporary Neo-Classicism. In fact the development of his mature aesthetic principles took considerably longer than the maturing of his style. From 1789, with *Songs of Innocence*, Blake's individuality as an artist is unmistakable, and with the large colour prints of 1795 he had reached a position which marks him off completely even from such imaginative and forceful contemporaries as Fuseli and Barry. In 1799 however he was still flattering himself of being capable of painting cabinet pictures not 'unworthy of a Scholar of Rembrandt & Teniers' (see No.141) and it was not until the *Descriptive Catalogue* of his own exhibition of 1809 and writings contemporary with this that his own personal aesthetic theories were fully developed. Indeed, these theories were only reconcilable with his actual artistic practice because of a further development in his style, away from the forcefulness of the mid 1790s. Much damage is done to the appreciation of Blake's earlier art by seeing his whole output as a monolithic creation moulded by the theories he expounded in his later years. Blake himself may have helped this process, by reading back into his own account of his early days the views of his maturity. For instance, his work in Westminster Abbey as an apprentice to James Basire was neither as revolutionary nor as profound an influence on his early work as in 1805 he led his first biographer Benjamin Heath Malkin to suppose (see No.1).

Blake's fully developed aesthetic theories are found in his annotations to Reynolds' *Discourses*, largely made *c*.1805–8, the *Descriptive Catalogue* of 1809, his description of his picture of 'The Last Judgment', drafted in 1810, and certain later writings such as the inscriptions on the 'Laocoön' print of *c*.1820 (No.315). These are more fully set out in the appropriate sections of the catalogue; because of the changing nature of Blake's views it is all the more important to see them in their chronological setting. Very simply, however, he can be said to have moved from the general Neo-Classical position which looked back to the art of antiquity as the ideal, to considering the great works of antiquity merely as a reflection of far greater but now vanished Hebrew works of art, themselves only directly known from the biblical description of the cherubim in the holy of holies in the Temple of Solomon (1 Kings 6:23–8). True art was thus indivisibly linked with true religion. Not only 'Grecian' but also 'Hindoo' and Egyptian art reflected lost originals. Blake derived certain elements, such as the form of the halo of 'The Spiritual Form of Pitt' (No.206), from engravings of Buddhist art; similarly plates 46 and 53 of *Jerusalem* (Nos.269 and 270), derived motifs from oriental art.

For Blake, as for the Neo-Classicists, the classical tradition and the Gothic were united in their basic principles. In his mature writings Blake made a very clear distinction between linear and painterly art, and, as he claimed both Raphael and Michelangelo had done before him, he 'contemned and rejected' painterly art 'with the utmost disdain'. He set the Florentine school against the Venetian, the early Flemish primitives against Rubens and Rembrandt, and the technique of tempera or fresco (which he tended to muddle together) against that of painting in oils. As he said of his own paintings 'The Spiritual Form of Pitt' and 'The Spiritual Form of Nelson' (Nos.206 and 205), 'Clearness and precision have been the chief objects in painting these Pictures. Clear colours unmudded by oil, and firm and determinate lineaments unbroken by shadows, which ought to display and not to hide form, as is the practice of the latter Schools of Italy and Flanders.' 'Colouring does not depend on where the Colours are put, but on where the lights and darks are put, and all depends on Form or Outline. On where that is put; where that is wrong, the Colouring never can be right; and it is always wrong in Titian and Correggio, Rubens and Rembrandt. Till we get rid of Titian and Correggio, Rubens and Rembrandt, We never shall equal Rafael and Albert Durer, Michael Angelo, and Julio Romano.' Interestingly, Blake makes absolutely no allowance for Rembrandt's deep insight as a religious painter, nor for his position as a rebel, misunderstood by his materialistic contemporaries; in these respects style, not content or context, was the sole criterion.

Blake's attitude to Reynolds was more complex. Despite opening his annotations to Reynolds' *Discourses* with 'This Man was Hired to Depress Art', Blake agreed with much that Reynolds said, particularly over such things as the superiority of history painting over all other genres and the praiseworthiness of Raphael and Michelangelo. What he attacked were Reynolds' deviations from strict academic doctrine and what he regarded as jibes at the imaginative qualities of Mortimer, Barry and Fuseli (perhaps significantly, Benjamin West, whose Neo-Classical subject pictures lie behind many of Blake's earliest works, but who succeeded Reynolds as President of the Royal Academy, was only once mentioned by Blake and then because of his equivocations over the respective merits of the engravings of Woollett and the more linear Basire). Blake's most profound difference from Reynolds was over how one should apprehend the ideal forms that both agreed were the fundamental basis of art. Both advocated copying the best masters: 'to learn the Language of Art Copy for Ever is my Rule', said Blake. However, rather than advocating that the artist should seek perfection through studying the details of nature, which were of necessity imperfect, and gradually refining from these the more perfect whole unknown in nature, Blake held that the artist could apprehend ideal beauty without reference to nature at all. 'Knowledge of Ideal Beauty is Not to be Acquired. It is Born with us. Innate Ideas are in Every Man Born with him; they are truly Himself. The man who says that we have No Innate Ideas must be a Fool & Knave, Having no Con-Science or Innate Science.' This Platonic rather than Aristotelian concept was closer to

High-Renaissance and Mannerist theory than to what was common in the seventeenth and eighteenth centuries.

For Blake colour was subservient to form. At its best however his colouring is, like his imagery and formal composition, of the greatest beauty. Again, he developed from the conventional colouring of the Neo-Classicists to something much more personal. Neo-Classical colouring is basically representational though without any attempt to imitate through brushwork and subtle relations of tone the exact semblance of shade and texture. Blake moved steadily away from even this qualified reality to create a largely non-representational, expressive or hieratic style of colouring. Often, particularly from about 1803, when his compositions became more symmetrical, the colouring of the figures supports this symmetry or acts as a counterpoint to it. Sometimes colour is used symbolically, for instance the red and blue robes of Dante and Virgil in the illustrations to Dante (see No. 319). At its best Blake's colouring is capable of every gradation from extreme delicacy, as in some of the biblical watercolours and the Dante illustrations (for example Nos. 161 and 333), to the sonorous oppressive tones of other of the biblical watercolours, the tempera paintings and above all the large colour prints of 1795. This end of the scale called for new textures and even new techniques. The first half of the 1790s saw, in his books and therefore in direct relationship with the development of his writing, the creation of a unique form of colour printing that led first to independent works in this medium and then to his own particular form of tempera. Later however this particular line of development was abandoned, in parallel with the evolution of his aesthetic theories.

So far Blake's art has been discussed as if divorced from his poetry and thought. Indeed, the appreciation of his visual works, though clearly dependent on a knowledge of his writings, has often been bedevilled by a failure to distinguish properly between his work in the two media. One cannot read Blake's pictures as one reads his poems, translating each image into purely verbal terms. Each medium requires its own approach, and Blake above all, because of the very fact that he was equally proficient in either, must have realised the differences between them and consciously used one or other for particular ends.

This said, it is important to accept that Blake saw all art, in whatever medium, as the product of an indivisible Poetic Genius that acted through artists to expound and clarify eternal truths. The true artist, not the priest, was man's closest link with God. Blake explained his role in *Jerusalem*:

> *. . . I rest not from my great task!*
> *To open the Eternal Worlds, to open the immortal Eyes*
> *Of Man inwards into Worlds of Thought: into Eternity*
> *Ever expanding in the Bosom of God, the Human Imagination.*

The ultimate purpose and message both of Blake's visual work and of his writings were the same; only the means of expression differed. In addition much of the imagery is the same, or at least overlaps. The poem *Urizen*, for instance, is full of 'vast clouds of blood', 'depths of dark solitude', 'books formd of metals', 'pale visages', 'cataracts of fire, blood, & gall', 'flames of eternal fury', and so on, and so are Blake's illustrations to that book (see Nos. 73–83). But not even the illustrations to Blake's own books are direct translations of the text into pictorial images. The illustrations often parallel, supplement or even contradict the text, for a greater richness and depth of expression. The unity of Blake's illuminated books–text and illustrations by the same artist–is a unity of equals, not of servant and master; neither however is it an indivisible whole to be appreciated in a single, undifferentiated apprehension. Similarly Blake's illustrations to other writers (the Bible, Milton, Dante above all) gloss their texts according to Blake's views on the issues involved. Dante, for instance, had views on man's salvation very different from Blake's, so Blake's illustrations often criticise or negate Dante's intentions (see Nos. 334–5 and 339).

For Blake art was only justified if it was didactic. One cannot therefore isolate visual qualities from content. But one must beware the overt literary approach and realise that verbal explanations can only hint at the central visual experience. Therefore, the explanations in the catalogue entries are not only of necessity short and somewhat superficial but at best can only act as stimuli to the visual appreciation of Blake's message.

As a background one can set out some of Blake's main tenets. Although he was fundamentally a non-conformist Christian his thought includes elements from a much wider range of sources than the Bible, both Christian and non-Christian, including the Apocrypha, Milton, Paracelsus, Emanuel Swedenborg, Jakob Böhme, and Neo-Platonism as introduced into this country by Thomas Taylor. Facile as it is to deduce either an artist's personal predicament or his philosophy directly from the content of his works, in Blake's case there do seem to be much closer parallels than usual, with a strong element of autobiography. It is therefore justifiable to suggest that the failure of political radicalism in the 1790s led to the Christian element in Blake's thought reaching a low point in the mid 1790s. This element gradually revived as he introduced Christian parallels into his illustrations to the *Night Thoughts*, 1795–7 (see Nos. 122 and 124) and into his own unfinished manuscript of *Vala or the Four Zoas*, *c.*1796–1807, and more obviously when he began his series of illustrations to the Bible in 1799. For Blake ideally, in eternity, 'We are all coexistent with God–Members of the Divine Body–all partakers of the divine nature', so Blake told Crabb Robinson in 1825; Christ 'is the only God . . . And so am I and so are you.'

Blake saw man's predicament in the material world as a division between the various elements that in eternity ideally complement each other but which in division fall to warring against each other. He saw the biblical Fall in this light, as merely one of a series of fallings into division. The Creation itself was another, giving over-emphasis to the material aspect of man. Paradoxically this was also a stage towards redemption; all giving form to error, all defining of error, was a stage in understanding it and therefore in being able to overcome it. The prime agent in overcoming error was not however the intellect or reason, but the imagination. Indeed, although the reason ranked equally with the imagination, the emotions and the natural senses as the four main elements into which the fallen man was divided, Blake was particularly suspicious of the faculty of reason, equating it with the oppression of the imagination that resulted from the unenlightened exercise of any authority, in particular religious or political. Further divisions, such as the creation of woman and the propagation of children, represented further stages of the Fall.

These concepts were developed by Blake into what can be termed his own mythology, the concepts acquiring personal identities and names rather like the protagonists in Wagner's *Ring* though without their background in northern mythology; a possible source for the general idea and structure of Blake's myth may have been the so-called writings of Ossian, not then fully recognised as the fabrications of Macpherson (in fact Blake, in his annotations of 1826 to Wordsworth's poems, wrote 'I believe both Macpherson & Chatterton, that what they say is Ancient, Is so'). However, Blake's personifications are constantly changing and developing and appear differently qualified in different guises, so any attempt to set them out in a system is of necessity misleading. Far better indeed to build on Blake's beloved 'minute particulars', as is attempted in some of the catalogue entries. A brief general summary, however, is that Blake divided the four elements of man into Los, the imagination and eventual source of redemption; Urizen, the reason and also the vengeful Jehovah of the Old Testament as opposed to the merciful Christ of the New; Tharmas, the senses; and Luvah, the emotions. These, of whom the first two are the most important, are the four Zoas, the Greek name for the four beasts of the Book of Revelation (a typical example of the cultural cross-references in Blake's thought). Each of them can exist in a fallen or in a redeemed state, and they often acquire different names according to which state they are in (for instance Urthona is Los in his spiritual state). Each also has an emanation, a female offshoot who not only represents a further stage of division but also makes things worse by attempting to dominate her male counterpart. The most important of these is Los's emanation, Enitharmon, who also represents Pity, for Blake an impure and destructive emotion (see No.80). Yet another stage of division occurs when Los and Enitharmon give birth to Orc, the spirit of energy, another important force in the achievement of salvation but one which alarms not only Urizen, who sees his authority threatened, but also Los himself, partly out of jealousy of Enitharmon's love for her son; thus love too can become an impure emotion. Many of Blake's writings, particularly *Urizen, Vala or the Four Zoas* and *Jerusalem*, deal with the conflicts between these personifications of man's divided self. An apocalyptic Last Judgment and end of the world, expressed in terms closely paralleling the Book of Revelation, herald a final solution.

Places, seen as states of being, are also important in Blake's fully developed myth. Again to simplify: immediately below Paradise, the state of eternal undivided unity, is Eden, the highest state of man's being as an individual, a place of active mental strife, and the gateway to eternity. In contrast Beulah, although a state of delight and peace, is passive, where the pursuit of pleasure can lead to one falling into Ulro or despair. The benign elderly couple Har and Heva (see No.41) are typical inhabitants of Beulah, and the Vales of Har in *Tiriel* are an anticipation in Blake's early writings of his later Beulah. The Garden of Eden before the Fall was seen by Blake in the same light (see No.221). Ulro is Blake's Hell; Generation is a stage above, representing man's earthly existence in a fallen state. In each state the degree of vision is different, from the single vision of Ulro to the two- and threefold vision of Generation and Beulah, and then to the four-fold vision of Eden.

In *Jerusalem*, c.1804–20, the use of place names goes much further (see p.127), and they are also used for a further class of personage. 'Jerusalem' herself is a character, the female emanation of Albion, the ancient man who stands both for mankind in general and, as his name suggests, for England in particular; it must always be remembered that Blake, like Hogarth, was exceedingly conscious of his Englishness. Jerusalem is less negative than most emanations, representing liberty and Man's desire for salvation through Christ; at the end of *Jerusalem* she is re-embodied in Albion through Christ's Crucifixion. Babylon is the contrary principle to Jerusalem, associated through the Protestant tradition of the Whore of Babylon with oppressive religion and particularly with the Church of Rome.

Other historical events and characters, the American and French Revolutions in particular, fall effortlessly into place within Blake's mythological structure. No element was too alien for him to use as part of his mythic vocabulary, so that what at first sight may look like an absurd *mélange* of disparate elements is in fact a complete system that can account for, and use, every aspect of man's life and history.

The mythology of Blake's writings is paralleled in Blake's visual art, though visual identifications have to be made with even greater caution than in the shifting world of Blake's written myth. Orc, a child or young man amidst flames, the Apollo-like Los, and Urizen, the horrific bearded old man, can be recognised both in Blake's illustrations to his own writings and in other works. For instance, the equation of Urizen with the vengeful, oppressive Jehovah of the Old Testament is as much a visual identification between the figure as he appears in *Urizen* and as he appears in Blake's illustrations to the Bible as it is a written one. But not every old man with a beard is Urizen, Urizenic or even nasty. Context is vital, and simple equation of type with type makes for gross over-simplification. This is true the other way round as well. Blake's condemnation of unenlightened reason finds one of its greatest expressions in the colour print 'Newton' (No.92). However, Newton is not shown as Blake's old man type of Urizen at all, though there are close links with 'The Ancient of Days' (see No.66) in which it is Blake's Urizen-Jehovah who wields the same pair of compasses (or 'dividers', a pun that may well be justified in this case). As companion to 'Newton', itself an extraordinary though highly Blakean use of an historic figure in his own personal myth, Blake expressed the material man, subject to the senses, in the much more obvious biblical parallel of

'Nebuchadnezzar' (No.91). Indeed, the whole series of large colour prints of 1795 is typical of Blake's amazing ability to unify disparate elements, in this case subjects from such diverse sources as the Bible, Shakespeare, Milton, his own writings and history, and human figures, whether real or imaginary, with abstractions such as Pity (see Nos.85–103).

In his most successful works the general message is conveyed through visual means; one's identification of Blake's personifications merely confirms what is visually apparent. The best of the large colour prints of 1795 are typical. 'Newton', despite showing a physically-ideal handsome young man, is obviously condemnatory of his slavish drawing of an abstract diagram with his compasses; the 'Elohim Creating Adam' (No.85) is clearly an extremely negative view of the biblical Creation; 'God Judging Adam' (No.87) is a scene of horror and oppression, and equally clearly not the passing on of the mantle of inspiration that it was once thought to be. In other cases, content and visual impact are mismatched as a result of Blake's failure to find a suitable image; such is the case of 'Samson Subdued' (No.167). Very occasionally one is left baffled by an apparent contradiction between the success of a work in purely visual terms on the one hand and what it actually expresses on the other. 'Beatrice Addressing Dante from the Car' (No.334), as has been demonstrated from the various ways in which it differs from Dante's text, is a criticism of all that Beatrice, Dante's symbol for the Church, stands for, yet the design is so positive in its glowing colours and balanced yet energetic design that one would never recognise without prompting the criticism that it embodies. Art can express negative concepts while being visually stimulating, as in Goya's 'Horrors of War' or in Blake's 'Nebuchadnezzar', but the contradictions of 'Beatrice Addressing Dante from the Car' seem to represent, against all one's sense of visual enjoyment, a total failure of communication. In fact, one still finds oneself straining to upset the evidence, however clear-cut it seems to be.

Blake's personal philosophy was not a retreat from everyday reality, nor did his visions mean that he was completely other-worldly, despite repeated suggestions even during his lifetime that he was insane. In fact, particularly during his younger days, he was deeply committed politically. He was against oppressive authority not just philosophically but in practice, rejoicing at the American and French Revolutions. He was on the fringe at least of the prominent group of radicals that included the publisher Joseph Johnson, Mary Wollstonecraft and Thomas Paine. Gilchrist said that Blake 'was an ardent member' of the group though there is no hard evidence for this. However, he was certainly associated with Johnson, whom he probably met through his friend Fuseli. Fuseli, typically of the 'advanced artist', then as now, had radical sympathies, as had Mortimer, Barry, Romney and Flaxman (even West, though largely occupied in painting for the King, covertly supported his countrymen; Reynolds and Copley on the other hand were royalists and 'Patriots'). Blake's apocalyptic *The French Revolution, a Poem in Seven Books* was actually set up in type to be published by Johnson in 1791 but, perhaps because of the Terror in France and repression in England, was never published. *America*, 1793, and *Europe*, 1794, also dealt with contemporary or near contemporary events, though Blake's illuminated printing meant that only a very limited number of copies were produced, and the growing obscurity of his verse may in part have reflected a retreat from too public a political role. Certainly, when it came to the relatively trivial incident of his throwing a drunken soldier out of his garden at Felpham in 1803, it seems more than coincidence that the affair was built up into a charge of sedition. It is probable that his selection of subjects from English history in about 1779, and again as reflected in his Prospectus of 1793, was consciously radical and even feminist (see Nos.16 and 19). Even as late as the Visionary Heads of *c*.1819 he seems to have had a particular *penchant* for fighters against oppression such as Cassibelane, Boadicea, Caractacus, Wat Tyler and Owen Glendower. Gilchrist reports a friend of Blake as saying that he asserted 'the curious hypothesis "that the Bonaparte of Italy was killed, and that another was somehow substituted . . . who was the Bonaparte of the Empire!"'.' One is reminded of Beethoven's tearing out his dedication of the 'Eroica' Symphony to Bonaparte on hearing that he had declared himself Emperor in 1804, and this story makes one all the more sorry that Blake's 'Spiritual Form of Napoleon', a probable companion to 'The Spiritual Form of Pitt' and 'The Spiritual Form of Nelson', has disappeared.

It was Blake's political commitment that made it so easy for him to incorporate figures like Pitt and Nelson into his own imagery and mythology. Similarly, figures like Locke and Newton could be included without distortion in his writings as part of the codification of error that would lead to its destruction. Even contemporaries of little importance save that they had offended Blake in some way, such as the soldier Schofield and Blake's well-meaning but maddening patron William Hayley, could appear on one of the plates of *Jerusalem* as 'Skofeld' and 'Hyle' (see No.275).

Blake's life was a continuous struggle against misunderstanding and poverty. Engraving, usually after the work of others, was more profitable than his own work, but he was constantly passed over or involved in schemes that for one reason or another disappointed his expectations, such as the illustrations to *Night Thoughts* and *The Grave* (see Nos.104–24, 152). What work he did get was largely through his friends, Fuseli, Flaxman and Cumberland, and even such relationships as these often soured. His dealings with possible patrons for his original works were equally hazardous, as can be seen from his correspondence with the Rev. Dr Trusler, who expected to dictate the actual composition of the works he had commissioned (see No.141), and the patronage of William Hayley who tried to direct Blake into more economically viable projects at the expense of his own imaginative work (see p.78). Three patrons stand out for their faith in Blake: the minor civil servant Thomas Butts, for whom Blake executed a series of illustrations to the Bible, the Book of Job and Milton from *c*.1799 onwards (see Nos.134–40, 159–196, 216–27 and

231–50); the Rev. Joseph Thomas who commissioned the first sets of Milton designs (see p. 112); and John Linnell, the young painter who, in Blake's last years, commissioned a second set of Job watercolours and the engravings, the Dante illustrations, and much else besides (see p. 133).

Linnell was also the agent through whom a group of young admirers, many of them artists, gathered around Blake in his last years, in particular Palmer, Calvert and Richmond (see p. 133), whose early works owe much to Blake. But what Palmer and his friends took from Blake was only a very small part of the full significance of his art. Palmer and Calvert drew particularly from the miraculous but untypical woodcut landscapes illustrating Thornton's *Virgil* (Nos.287–303). Moreover Palmer, far from sharing Blake's deeper beliefs, was a High Church Anglican who campaigned against the Reform Bill of 1832, while Calvert reverted to what his friends termed 'paganism'. Richmond at least drew his early inspiration from Blake's figure style but later concentrated on portraying his eminent contemporaries. A deeper kinship with Blake was perhaps felt by Dante Gabriel Rossetti, like him both poet and painter, inspired by Dante and, though in a very different way from Blake, a visionary and mystic. While the influence of the Virgil woodcuts persisted, by way of Palmer and Calvert, into the twentieth century in the early works of such artists as Paul Nash and Graham Sutherland, the tradition of the visionary poet-painter was less easily assimilated; of later artists perhaps only David Jones has developed this aspect of Blake's legacy. Blake however had an intensity of vision, an imaginative scope, and a multiplicity of means of expression beyond any followers, indeed beyond most men. Of his greatness as a complete man there can be no doubt; nor, it is here claimed, should there be any doubt about his greatness as an artist.

Catalogue

Explanations

dates

Dates are given following the title of each work with varying degrees of certainty according to whether the date is documented or inferred from the evidence summarised in the entry. In the case of the illuminated books a date following the form '1789/c.1800' means that the plates were etched in 1789 but that the colouring can be dated to about 1800.

media

The question of Blake's media is a complex one. For Blake's own form of tempera, which changed radically in his last years and which he sometimes called 'fresco', see pp.75 and 142. His prints were produced by a variety of techniques. His relief etchings, sometimes called stereotypes or woodcuts on pewter, were printed from the raised, unetched areas of the plate. His line engravings, which nearly all involved etching with acid as well as actually engraving into the surface of the plate, were normally printed in intaglio, that is by first inking the plate and then wiping the ink off so that only the incised lines printed, not the raised areas. However, some plates of *Milton* and *Jerusalem*, though engraved and etched in the normal way, were printed in relief, so that the engraved or etched lines show up as white; this technique is sometimes referred to as white-line engraving. After printing the illustrations to his books, Blake normally coloured them by hand. However, the pages of the books, or separate plates from the books, were sometimes, particularly in about 1795, coloured not in watercolour but in Blake's own colour-printing process, for which see p.48.

dimensions

The dimensions are given in inches followed by centimetres in brackets; height precedes width. In the case of engravings the actual image size is given, together with the platemark save in the fairly frequent cases where this has been lost through trimming.

inscriptions

Inscriptions are presumed to be by Blake unless otherwise stated. For engravings the quoted signatures and inscriptions are printed as part of the engraving unless otherwise stated. The term '"WB inv" as monogram' signifies Blake's characteristic monogram, reproduced below, even in cases where the characters are not actually linked.

quotations

Quotations from Blake's writings normally follow his somewhat idiosyncratic spelling and use of capital initials, but punctuation has sometimes been added or altered in the interest of clarity.

Blake's monogram, reproduced actual size from
The River of Life, c.1805 (Tate Gallery 5887)

213 *The Last Judgment*, 1808 (entry on p.110)

Apprenticeship and Early Work, c.1775–85

Blake's training as an artist was long, conventional and largely confined to the 'lowly' art of engraving. Later however it was to fall into place as a significant background to much of his work and artistic theory, but one must remember that even by the time of the first biographical account of Blake's early career, Benjamin Heath Malkin's introductory letter to his *Father's Memoirs of his Child*, published in 1806 and based on a close friendship with Blake, Blake's opinions had crystallised into a form very different from those that had governed his earlier artistic activity.

At the age of ten Blake entered Henry Pars's drawing school in the Strand where he copied from Antique casts, examples of which his father also bought for him to work from at home. Five years later, in 1772, he was apprenticed to the engraver James Basire, whose sound but old-fashioned technique gave Blake a grounding which he was to use in commercial work but on which he could also base his own much more experimental, highly personal engraving technique. Finally, in 1779, he entered the Royal Academy Schools. He exhibited with the Royal Academy for the first time the following year, illustrating a subject from English history, 'The Death of Earl Goodwin', an essay in history painting, regarded in academic circles as the highest genre of painting.

At the Academy, as at Pars's drawing school, Blake was set to drawing from the Antique and also from life. A number of anecdotes speak of his rejecting this accepted mode of teaching, but these partly reflect his later preoccupations.

Most significant, perhaps, is the story of his rage when Moser, the Keeper, tried to divert him from studying prints after Raphael and Michelangelo to studying those of Rubens and Le Brun; just as in the case of Blake's later annotations to Reynolds' *Discourses*, what really seems to have annoyed him was the desertion of true academic principles by those who should have most defended them. Much of what was taught in Royal Academy circles he accepted and set himself to achieve, not only that history painting was the highest form of art but that the suitable mode for expressing this was based on the art of Antiquity and the Renaissance. If this could be combined with the current patriotic interest in early English history, as in his first exhibit, 'The Death of Earl Goodwin', so much the better.

Blake's work for Basire led to the other great formative influence on his art, his copying of the tombs and other mediaeval works in Westminster Abbey (see Nos.1–5). This too was a reflection of contemporary taste; interest in the achievements of the English past led to the publication of a number of large antiquarian folios including two in which Basire was directly concerned, Richard Gough's *Sepulchral Monuments in Great Britain*, published from 1786 onwards, and the Society of Antiquaries' *Vetusta Monumenta*, published in 1789. The stress in Gothic on clear outlines, flowing line and symmetrical composition was readily reconcilable with Neo-Classicism but even more important was Blake's contact with the spiritual content of an art based on faith. It was not irrelevant that, according to anecdote, one of the first places where Blake saw a vision was Westminster Abbey.

Meanwhile the true individuality and quality of Blake's art was already making itself apparent. Blake's dating of his works must be viewed with caution; he had a habit of pre-dating works unparalleled until its adoption by some of the pioneers of the modern movement. However, it seems clear that the original form of 'Glad Day' dates from about this time, 1780 (see Nos.9–11). Here Blake shows himself in the main European tradition of figurative art, expressing through the human figure a positive affirmation of the centrality of the individual soul. This image remained as a central one with Blake, to be re-used at least twice later in his career in ever more personal contexts as he developed his personal philosophy. He also used it in a more general way as the basis for a recurrent image of ecstasy, as in one of the most striking of the illustrations to *Jerusalem*, c.1804–20 (see No.272).

---

1   *Henry III, Head and Shoulders from his Effigy in Westminster Abbey* c.1774–5

Pencil, oval, $13\frac{3}{8} \times 11\frac{1}{2}$ (34 × 29.2) on paper $19\frac{1}{4} \times 12$ (48.8 × 30.5).
Inscr. 'JBasire ['JB' as monogram]. del.' and 'K. Henry III'.
Bodleian Library, Oxford

The evidence for Blake's authorship of a group of drawings after the monuments in Westminster Abbey comes in Benjamin Heath Malkin's introductory letter to his *Father's Memoirs of His Child*, 1806, for which Blake's drawing for the frontispiece was engraved by R. H. Cromek. Malkin, in linking the genius of his infant son with that of Blake, gives a biographical and critical account of the latter, apparently derived from Blake's own account.

After two years of his apprenticeship to James Basire the engagement of

1

2

3

two other apprentices destroyed the harmony of Basire's studio and Blake was sent out, by way of escape, to make 'drawings from old buildings and monuments, and occasionally, especially in winter, in engraving from those drawings. This occupation led him to an acquaintance with those neglected works of art, called Gothic monuments . . . The monuments of Kings and Queens in Westminster Abbey, which surround the chapel of Edward the Confessor, particularly that of King Henry the Third, the beautiful monument and figure of Queen Elinor, Queen Philippa, King Edward the Third, King Richard the Second and his Queen, were among his first studies. All these he drew in every point he could catch, frequently standing on the monument, and viewing the figures from the top. The heads he considered as portraits; and all the ornaments appeared as miracles of art, to his Gothicised imagination'; we must remember that this was written thirty years later, when Blake was newly convinced of the superiority of Gothic art.

Pen and wash drawings of the tombs mentioned by Malkin, and pencil drawings of the heads like this example and No.2, were engraved for Richard Gough's *Sepulchral Monuments of Great Britain* and published in 1786 and 1796. Although usually 'signed' by James Basire this would have been normal practice for apprentice work and there seems no reason to doubt either Malkin's account, or that, as well as the drawings, at least some of the engravings were done by Blake as part of learning his trade.

Henry III died in 1272 but was reburied by Edward I in a grander tomb c.1280. The gilt bronze effigy, of which this drawing shows the head and shoulders, is by William Torel, 1291.

2 Queen Eleanor, Head and Shoulders from her Effigy in Westminster Abbey c.1774–5

Pencil, oval, $13\frac{1}{4} \times 11\frac{5}{8}$ (33.6 × 29.5) on paper $19\frac{1}{4} \times 12$ (48.8 × 30.5).
Inscr. 'JBasire ['JB' as monogram]. del.' and 'Queen. Eleanor'.
Bodleian Library, Oxford

See No.1. Queen Eleanor, wife of Edward I, died in 1290 at Hardby in Lincolnshire and the resting places of her funeral *cortège* back to London were marked by the erection of the Eleanor Crosses. Her effigy, like that of Henry III, was made by William Torel in 1291.

3 Side View of the Tomb of Countess Aveline 1775

Pen and sepia wash, $12\frac{3}{8} \times 9\frac{3}{16}$ (31.4 × 23.3) on paper $14\frac{13}{16} \times 10\frac{3}{4}$ (37.6 × 27.3).
Inscr.'JBasire ['JB' as monogram] del. 1775.', 'Tomb of Aveline first wife of Edmund Crouchback Earl of Lancaster on the N. side of the Altar Westminr. Abbey. Vet. Mon. Vol.11. pl.29' and with dimensions, 'foot 7.1 8.½' wide and 'foot 10:1 10:' high.
Society of Antiquaries of London

Malkin continued his account of Blake's work at Westminster Abbey (see No.1) as follows: 'He then drew Aymer de Valence's monument, with his fine figure on the top. Those exquisite little figures which surround it, though dreadfully mutilated, are still models for the study of drapery. But I do not mean to enumerate all his drawings, since they would lead me over all the old monuments in Westminster Abbey, as well as over other churches in and about London'. Three drawings of the tomb of Aymer de Valence, engraved for Richard Gough's *Sepulchral Monuments*, are in the Bodleian Library, Oxford, and provide a yardstick by which further tomb drawings such as this one can be attributed to Blake. The 'signature' of James Basire was no more than standard workshop practice and was almost certainly added at the same time as the inscription referring to volume II of *Vetusta Monumenta*, published in 1789, in which the engraving after this drawing, probably also done by Blake, appears as plate 29.

The engraving had already been used as plate I in Sir Joseph Ayloffe's *An Account of Some Ancient Monuments in Westminster Abbey*, 1780. This monument was one of those temporarily uncovered in the presbytery of Westminster Abbey in the summer of 1775; by 1778 they were again concealed, though they are visible today. As well as this side view of the tomb, there are drawings also attributed to Blake of the effigy seen from above and of four details; there are replicas of these among the drawings done for Richard Gough in the Bodleian Library.

Countess Aveline died in 1272, but her monument dates from the same time as that of her husband Edmund Earl of Lancaster, who died twenty years later.

4

4   *King Sebert, from the Wall-Painting above his Monument* 1775

> Pen, watercolour and gold, $12\frac{7}{16} \times 4\frac{3}{4}$ (31.5 × 12) on paper $15\frac{11}{16} \times 10\frac{1}{4}$ (39.8 × 26).
> Inscr. 'JBasire ['JB' as monogram]. del.', 'Figure supposed to be that of King Sebert on the North front of his Tomb. Westmin.ʳ Abbey vide Vetutst [the second 't' crossed out]. Mon. Vol. II. pl. 33.' (now covered) and with dimensions, 'foot 2: I 8' wide and 'foot 7. I 2' high.
> *Society of Antiquaries of London*

The monument of Sebert or Sigebert, King of the East Angles (fl.637 A.D., a legendary convert to Christianity and founder of Westminster Abbey) was built *c*.1308. The paintings are perhaps by Thomas of Durham. The north side, like the tomb of Countess Aveline, was uncovered in summer 1775.

For the supposed signature of Basire see No.3. As the inscription states, an engraving after this drawing (probably also done by Blake) was included in Volume II of *Vetusta Monumenta*, 1789, as plate 33, having already been published in Ayloffe's *Account* in 1780. There are further drawings also attributed to Blake of the north side of the whole monument and also of details, as well as replicas among the Gough drawings in the Bodleian Library. See also No.5.

5

5   *Henry III, from the Wall-Painting above the Monument of King Sebert* 1775

> Pen, watercolour and gold, $12\frac{7}{16} \times 4\frac{3}{4}$ (31.5 × 12) on paper $15\frac{11}{16} \times 10\frac{1}{4}$ (39.8 × 26).
> Inscr. 'JBasire ['JB' as monogram]. del.', 'Figure supposed to be that of Henry III, as painted in the N. front of the Monument of King Sebert in Westmin.ʳ Abbey. Vetust. Mon. Vol. [cut by trimming of paper] (now covered) and with dimensions, 'foot 2: I 8' wide and 'foot 7. I 2' high.
> *Society of Antiquaries of London*

'Henry III' was presumably painted as a pendant to 'King Sebert' on account of his importance in the rebuilding of the Abbey. This drawing was engraved on the same plate as No.4, and again there is a replica among the Gough drawings in the Bodleian Library.

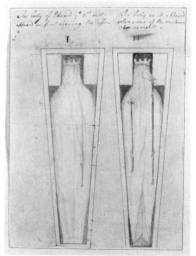

6

6   *The Body of Edward I in his Coffin: two rough drawings* 1774

> Pencil, each drawing approx. $6\frac{1}{2} \times 2\frac{1}{4}$ (16.5 × 5.5) on paper $7\frac{7}{8} \times 5\frac{5}{8}$ (20 × 14.3).
> Inscr. 'I The body of Edward yᵉ 1ˢᵗ as it appeared on first opening the Coffin', and 'II The body as it appeared when some of the vestmen[ts] were remov'd', and with the inside dimensions of the coffin, '6-7' long, '2-7' across at top, '1-10' across at bottom and '2-3' across half way down; the width of the coffin walls is given as '3'.
> *Society of Antiquaries of London*

According to the minutes of the Society of Antiquaries, the tomb of Edward I in Westminster Abbey was opened by Sir Joseph Ayloffe on 2 May 1774, 'In the Presence of a select Party, chiefly members of this Society'. Richard Gough was there and proposed that Basire should be present, but it was not thought necessary, 'so little did we expect to find what we did find'. The tomb was open for about an hour during which time Gough did some rough drawings of the king's sceptres. There were thus no official drawings of the body, but the style of the drawing, and the handwriting, support the possibility that Blake, working in the Abbey at the time, did these two sketches. See also No.7.

Ayloffe's account of the opening was published as a separate pamphlet and in *Archaelogia*, vol.III, 1786, pp.376–413, but without illustrations. This drawing follows his description closely. Ayloffe's account also includes such macabre details as that the corpse had turned 'a chocolate colour, approaching black. The chin and lips were intire, but without any beard'. The corpse was in good condition, having been specially preserved following Edward I's death on a campaign against the Scots.

7

7   *The Body of Edward I in his Coffin: two finished drawings* c.1774

Pen and sepia wash, each drawing approx. $4\frac{1}{2} \times 7\frac{3}{4}$ (11.5 × 19.5) on paper $9\frac{5}{16} \times 17\frac{15}{16}$ (23.6 × 45.6).
Inscr. 'Scale of 7 feet' and '1' up to '7'.
Society of Antiquaries of London

Although Ayloffe's account of the opening of Edward I's coffin was published without illustrations, these may have been planned. In any case this drawing, based on No.6, is typical of the finished drawings produced in Basire's studio and is close to the tomb drawings attributed to Blake. The artist has added detailed drawings of the two sceptres, presumably based on the 'rude sketches . . . scrawled' by Richard Gough at the time.

8   *Academy Study* c.1779–80

Black chalk, $18\frac{7}{8} \times 14\frac{9}{16}$ (47.9 × 37).
Trustees of the British Museum, London

This life study is usually accepted as having been done during Blake's period of study at the Royal Academy, 1779–80. It may well be, as has been suggested, a study of Blake's younger brother Robert or even of himself, but there is no evidence for this.

8

9   *Study for 'Albion Rose' or 'Glad Day'* c.1780

Pencil on paper, irregular, $8\frac{1}{8} \times 11\frac{3}{8}$ (20.6 × 28.8).
Victoria and Albert Museum, London

This is the first stage in the evolution of the famous design commonly known as 'Glad Day' though more correctly, on account of the inscription on the engraving, as 'Albion Rose' or 'The Dance of Albion'. On the back is a drawing of the same figure seen from behind (fig.1).

This is a case where one has to treat Blake's own dating with caution. The only known uncoloured state of the engraving is signed, on the only surviving untrimmed copy, 'WB inv 1780' (see No.11), but the technique and the reference to Albion in the caption below the print suggests a date considerably later, say *c.*1800. Presumably the date '1780' refers either to an earlier state of the engraving, now lost, or to the original conception of the figure, i.e. this drawing.

The pose of the figure is derived from the famous 'Vitruvian Figure', used by the Roman architect Vitruvius and Renaissance followers such as Vincenzo Scamozzi to demonstrate the proportions of the human figure. In these diagrams, the figure stands within a circle, itself within a measured-out square: man is shown as the measure of a mathematically proportioned universe. This is a concept that places Blake right in the midstream of the humanist, rational, academic tradition, however much he might later rebel against its restricted vision. It has been further suggested that this drawing, showing the front and the back of the same figure, may be based on an eighteenth-century engraving after a bronze statuette of a fawn found at Herculaneum. Again such a dependence on an Antique would be nothing unusual for a late eighteenth-century art student.

Even apart from its reappearance as a colour print and as a later engraving (see Nos. 10 and 11), this figure was to recur throughout Blake's later works as a motif of ecstasy (see Nos. 272 and 274). In such cases, the precise source is less important than the fact that Blake, like his contemporaries, was using a common language of expressive formulae, using not just facial expression (as in Le Brun's famous plates, so despised by Blake when he was an Academy student) but the whole body.

In its later form, the design has parallels in Blake's poems *Milton* and *Jerusalem*. Here, the image can be related to Blake's dramatic fragment 'King Edward the Third', published in his *Poetical Sketches* in 1783; these sketches, however, were published as 'the production of untutored youth, commenced in his twelfth, and occasionally resumed by the author till his twentieth year', i.e. c.1769–77:

> Good morrow, brave Sir Thomas; the bright morn
> Smiles on your army, and the gallant sun
> Springs from the hills like a young hero
> Into the battle, shaking his golden locks
> Exultingly; this is a promising day.

Thus Blake was able to use a traditional motive derived from Antiquity in a design related to his interest in English history, here paralleling a dramatic poem in which he would have seen himself as the heir of Shakespeare. The image can thus be seen as absolutely central in Blake's consciousness as an artist.

Fig. 1 William Blake
Reverse of Study for 'Albion Rose'
*or 'Glad Day', c.*1780 (No.9)
(Victoria and Albert Museum)

10   *Albion Rose or Glad Day* c.1795

Colour-printed line engraving finished in pen and watercolour,
$10\frac{13}{16} \times 7\frac{15}{16}$ (27.5 × 20.2) on paper $13\frac{5}{8} \times 9\frac{11}{16}$ (34.5 × 24.6).
Trustees of the British Museum, London

This colour-printed version of the composition comes from the so-called 'Large Book of Designs'; the only other known colour-printed copy, in the Huntington Library, is watermarked 1794. Thus this version is paradoxically earlier than the only known copies of the print uncoloured, supporting the probability that there was an earlier, now untraced state of the engraving probably dating from 1780 (see Nos.9 and 11).

11   *Albion Rose or Glad Day* c.1805

Line engraving, $10 \times 7\frac{3}{8}$ (25.3 × 18.8); plate-mark
$10\frac{3}{4} \times 7\frac{3}{4}$ (27.2 × 19.7).
Inscr. 'WB inv 1780' and with traces of the inscription known from the only known untrimmed copy of the print, 'Albion rose from where he labourd at the Mill with Slaves'/'Giving himself For the Nations he dancd the dance of Eternal Death'.
Trustees of the British Museum, London

The complete inscription is only found on the copy of the print in the Rosenwald Collection; traces of the first two letters 'Al' can just be seen at the bottom of this example. Despite the date '1780' the reference to Albion has no parallels in Blake's writings until the late 1790s, and the closest parallels, identifying Albion with the personality and people of England and making reference to the 'Satanic Mill', are in his poems *Milton*, c.1804–8 and *Jerusalem*, c.1804–20. Technically, the engraving also fits better with the works of c.1805. The bold outlining of the forms of the

10

11

figure, set against the linear conventions used to indicate the sky, **represents a major step beyond the great virtuosity but conventionality of** the use of various linear patterns all over the entire surface of the large 'Job' and 'Ezekiel' prints of the mid 1790s (Nos. 32 and 33). The date therefore presumably refers to an earlier state, or to Blake's original drawing, No. 9.

The risen Albion stands with one foot on the worm, a symbol of materialism, while a bat-winged spirit of evil flies away. The 'dance of Eternal Death' and the pose refer with typically complex meaning to the Crucifixion as the Christian Triumph (again a concept only developed in Blake's writings in the later 1790s, perhaps in part reflecting his encounter with the term in Young's *Night Thoughts* which he illustrated in 1795-7).

12 *Warring Angels: Michael Contending with Satan* c.1780-85

Pen and grey wash over pencil, $9\frac{1}{2} \times 13$ (24.2 × 33).
Bolton Museum and Art Gallery

This drawing, which only turned up in 1976, is one of four related sketches, eventually used by Blake for one of his illustrations to Young's *Night Thoughts*, c.1795-7; see No.121. However, only the fragmentary drawing in the British Museum can be as late as the 1790s. This example, like that from the Graham Robertson collection and that now in the Philadelphia Museum, is typical of a whole group of drawings of the late 1770s and early 1780s. The use of pen and wash in this way, ultimately derived from sixteenth-century Italian artists and from Poussin, was common to the imaginative Neo-Classical British artists among whom Blake grew up, for instance Flaxman, Fuseli and Romney (see figs. 2 and 3).

Despite its eventual use in the *Night Thoughts* illustration, the composition, of which this drawing represents the third known stage, probably began as an illustration to Milton's *Paradise Lost* (in this case to Book VI), as did a number of other composition studies of this time. In fact, Blake's drawings of the early 1780s anticipate many of his later preoccupations; for *Paradise Lost* see Nos. 216-30.

13 *Young Woman Reclining on a Couch* c.1780-85

Pen and grey wash over pencil, irregular, $9 \times 13\frac{3}{8}$
(22.8 × 33.9).
Private collection, England

The graceful but serious figure wears a delicate crown and writes in a book, but the exact subject is unknown. This is another of the group of early pen and wash drawings, and is particularly close to several that deal with themes of mortality anticipating Blake's later illustrations to Young's *Night Thoughts* and Blair's *The Grave*.

12

Fig. 2 George Romney, *The Rape of Kunaza*, c.1785-90 (Fitzwilliam Museum, Cambridge)

Fig. 3 John Flaxman, *Three Air-borne Figures* (Fitzwilliam Museum, Cambridge)

14 *Abias, Copy after Michelangelo* c.1780–85

> Pen and wash, irregular, $6\frac{1}{2} \times 4\frac{5}{8}$ (16.5 × 11.7) on paper
> $9\frac{5}{8} \times 6\frac{7}{8}$ (24.4 × 17.4).
> Inscr. on the back by Frederick Tatham, 'Drawn by Blake from the
> print by Michael Angelo vouched by Fred^k Tatham'.
> *Trustees of the British Museum, London*

13

One of seven copies from Giorgio Ghisi's engravings after figures, mainly of the Ancestors of Christ, from Michelangelo's frescoes on the ceiling of the Sistine Chapel. Like his friend Fuseli, Blake at this time probably admired Michelangelo as an exponent of the more emotional, Dionysiac element in classical art, deriving from such things as the 'Laocoön' group (see No.315); in this he differed from the strict Academicians on the one hand, who saw Michelangelo as a disturbing influence, and the extreme Neo-Classicists on the other, who looked to Antique art for restraint and purity of expression. Michelangelo, as known through engravings, was always a strong influence on Blake's figures and even in some cases on his compositions (see Nos.211–13) though what would have happened had Blake himself ever visited Italy and seen the originals is difficult to imagine (such a trip nearly occurred: in 1784 John Hawkins of Cornwall was 'so convinced of his uncommon talents that he is now endeavouring to raise a subscription to send him to finish his studies in Rome'; see Chronology p.157).

Like many of his early figure studies, this one remained in Blake's repertoire and, transformed with a new energy but still representative (as in the original Michelangelo conception of the Ancestors of Christ) of a twilight zone in Man's evolution, reappeared in the famous colour print of 'Newton', No.92.

14

15 *Aminadab, Copy after Michelangelo: The Reposing Traveller* c.1780–85

> Pen and wash, irregular, $5\frac{13}{16} \times 3\frac{3}{4}$ (14.5 × 9.5) on paper
> $9\frac{5}{8} \times 6\frac{13}{16}$ (24.4 × 17.3).
> Inscr. 'The Reposing Traveller', and by Frederick Tatham, 'Blakes
> writing & Drawing', and, also by Tatham on the other side, 'drawn
> by William Blake from Michael Angelo vouched by Fred^k Tatham'.
> *Trustees of the British Museum, London*

Another of the copies from Ghisi's engravings after the Sistine Chapel ceiling. Blake however did not copy merely to establish an expressive figure style. In this case he also placed the figure within the context of his own ideas: the Traveller was his image for the artist, searching for enlightenment through experience. A similar transformation occurred, though probably as a later afterthought, to another of his copies after Michelangelo, the engraving after a figure from the 'Crucifixion of St. Peter' in the Cappella Paolina. First 'Engraved when I was a beginner at Basires', c.1773, it was later reissued with the retrospective date '1773' and the caption, 'This is one of the Gothic Artists who Built the Cathedrals in what we call the Dark Ages...'; this second state probably dates from c.1810. It is probably not too fanciful to suggest that Blake saw Michelangelo's Aminadab, one of the Ancestors of Christ in the twilight zone of the Sistine Chapel lunettes, as the searching artist in repose; as compared with the Ghisi engraving the figure is given a new alertness of pose and gaze.

16 *The Penance of Jane Shore* c.1779

> Pen and watercolour over pencil, irregular, $5\frac{1}{4} \times 7\frac{1}{4}$
> (13.3 × 18.4).
> *Mrs S. Caird*

Either this early watercolour or the later, larger version (No.17) was included by Blake in his exhibition of 1809–10 with the note, 'This

15

16

Fig.4 after Gavin Hamilton, *Andromache Bewailing the Death of Hector*, engr. by Cunego 1764 (British Museum)

Fig.5 Benjamin West, *Cleombrotus Ordered into Banishment by Leonidas II, King of Sparta*, 1768 (Tate Gallery)

17

Drawing was done above Thirty Years ago, and proves to the Author, and he thinks will prove to any discerning eye, that the productions of our youth and of our maturer age are equal in all essential points.' Both Gilchrist, in his *Life of William Blake*, 1863, and William Rossetti, in his list catalogue in volume II of the same book, assume that it was the later version that was shown, in which case Blake was being rather disingenuous. Certainly, although the existence of the two versions demonstrates that an early composition could remain valid for Blake in later years, the smaller watercolour is hardly equal to the other in quality.

The date suggested by the *Descriptive Catalogue* to Blake's exhibition is reinforced by the fact that this is one of about ten similar small watercolours of English history, one of which, 'The Death of Earl Goodwin' now in the British Museum, was either exhibited by Blake at the Royal Academy in 1780 or was a sketch for that exhibit. The series includes such legendary events as 'The Landing of Trojan Brutus in England' and 'Lear and Cordelia in Prison' (Tate Gallery; Blake is here illustrating history rather than, directly, Shakespeare), but is remarkable for the emphasis on moral virtues rather than deeds of glory. In fact, Blake seems deliberately to have chosen certain episodes the historical accuracy of which had been doubted by eighteenth-century historians. An example is 'The Death of Earl Goodwin', seen as a divine judgment for Goodwin's false denial of complicity in the death of Edward the Confessor's brother Alfred.

Similarly, 'The Penance of Jane Shore' illustrates the victory of innocence over despotic power. Jane Shore, the mistress of Edward IV, was noted for her beauty and goodness, but on Edward's death in 1483 she was imprisoned and accused of harlotry by the future Richard III. Condemned to do penance in St. Paul's, she was taken there in a white sheet, a wax taper in her hand. However, 'she behaved with so much modesty and decency, that such as respected her Beauty more than her fault, never were in greater admiration of her, than now' (so wrote the eighteenth-century historian Rapin de Thoyras).

In style, this watercolour is an immature essay in the manner of Neo-Classical history painting, developed by Gavin Hamilton in Rome in the 1760s and introduced to England by Benjamin West in such works as the Tate Gallery's 'Cleombrotus' of 1768 (fig.5). That Blake, while putting on record his admiration for the more imaginative Neo-Classical history paintings of James Barry, John Hamilton Mortimer and Henry Fuseli, never referred to West save once, in passing, nor to Hamilton, probably reflects his later aversion to the negative aspects of the stricter forms of the movement, and also to the fact that West, painter to the King and later President of the Royal Academy, represented the establishment.

This drawing seems to have entered the possession of the Verney family by the 1860s, perhaps as a wedding present from the Richmond family.

17 *The Penance of Jane Shore* c.1793(?)

Pen and watercolour, sized, $9\frac{5}{8} \times 11\frac{5}{8}$ (24.5 × 29.5).
Tate Gallery, London

See No.16. This version of the composition is inscribed on the back by Henry Cunliffe, who bought it at the sale on 29 April 1862 of Mrs Blake's *de facto* executor, Frederick Tatham, who inherited all that remained from Blake's studio. When the old heavy varnish was removed in 1972, it was found that the watercolour had been covered with a thin, much more translucent layer of size, a practice quite common in the late eighteenth and early nineteenth centuries. Gilchrist assumed that Blake was responsible, and it could possibly have been done at the time of his exhibition, in 1809, to give the watercolour greater presence.

The title 'The Penance of Jane Shore' appears in a list of titles from English history written in Blake's Notebook about 1793, at which time Blake was planning to publish 'The History of England, a small book of

Engravings'. That the Tate watercolour could date from about this time is suggested by its closeness in style to the engraving of 1793 of 'Edward and Elenor' (No.18). It certainly represents an immense advance in accomplishment from the tentative watercolour of *c.*1779. A pencil drawing in an English private collection shows Blake reworking the composition for the later version, which also suggests that a considerable time had elapsed.

18 *Edward and Elenor* 1793

Line engraving, 12⅛ × 18½ (30.8 × 45.9); plate-mark
14⅝ × 20⅜ (37.7 × 51.8).
Inscr. 'EDWARD & ELENOR', 'Painted and Engraved by William Blake' and 'Published 18th August 1793 by W Blake No 13 Hercules Buildings Lambeth.'
Trustees of the British Museum, London

This was listed in Blake's *Prospectus* of 1793 as 'Edward and Elinor [*sic*], a Historical Engraving, Size 1 ft. 6½in. by 1 ft. : price 10*s*. 6*d*.' In style, this is close to the watercolours of 'Jane Shore' and 'Queen Emma' (Nos.17 and 19), but in its conservative Neo-Classical composition, lacking the weight of the 'Job' and 'Ezekiel' engravings (Nos.31–3), it may derive, like the 'Jane Shore', from an earlier composition of *c.*1779–80. The composition is particularly close to that of John Hamilton Mortimer's 'Vortigern and Rowena', exhibited in 1779 (fig.6).

The subject is another example of female virtue. Eleanor of Castile accompanied her husband Prince Edward, later Edward I, to the Holy Land, where he was stabbed in the arm with a poisoned dagger by an assassin disguised as a Christian. Eleanor is traditionally said to have saved her husband's life by sucking the poison from the wound.

Fig.6 John Hamilton Mortimer
Vortigern and Rowena, exh. 1779
(Private collection)

19 *The Ordeal of Queen Emma* c.1793(?)

Pen and watercolour, 11⅞ × 18½ (30.2 × 47).
Private collection, England

Like No.17, this remained in Blake's possession and passed after his death to Frederick Tatham and thence to Henry Cunliffe and W. Graham Robertson. Similarly, it seems to be a product of Blake's return to subjects from English history in about 1793. Almost exactly the same size as the engraving of 'Edward and Elenor' (No.18), it too was perhaps intended to be engraved.

Like Jane Shore, Queen Emma was popularly set up as an example of the woman unjustly accused by a royal tyrant, in this case her son, Edward the Confessor. According to Rapin de Thoyras, 'Besides his hatred to Goodwin and his own Wife, he cherished in his Breast against his Mother a desire of Revenge, which agreed no better with the Maxims of the Gospel', and accused her of adultery and complicity with Earl Goodwin in the murder of his brother Alfred. The trial 'consisted in obliging the Party accus'd to walk bare-foot and hood-wink'd over nine red-hot Plough-shares'. Needless to say, the Queen emerged unscathed.

Blake the Neo-Classicist, c.1780–90

The climax of Blake's early development as an artist occurred in the middle of the 1780s. His early tentative attempts at Neo-Classical history painting, coupled with his practice of drawing in pen outlines, finished with wash, culminated in a group of powerful designs with large-scale figures, controlled by great sweeping outlines and arranged in relief-like compositions. Three watercolours dealing with the story of Joseph in Egypt were exhibited at the Royal Academy in 1785 (Nos.28–30; these, with a lost picture of Gray's *Bard*, represent Blake's most ambitious attempt to make his mark at the Academy). Similar in style and probably from more or less the same time are the preliminary drawings and first states of Blake's two massive engravings of Job and Ezekiel, even grander and more powerful than the 'Joseph' watercolours; amazingly, reworking ten years later strengthened these designs still further (see Nos.31–3).

These illustrations to the Bible were supplemented, in the form of two lost exhibits of 1784, by two rather more personal subjects dealing with the horrors of war; these were compositions which preoccupied Blake for twenty-five years, from tentative beginnings in about 1780 up to a group of watercolours of 1805 (see Nos.20–26). This reworking of a composition over a long period is typical of Blake's art; it is also useful in that comparison of the various versions demonstrates the development of Blake's style and abilities.

Probably from towards the end of the 1780s date the first series of illustrations to Blake's own writings, the wash drawings of subjects from his poem *Tiriel*, which is usually dated about 1789. Certain examples such as No.41 have something of the scale and monumentality of the mid-1780s; others, such as No.40, closer in detail to the texts they illustrate,

display the tighter more delicate style that characterises much of Blake's work in the later 1780s and early 1790s. This more intimate style had grown up beside the other, partly as a result of Blake's activities as a commercial engraver, reflecting another aspect of Neo-Classicism, the French inspired 'sensibility' of such artists as Angelica Kauffmann and Blake's friend Thomas Stothard; this accorded with the mood of much of Blake's early lyrical poetry. An obvious source of this aspect of Blake's early style is his own engravings after Watteau and Stothard (see Nos.37–8). These are reflected both in the more decorative of the *Tiriel* illustrations and in certain small jewel-like, highly coloured watercolours of the same period such as 'Age Teaching Youth' (No.39). The style also characterised the illustrations of Blake's first illuminated books (see Nos.42–6).

Fig.7 Nicholas Poussin, *The Death of Germanicus*, c.1627 (Minneapolis Institute of Arts)

20

20 Sketch for 'War Unchained by an Angel, Fire, Pestilence, and Famine Following' c.1780–84

Pen and indian ink, 7 × 8 11/16 (17.7 × 22.1).
Inscr., probably not by Blake, 'June 1783'.
Steigal Fine Art, Edinburgh

This drawing, typical of Blake's pen and wash drawings of the first half of the 1780s, seems to be a sketch for the lost 'War unchained by an Angel...' exhibited at the Royal Academy in 1784, and was itself lost until a few years ago. Also at the Academy in 1784 was a presumed companion, also untraced, though known in three later versions, of 'A Breach in a City, the Morning after the Battle.' 'War unchained by an Angel' does not seem to have been treated again after 1784, but 'Pestilence' was a recurrent theme in Blake's work from c.1779 to 1805 (see Nos.21–5), while 'Fire' and 'Famine' reappear as separate watercolours in 1805 (see No.26). The theme of war and its consequences obviously obsessed Blake during these years and is also, of course, an important theme in his Prophetic Books in the 1790s.

On the back, completely unrelated, are studies of a child done in preparation for Malkin's *Memoirs of his Child*, 1806.

21 *Pestilence: The Great Plague of London* c.1779–80

    Pen and watercolour, $5\frac{7}{16} \times 7\frac{5}{16}$ (13.8×18.6).

    Signed (?) 'WB' and inscr. 'Lord have m^{er} ['mercy'] on us' on door.

    Steigal Fine Art, Edinburgh

This watercolour, which only turned up in Scotland a few years ago, is one of the early series devoted to the History of England (see No. 16), and is also the first of a series of developments of the composition which occupied Blake up to 1805 (see Nos.22–5). It is fascinating to see that this theme, which became such an obsession with Blake, was first treated purely as an historical incident. Not only is this watercolour one of the group of early historical watercolours, but the title 'The Plague' appears in the list of historical subjects that Blake wrote in his Notebook in about 1793, following 'The Penance of Jane Shore' (see No.17) and immediately preceding 'The fire of London'.

    Motives from this watercolour also recur on plate 7 of Blake's illuminated book *Europe* of 1794: the Bellman, the door inscribed 'LORD HAVE MERC[Y] ON US' and the young man supporting the girl on the left.

22 *Pestilence* c.1780–84

    Pen and watercolour, approx. $7\frac{1}{4} \times 10\frac{3}{4}$ (18.5×27.5).

    Robert N. Essick

In 1784, Blake exhibited two watercolours of similar subjects at the Royal Academy, 'War unchained by an Angel, Fire, Pestilence, and Famine Following' (see No. 20) and 'A Breach in a City, the Morning after the Battle'. The actual exhibits seem to be untraced, though versions of both are known. This version of 'Pestilence', which only reappeared in 1976, probably dates from much the same time or slightly earlier, fairly soon after No.21 which it follows in nearly all details.

23 *Pestilence* c.1790–5

    Pen and watercolour, $12\frac{7}{16} \times 18\frac{15}{16}$ (31.6×48.1).

    Inscr. 'Pestilence'; a note on the back identifies this as one of the works bought by Lord Cunliffe at the Tatham sale in 1862.

    Bateson Collection

This is a largely new treatment of the subject of Nos.21 and 22, done as a companion to a version of 'A Breach in a City, the Morning after a Battle', now in the Carnegie Institute, Pittsburgh. The word 'Pestilence' seems to have been added in a different ink, suggesting that this watercolour preceded No.24. However, though the order in which these works were painted seems clear, the datings suggested here, though supported by comparison with other works, are partly notional.

24 *Pestilence* c.1795–1800

    Pen and watercolour, $12\frac{11}{16} \times 19\frac{1}{16}$ (32.2×48.4).

    Signed 'W Blake inv$d$' and inscr. 'Pestilence'.

    Bristol City Art Gallery

The inscribed title 'Pestilence' seems less of an afterthought than that on No.23 and the composition is slightly more advanced: fewer of the figures are seen in full profile, their features are more sharply defined and the third body on the right is distinctly shown. Again there is a companion version of 'A Breach in a City', now at the University of North Carolina, Chapel Hill.

25 *Pestilence* c.1805

    Pen and watercolour over pencil, $11\frac{7}{8} \times 17$ (31.2×43).

    Museum of Fine Arts, Boston, Mass.

The final, definitive version of the composition, painted for Blake's most important patron Thomas Butts. This time, the design is not paired with 'A Breach in a City', but is one of a set of four, with 'Fire', 'War' and 'Famine',

25

26

Fig.8 after Raphael
The Fire in the Borgo,
engraving by Volpato
(Victoria and Albert Museum)

all from the Butts collection and the last two of which are dated '1805' (Pierpont Morgan Library (No.26), Fogg Museum and Boston Museum respectively); 'War' is however a version of the composition of 'A Breach in a City', first exhibited in 1784. These four watercolours, though sometimes taken to have biblical references and to be part of the series of illustrations to the Bible done for Butts at the same time, are more likely to form a distinct group, developed from the non-biblical works of the 1780s. The Mosaic 'Pestilence' is, in fact, the subject of another watercolour that is from the Bible series (see No.163).

The style is much crisper and less atmospheric than the versions here dated to the 1790s, representing a return to Neo-Classicism, though now in a completely personal manner.

26 *Fire* c.1805

Pen and watercolour, $12\frac{7}{8} \times 16\frac{7}{8}$ (31.7 × 42.8).
Signed 'WB'.
Pierpont Morgan Library, New York, Gift of Mrs. Landon K. Thorne
With No.25, this is one of the four watercolours of the consequences of war painted for Thomas Butts c.1805; see also No.20. There are echoes of, though no specific derivations from, Raphael's fresco of 'The Fire in the Borgo' in the Stanza dell'Incendio in the Vatican (fig.8).

27 *The Witch of Endor Raising the Spirit of Samuel* 1783

Pen and watercolour, $11\frac{1}{8} \times 16\frac{5}{8}$ (28.3 × 42.3).
Signed '1783 W Blake inv' and inscr. 'The witch of Endor raising the Spirit of Samuel'; an inscription on the back identifies this as one of the works bought by Henry Cunliffe at the Tatham sale in 1862.
New York Public Library, Prints Division, Astor, Lenox and Tilden Foundations
1 Samuel 28:8, 12–20. Saul, frightened at the prospect of his forthcoming battle against the Philistines, goes in disguise to the Witch of Endor who summons up the ghost of Samuel; Samuel prophesies his defeat and death, whereupon 'Saul fell straightway all along on the earth, and was sore afraid'.

This dated work of 1783 helps to document Blake's increasingly accomplished Neo-Classicism. The curving draperies of the Witch of Endor are particularly close to the Greek vase paintings and reliefs that Blake had copied from d'Hancarville's *Cabinet de M. Hamilton* (Sir William Hamilton's collection) 1766–7 (Blake's copies are in the British Museum) and was later to engrave for his friend George Cumberland's *Thoughts on Outline*, 1796. The composition also contains elements from Raphael's fresco of 'Abraham and the Three Angels' in the Vatican Loggie, which Blake had engraved for *The Protestants Family Bible*, 1780–81. For a later watercolour of the same subject see No.169.

28 *Joseph's Brethren Bowing Before Him* Exh.1785
29 *Joseph Ordering Simeon to be Bound* Exh.1785
30 *Joseph Making Himself Known to his Brethren* Exh.1785

Pen and watercolour over pencil, each approx. $15\frac{15}{16} \times 22\frac{1}{16}$ (40.5 × 56).
Syndics of the Fitzwilliam Museum, Cambridge
Genesis 42: 3, 6–8. Genesis 42: 18–19, 24. Genesis 45: 1–4, 14. Joseph, having been sold into slavery by his brethren, eventually becomes governor of Egypt, whither his brethren come to buy corn in time of famine. They do not recognise Joseph but he, knowing them, accuses them of spying and detains Simeon pending the arrival of his youngest brother

Benjamin who had been left behind in Canaan. When they return Joseph finally, after further trials, reveals himself to them and falls weeping on Benjamin's neck.

Joseph's gift of prophecy had resulted in his being sold into slavery and Blake may well have been specially interested in the story of his revealing himself to his uncomprehending brethren. The setting, Egypt, was later if not already to be seen by him as the epitome of materialism in which, however, first Joseph, then Moses and finally Christ were nurtured.

Blake's Neo-Classicism is here seen at its strictest, closer to Antique reliefs and to the works of his friend John Flaxman than to West, Mortimer or even Barry. The poses of Joseph in the first and third watercolour have well-known Antique prototypes. The quality of Blake's line is already fully apparent, albeit in a rather impersonal manner.

These pictures may actually have been sold when they were exhibited at the Royal Academy in 1785. After a gap of some sixty-five years they turned up romantically 'at a broker's in Wardour Street, who had purchased them at a furniture sale in the neighbourhood' (so writes Gilchrist). They were then sold by 'An Old Established Printseller' (Walter E. Tiffin) at Sotheby's and by 1862 belonged to Lord Coleridge. Their original freshness of colour has recently been revealed by cleaning at the Fitzwilliam Museum. There are sketches for 'Joseph ordering Simeon to be bound' and 'Joseph making himself known to his Brethren' in an Italian private collection and in the Royal Collection at Windsor respectively.

The Complaint of Job

31 **First State** c.1786
32 **Second State** 1793
    Line engraving, $13\frac{11}{16} \times 19\frac{7}{16}$ (34.8 × 49.4); plate mark $18\frac{1}{8} \times 21\frac{1}{4}$ (46 × 54).
    Inscr. (No.31) 'Painted and Engraved by William Blake' and 'JOB'; there are traces of a further line or lines below but these have been trimmed; (No.32) 'Painted and Engraved by William Blake', 'JOB', 'What is Man That thou shouldest Try him Every Moment? Job vii C17 & 18v' and 'Published 18 August 1793 by W. Blake No 13 Hercules Buildings Lambeth' (last line is covered by mount).
    Private collection, England

Job 7: 17–18. Job, having lost his children and his possessions, and having been smitten with sore boils, asks God for justification: 'What is man that thou shouldest . . . try him every moment?' The theme of Job's sufferings was later to be illustrated by Blake in two series of watercolours and one of engravings, see Nos.191–204.

Despite arguments to the contrary, the first state of this engraving seems to date from the mid-1780s; more powerful still than the 'Joseph' watercolours exhibited in 1785, it is notionally dated *c.*1786. Three preliminary drawings are typical of Blake's pen and wash technique of the first half of the 1780s (Tate Gallery; untraced since Sotheby's sale, 17 December 1928, lot 138; De Young Memorial Museum, San Francisco).

The second state of the engraving, for which it seems reasonable, in this instance, to accept Blake's given date of '1793', strengthens the drama both by additional motives such as the lightning and the tears now streaming down Job's cheeks and by increasing the contrasts of light and texture. The head of Job has been given greater prominence by being re-engraved to make it wider. The increased drama stresses the tendency already apparent in the first state to move beyond the highly controlled classicism of the Joseph watercolours; here the influence can be felt of the more imaginative of Blake's contemporaries, Fuseli and, even more, Barry (see fig.9).

Both states are magnificent examples of Blake's exploitation of the conventions of traditional engraving techniques, to a certain extent

Fig.9 James Barry, *King Lear Weeping over the Dead Body of Cordelia*, 1786–8 (Tate Gallery)

embodying the 'absurd Nonsense about dots and Lozenges & Clean Strokes' that Blake was later to criticise in his draft 'Public Address' on 'The Canterbury Pilgrims', *c*.1810 (but these were even more apparent in the work of fashionable engravers such as Woollett and Schiavonetti). The second state almost parodies the technique in its extravagant contrasts of tones and textures.

33 *The Death of Ezekiel's Wife* c.1786/1794

Line engraving, $14 \times 18\frac{15}{16}$ (35.5×48.1); platemark $18\frac{5}{16} \times 21\frac{7}{16}$ (46.5×54.5).
Inscr. 'Painted & Engraved by W Blake', 'EZEKIEL.', 'I take away from thee the Desire of thine Eyes, Ezekiel xxiv c 16' and 'Published October 27 1794 by W Blake N° 13 Hercules Buildings Lambeth' (last line is covered by mount).
Private collection, England

Ezekiel 24: 15–18. Ezekiel, having that morning preached the Lord's command neither to mourn nor weep for the dead, is faced by his own wife's death the same evening.

Companion to the second state of 'The Complaint of Job', No.32. That there was probably an earlier state of the 'Ezekiel' print, paralleling that of the 'Job', is suggested by the existence of preparatory drawings similar in style and character to those for the 'Job' (private collection, USA; Philadelphia Museum).

The power of this design is even greater than that of the second state of the 'Job' engraving; the next year, 1795, was to see the magnificent series of large colour prints which match this design in impact but in a much more personal manner. Here the power is achieved through a very disciplined composition: the figures are either full-face or in profile and are held together by a very strict rectilinear framework. As in the case of 'The Complaint of Job', the restraint of the composition throws into higher relief the expressive quality of the protagonist's face, the hands, and the folds of the draperies.

34 *Macbeth and the Ghost of Banquo* c.1785

Pencil, irregular, $14\frac{7}{8} \times 20\frac{9}{16}$ (37.8×52.2).
Private collection, England

Macbeth, Act III, scene 4. The Ghost of Banquo, murdered at Macbeth's orders, appears seated in his place at the banquet to which Macbeth had invited him. Macbeth stands aghast on the left, with Lady Macbeth seated behind him. Blake seems to have identified himself as Banquo, whose profile is remarkably like his own.

This bold, large-scale drawing, with the dramatic effect of Macbeth's hands upraised with spread fingers, is close in impact and in manner of composition to the large print of Ezekiel, the only known state of which is dated 1794, but which is almost certainly based on a drawing of *c*.1786 (see Nos.31–3).

On the back is an earlier drawing, *c*.1780, of an unidentified historical subject.

35 *The Approach of Doom* c.1787–90

Relief etching, $11\frac{11}{16} \times 8\frac{1}{4}$ (29.7×21).
Trustees of the British Museum, London

This extraordinarily bold engraving, such a contrast to the equally imposing but highly finished 'Job' and 'Ezekiel' prints, Nos.31–3, is probably one of Blake's first experiments in relief etching, used mainly by Blake for his illuminated books (see p.44). Blake exploits the technique to produce even greater contrasts of tone, making the figures stand out far more clearly. His claim that the technique was revealed to him by his dead brother Robert in a vision is, in a sense, supported here by the fact that the

10 *Albion Rose or Glad Day,* c.1795 (entry on p.31)

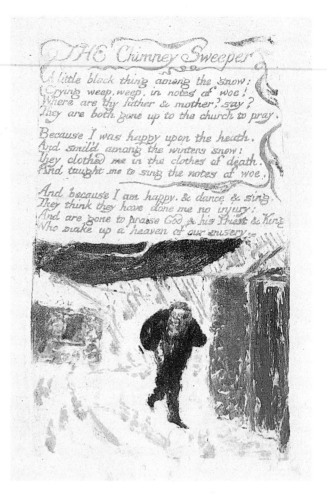

composition is based on one of his brother's drawings, No. 36. The copper plate from which this was printed was cut up and used by Blake again for *Urizen*, 1794 (see No. 82); the backs of these fragments seem already to have been used for *The Marriage of Heaven and Hell*, including some of the earlier pages etched in 1790. 'The Approach of Doom' was therefore presumably engraved between Robert Blake's death in February 1787 and 1790. The title 'The Approach of Doom' is not Blake's or his brother's and one cannot be sure whether there is any specific subject.

This unique copy of the print was acquired by the British Museum, together with Robert Blake's drawing, from H. H. Gilchrist, the son of Blake's biographer Alexander Gilchrist.

ROBERT BLAKE (1767(?)–1787)

36 *The Approach of Doom* c. 1785

Pen and sepia wash, $13\frac{3}{16} \times 18\frac{11}{16}$ (33.5 × 47.5).
Trustees of the British Museum, London

This drawing by William's brother Robert was developed by William in his engraving, No. 35. Robert was William's youngest and favourite brother. He is presumably the Robert Blake who entered the Royal Academy Schools in April 1782, when his birthdate was recorded as 4 August 1767, though he could just possibly have been an otherwise unrecorded brother noted, as 'Richard', as having been born on 19 June 1762. He died early in February 1787 at their parents' home in Broad Street, Golden Square, having been nursed by William who stayed by his bed for the last fortnight of his life; he was buried on 11 February.

Attributions to Robert depend on the descriptions of Alexander Gilchrist, who saw a group of Robert's drawings belonging to Frederick Tatham. He describes them as 'naif and archaic-looking; rude, faltering, often puerile or absurd in drawing; but . . . characterized by Blake-like feeling and intention. . . . True imaginative *animus* is often made manifest by very imperfect means'. Two of the drawings described by Gilchrist have been identified, this being one of them: 'a group of ancient men stand silent on the verge of a sea-girt precipice, beyond which they gaze towards awe-inspiring shapes and sights unseen by us. This last motive seems to have pleased Blake himself. One of his earlier attempts, if not his very earliest, in that peculiar stereotype process he soon afterwards invented, is a version of this very composition.'

After WATTEAU

37 *Morning Amusement* 1782

After WATTEAU

38 *Evening Amusement* 1782

Stipple engravings, each oval, approx. $9\frac{7}{8} \times 11\frac{7}{8}$ (25 × 30); platemarks $13 \times 14\frac{1}{4}$ (33 × 36).
Inscr. (No. 37) 'Watteau pinx!', 'W.. Blake sculp!', 'MORNING AMUSEMENT', 'From an Original Picture in the Collection of M.ʳ A.. Maskins', 'Pubᵈ August 10ᵗʰ 1782 by Thoˢ Macklin Nº 39 Fleet Street'; (No. 38) 'Watteau pinx!', 'W.. Blake fecit', 'EVENING AMUSEMENT', 'From an Original Picture in the Collection of M.ʳ A.. Maskin.', 'Pubᵈ as the Act directs August 21..1782 by T.. Macklin, Nº 39 Fleet Street.'
Private collection, England

Two examples of Blake's early commercial work, engraving for the print-sellers. In the 1780s Blake did similar reproductive prints after his friends Thomas Stothard and Richard Cosway and also after George Morland. Versions of the two Watteau paintings can be seen in the Wallace Collection.

37

38

39

39 *Age Teaching Youth* c.1785-90

Pen and watercolour, $4\frac{1}{4} \times 3\frac{1}{8}$ (10.8 × 8).
Tate Gallery, London

This delicate little watercolour with its jewel-like colouring probably dates from the later 1780s. The decorative pattern of the boy's garment is also found in some of the *Tiriel* illustrations such as No.41. In so far as one is justified in reading ideas expressed by Blake in his later writings into his early works, this watercolour may illustrate the subjection of the unfettered inspiration of youth to the restrictive book-learning imposed by the old. On the other hand, the parallel with the title page of *Songs of Innocence* (fig.10 on p.48) suggests that this is to read too much into an innocent scene.

40 *Tiriel Supporting the Dying Myratana and Cursing his Sons* c.1789

Pen and grey wash, $7\frac{5}{16} \times 10\frac{11}{16}$ (18.6 × 27.2)
Yale Center for British Art, New Haven, Connecticut (Paul Mellon Collection)

This is the first of twelve illustrations to *Tiriel*, which was apparently Blake's first verse prophecy; unpublished either in ordinary letterpress or Blake's illuminated printing, the manuscript, now in the British Library, is not even titled, Tiriel being the name of the chief protagonist. Nor is the date established, though the very fact that this series of finished wash drawings seems to anticipate normal engraved illustrations, at right-angles to the text, suggests that it dates from before the *Songs of Innocence* of 1789. The style of the illustrations seems to represent a certain relaxation after the monumental Neo-Classicism of the mid 1780s, which supports a date late in the decade.

The drawings are now dispersed, three being untraced. In the later nineteenth century at least four of the series, including this one, belonged to the Pre-Raphaelite collector James Leathart.

The blind Tiriel is a rather Lear-like character, expelled from his palace by his sons. An important stage in his redemption is when he asks the Blakean question,

Why is one law given to the lion and the patient Ox
Dost thou not see that men cannot be all alike,

an anticipation of the maxim 'One Law for the Lion & Ox is Oppression' in *The Marriage of Heaven and Hell*, 1790-93. In this scene Tiriel returns to his palace with his dying wife Myratana and curses his sons for causing her death, to which Heuxos, the eldest, replies,

His blessing was a cruel curse. His curse may be a blessing.

The pyramids, which came to signify for Blake the oppression of Pharaonic despotic tyranny, are not in the text but are a typical gloss by which Blake used his illustration to supplement the imagery of his verses. Similarly with the attributes of the three sons: the crown of Heuxos, King of the West, the embodiment of material power, the laurel wreath of the second son, apparently representing poetry, and the vine leaves of the third, representing sensual pleasures, all in the debased state brought about by Man's division in the Fallen World.

41 *Har and Heva Asleep with Mnetha* c.1789

Pen and grey wash, $7\frac{1}{2} \times 10\frac{15}{16}$ (19 × 27.8).
Private collection, England

Another of the illustrations to *Tiriel*. Har and Heva, Tiriel's parents, and Mnetha, his grandmother, inhabit an earthly paradise, the Vales of Har, in a state of unenlightened innocence. The name Mnetha probably derives from Mnemosyne, the Greek goddess of memory, and Har and Heva probably represent a limited vision of art based on memory, art breeding exclusively on art. Despite their negative role in the poem, however, they are shown, in this drawing and in the second design of the series, 'Har and Heva bathing, Mnetha looking on' (Fitzwilliam Museum, Cambridge), in a sympathetic manner. In fact these two drawings, unlike the other surviving examples, are difficult to relate closely to any specific lines in the text; the closest to this example is the first general description of Har, Heva and Mnetha,

> *Playing with flowers & running after birds they spent the day*
> *And in the night like infants slept delighted with infant dreams.*

The two drawings of the innocence of Har and Heva are also distinct in style from the rest of the series, the figures being larger in scale and more monumental and the general treatment rather looser. To a certain extent this dichotomy echoes the divergent strands of Blake's early Neo-Classicism, the monumental severity of the Joseph watercolours and the 'Job' and 'Ezekiel' prints, Nos.31–3, on the one hand and the more decorative Neo-Classicism, derived from Watteau and Stothard, that marks the illustrations to *Songs of Innocence* and which is also found in certain watercolours such as No.39.

40

41

The Early Illuminated Books and Contemporary Book Illustrations, 1789–91

Blake's illuminated books are unique in that they combine text both written and printed by the poet with illustrations by the same artist. This was achieved by printing both the text and the outline of the illustrations in relief etching or stereotype (printing from the raised, unetched surface of the plate). Blake claimed that the process had come to him in a vision from his younger brother Robert after his death in 1787, but it was also in the air at the time; indeed the experiments of Blake's friend George Cumberland are referred to in Blake's manuscript *An Island in the Moon* of *c.*1784. Blake would then colour the illustrations by hand, usually on selling a copy of the book, with the result that each copy is different, particularly as he went on colouring his books throughout the rest of his life. Blake's time at Westminster Abbey may have given him both the general idea and a pattern for the actual design of the pages in his books, in that it would have given him the chance to see a number of mediaeval illuminated manuscripts. However, there are also a number of similarities with contemporary children's books and song books such as Joseph Ritson's *English Songs*, 1783, for which Blake had done some of the engraved illustrations; also prayer books and devotional works that revived the mediaeval tradition. There are particularly close parallels to the *Songs of Innocence* in certain French *Livres de Piété* of the later eighteenth century. Blake's books have not only illustrations occupying part of the text pages but also border decorations and even decorations between the lines. These differ from their prototypes in that they are closely integrated with the message of the text, though not always as direct illustrations; often in fact they are rather a supplement or a complement to the text.

Blake's first illuminated books are the tentative and very small *All Religions are One* and *There is no Natural Religion.* These seem to have been etched in 1788 though the earliest surviving copies, all more or less incomplete, date from about five years later. The series really starts with *Songs of Innocence* and *The Book of Thel*, both of 1789. The style of the illustrations to these books is close to the decorative Neo-Classicism of the late 1780s. Particularly when coloured with the delicate washes of the earliest copies, they have a freshness and delicacy very much in tune with the 'Age of Sensibility' and at a far remove from the power of the independent watercolours and engravings of the mid 1780s.

Similar among Blake's conventional book illustrations are those to Mary Wollstonecraft's *Original Stories from Real Life*, published in 1791. The comparative tameness of the illustrations belies the political context of this work; like many other Neo-Classical artists at this time Blake sympathised with the ideals of the American and French Revolutions and was one of a group gathering round the radical publisher Joseph Johnson which included not only Mary Wollstonecraft and her husband William Godwin but also Joseph Priestley and Tom Paine; in fact it was Blake who was supposed, as a result of a visionary premonition, to have tipped off Tom Paine to make his escape from being arrested in 1792. Unlike his later followers such as Samuel Palmer, Blake was always a 'Liberty Boy'. However, after the September Massacres of 1792 this radical group split up and Blake's republican sentiments went underground. His poem *The French Revolution*, which was to have been published by Johnson in 1791, got no further than page proofs.

42

43

44

'Songs of Innocence' 1789/c.1800

42 **Frontispiece: page 2**
43 **'Holy Thursday': page 19**
44 **'Night', page 1: page 20**
45 **'Infant Joy': page 25**
46 **'On Another's Sorrow': page 27**
Relief etchings finished in watercolour, approx. $4\frac{1}{2} \times 2\frac{3}{4}$ (11×7)
on paper approx. $8\frac{1}{4} \times 5\frac{3}{4}$ (21×14.5).
Private collection, England

The page numbers given above come from the standard numbering now generally adopted for the *Songs*, though the actual order varies from copy to copy. The book is dated 1789 but these pages were probably coloured rather later. They come from a copy (R) that apparently belonged to the first Baron Dimsdale; if so they must have been coloured before his death in 1800, though the colouring of the text in addition to the actual designs and the use of gold on some of the pages is usually taken as a sign of a later date. The book is said to have been rescued from a bonfire in the late 1890s and only nine pages survive.

The poems of *Songs of Innocence* are in the pastoral mode, ostensibly poems for children though with a wider, if generally unsophisticated audience in mind. The graceful decorations are well attuned to the poems and themselves follow the pastoral mode of such an artist and book illustrator as Blake's friend Thomas Stothard, as well as the other sources mentioned above, p.44.

The frontispiece illustrates the 'Introduction' on page 4, which sets out the context of the *Songs of Innocence*:

> *Piping down the valleys wild*
> *Piping songs of pleasant glee*
> *On a cloud I saw a child*
> *And he laughing said to me*
>
> *Pipe a song about a Lamb*
> *So I piped with merry chear*
> *. . .*
>
> *Piper sit thee down and write*
> *In a book that all may read*
> *. . .*
>
> *And I wrote my happy songs*
> *Every child may joy to hear.*

45

The poet with his pipe strides forth (the 'Traveller' again) gazing up at a soaring putto or cherub, signifying inspiration. On the title-page (not exhibited; see fig.10 on p.48) two children stand at the knee of their nurse (to judge by her cap); the fact that they are looking at books seems to have no pejorative connotation (but c.f. No.39). The poem 'Holy Thursday' describes the annual march of charity-school children to St. Paul's. Again it is not quite clear whether the piety is altogether innocent of ironic overtones; Blake may have intended to contrast the flames of inspiration that start up from the 'L' of 'HOLY' with the clinging vine that spreads from the 'Y' of 'THURSDAY'. The small figure leaping up from 'the voice of song' contrasts with the rather ominous bird below the last, warning line.

In 'Night' Blake describes how angels keep watch over every sleeping creature. On the second page, alas destroyed in this copy, he goes on to say that if the angels fail to protect the sheep from the wolves and tigers the victims will find a new dispensation in heaven, where the pitying lion will lie down with the bleating lamb. In this miraculously delicate design the angels can be seen in the tree and in the left-hand margin, while a lion crouches in wait at the foot of the tree.

The tiny figures within the flower of 'Infant Joy' may have their origins in an illustration by Stothard, though they also recall the delightful

46

watercolour of 'Oberon and Titania in a Lily' (Philip Hofer Collection), itself based on a drawing by Blake's younger brother Robert, who had died two years earlier. Here the illustrations magically contrast the smiling two-day-old-joy in the womb-like open blossom with the sterile hanging blossom on the right.

'On Another's Sorrow' concludes the *Songs of Innocence* with a hymn to shared joys and shared sorrows. The joys are expressed in the ebullient foliage and tendrils that thrust into the text from the right-hand margin. The piper of the frontispiece reappears at the bottom of the constricted left-hand marginal decorations, which contain tiny figures of supplication and sorrow. The contrast between the two margins was to become, five years later, the contrast between the *Songs of Innocence* and the *Songs of Experience*.

47

47 *'The Book of Thel': plate 2* 1789/c.1794

Reissued as plate 23 of the 'Small Book of Designs'
Colour-printed relief etching finished in pen and watercolour, $2\frac{7}{8} \times 4\frac{5}{16}$ (7.4 × 11) on paper $10\frac{1}{4} \times 7\frac{7}{16}$ (26 × 18.9).
Trustees of the British Museum, London
From the first copy of the so-called 'Small Book of Designs'; see p.49. In *The Book of Thel*, 1789, the design forms the tailpiece to section I and shows the Lily bowing before Thel, before going off 'to mind her numerous charge among the verdant grass'.

48

48 *'The Book of Thel': plate 5* 1789/c.1794

Reissued as plate 22 of the 'Small Book of Designs'
Colour-printed relief etching finished in pen and watercolour, $3\frac{1}{4} \times 4\frac{1}{4}$ (8.2 × 10.8) on paper $10\frac{1}{4} \times 7\frac{1}{2}$ (26 × 19.1).
Trustees of the British Museum, London
From the first copy of the 'Small Book of Designs'; see p.49. Based on the sketch, No.49.

49 *Two Sketches for 'The Book of Thel'* c.1789

Pencil, two drawings each approx. $6 \times 4\frac{1}{2}$ (15 × 11.5) on paper $8\frac{13}{16} \times 12\frac{1}{2}$ (22.4 × 31.7).
Inscr. by Frederick Tatham, 'By William Blake attested by Frederick Tatham'.
Private collection

49

This is a fascinating and unique example of Blake setting out the effect of a page-opening in one of his illuminated books, complete with indications of the lines of text as well as the illustrations. It shows plates 4 and 5, section III of *The Book of Thel*, 1789. In the event Blake moved the drawing on the left to replace that on the right (see No.48), presumably to improve the balance; his new headpiece for plate 4 is a lighter, more delicate composition.

The setting of *The Book of Thel* is the same 'Vales of Har' as those in which Tiriel's parents lived in perpetual Innocence (see No.41). The maiden Thel confronts, but finally flees from Experience in the shape of various embodiments of natural propagation, a Lily-of-the-Valley, a cloud, a worm and a clod of clay. The design on the left shows Thel leaning over the 'Matron Clay' and the worm; that on the right, Thel either entering or fleeing from the house of Clay, over which fly her 'sighs' and 'moans'.

Illustrations to Mary Wollstonecraft's 'Original Stories' c.1790

50 **'Look what a Fine Morning it is': for plate 1**
Pen and sepia wash, approx. $5\frac{1}{16} \times 2\frac{5}{8}$ (13 × 6.5) on paper $5\frac{1}{4} \times 2\frac{3}{16}$ (13.3 × 6.8).

51 **'Indeed We are Very Happy': for plate 3**
Pen and sepia wash, approx. $4\frac{3}{8} \times 2\frac{5}{8}$ (11 × 6.5) on three pieces of paper $5\frac{9}{16} \times 2\frac{5}{8}$ (14 × 6.7).

52 **The Ruined House: 'Be Calm, My Child': for plate 4**
Pen and sepia wash, approx. $5\frac{1}{8} \times 2\frac{1}{2}$ (13 × 6.5) on paper $5\frac{1}{8} \times 2\frac{11}{16}$ (13 × 6.8).

53 **'Oeconomy and Self-Denial are Necessary': for plate 6**
Pen and sepia wash, approx. $5\frac{1}{2} \times 2\frac{1}{2}$ (14 × 6.5) on paper $5\frac{9}{16} \times 2\frac{5}{8}$ (14.2 × 6.7).
Library of Congress, Washington (Rosenwald Collection)

Mary Wollstonecraft's *Original Stories* had been first published in 1788 without illustrations but Blake's friend the radical publisher Joseph Johnson commissioned him to illustrate a new edition published in 1791. Blake engraved six plates, for five of which there are surviving drawings: five further drawings were not used. There was a new edition with Blake's engravings in 1796.

The tone of the book is conveyed by its full title: *Original Stories from Real Life; with Conversations, Calculated to Regulate the Affections and Form the Mind to Truth and Goodness.* The sentiments, though rather more didactic than those of *Songs of Innocence*, were designed to appeal to much the same audience, and Blake's illustrations are generally similar in their dependance on the tradition of late eighteenth-century book illustration. Some of the grimmer subjects, such as 'Oeconomy and Self-Denial are Necessary', drew forth illustrations that anticipated those in *Songs of Experience.*

50

51

52

53

The Prophetic Books, 1793–6

Blake's development in the first half of the 1790s has an internal momentum that seems to have driven him relentlessly on to what were perhaps his greatest, and certainly his most powerful, works, the large colour prints of 1795 (Nos.85–103). Seldom can form and content be seen working together so closely to forge a new style with a new technique and a new forcefulness of expression.

The development at first took place within the confines of the illuminated books, but eventually broke out in separate works of art. A convenient demonstration of the development of Blake's style occurred when he supplemented his *Songs of Innocence* with the *Songs of Experience* of 1794. These followed the unparalleled ironic wit of *The Marriage of Heaven and Hell* of 1790–93. The lessons of experience and the destruction of all political hope following the distortion of the aims of the French

Fig.10 William Blake
Title-page of 'Songs of Innocence',
1789 (British Museum)

Fig.11 William Blake
Title-page of 'Songs of Experience',
1794 (British Museum)

Revolution could no longer be laughed off, and the illustrations to the new poems, though preserving the general stylistic pattern of the earlier ones, reveal a new mood, spare rather than luxuriant, rectilinear rather than curvilinear (c.f. figs.10 and 11).

The growing seriousness of mood is paralleled by a growth in scale, both of actual page size and in the relationship of design to page. *Songs of Innocence*, followed by *Songs of Experience*, was printed from plates of approximately $4\frac{1}{2} \times 2\frac{1}{4}$ in. In the same year as the former, 1789, Blake evolved a more or less standard $6\frac{1}{4} \times 4\frac{1}{4}$ in. size in *The Book of Thel*; this he followed in *The Visions of the Daughters of Albion*, 1793, *The Marriage of Heaven and Hell* of 1790–93, *Urizen*, 1794, *The Book of Ahania*, 1795 and *The Book of Los*, 1795. However, in 1793, in *America*, he increased this to $9\frac{1}{2} \times 6\frac{3}{4}$ in, retaining this larger format for *Europe*, 1794, and *The Song of Los*, 1795. At the same time the designs occupied more and more of the books. In *America* they often occupy half a page, and they take up even more in *Europe*, in which three pages are given over to designs alone. In *Urizen*, although the page size is smaller, this process continues, with many designs occupying three-quarters or even more of the pages where text appears at all, and a far greater number of full-page designs, ten out of twenty-eight pages. In addition, the designs are more self-contained; the luxurious interlinear decoration of the earlier books has disappeared.

At the same time Blake drastically altered the method by which he coloured the illustrations to his books. Up to and including the first copy of *Europe* to be coloured, the colouring was done in watercolour, but in *Urizen* and in other early copies of *Europe* he turned to the use of a form of colour printing. A very tentative form of this is found in copies of *All Religions are One* and *No Natural Religion* which also seem to date from 1794. The new technique was also used for the copies Blake printed about this time of some of his earlier books, *Visions of the Daughters of Albion*, *The Marriage of Heaven and Hell* and *Songs of Experience* (see Nos.54–8).

The colour printing seems to have been done by applying thick, tacky pigments to the engraved plate from which the text and outlines had already been printed and then taking an impression. The colours seem to have been mixed with carpenter's glue, creating a very rich, textured, heavy effect similar to his later tempera paintings; he sometimes called this medium 'fresco'. The designs were then normally tidied up with pen and watercolour. The impact of the colour-printed illustrations in *Urizen* is unparalleled in Blake's books (see Nos.73–4). It is no coincidence that they accompany Blake's most negatively pessimistic expression of his views on man's predicament. Whereas in *America* the outbreak of revolution in that continent heralded a new dawn, and *Europe* also ended in the anticipation of revolution, *Urizen* concentrates on the Creation as a definition of material reality in its most horrific and negative form. The material opacity of the colouring of the illustrations could not be better attuned to this theme.

The dark splendour of *Urizen* all but exhausted Blake's literary creativity for the time. The following year saw only the three very short books, *The Song of Los*, *The Book of Ahania* and *The Book of Los*. In the last two of these Blake followed the logic of his technical development and printed the text completely separately in intaglio, recognising that his opaque colouring would completely obliterate any printed outlines. Meanwhile, the designs, which had already tended to take over the books from their texts, were given an independent existence of their own in the so-called 'Small' and 'Large Book of Designs', these being, as Blake later described them, 'a selection from the different Books of such as could be Printed without the Writing, tho' to the Loss of some of the best things' (see Nos.10, 47–8,

75–83). One set of the 'Small Book of Designs' used as its title-page the bottom half of the title-page from *Urizen*, including the printed date 1794. For a second, varied selection the same title-page was used but with the date altered to 1796 (see No.75).

After 1795 or 1796 Blake no longer seems to have used colour printing in his books. In part the reasons were technical in that, given the flexibility of the page, the heavy colours could easily crack; there was also a tendency for the medium to stain the paper before it was fully dry. More important, the process had led Blake further into independent designs, the large colour prints of 1795.

'Songs of Experience' 1794

54 'The Clod and the Pebble': page 32
55 'The Chimney Sweeper': page 37
56 'The Tyger': page 42
57 'The Human Abstract': page 47
58 'A Little Boy Lost': page 50
Colour-printed relief etchings, sometimes finished in watercolour, approximately $4\frac{1}{2} \times 3\frac{3}{4}$ (11 × 7) on paper of various sizes, very roughly $7 \times 4\frac{3}{4}$ (18 × 12).
Private collection, England

These pages are uniform in type of paper and style of colouring; though they were acquired from different sources they probably represent the remains of a single Copy G of *Songs of Experience*. The book is dated 1794 on the title-page and the use of colour printing suggests that this copy was one of the first to be coloured. It was also probably issued on its own, though most surviving copies were bound up with, and formed a single sequence with, *Songs of Innocence*, with a separate title-page half way through; certain pages were even transferred from the original *Innocence* to *Experience*.

54

The new title-page (not exhibited; see fig.11 on p.48) immediately establishes the new mood: while the words 'SONGS of' are still surrounded by flying figures, leaves and tendrils, 'EXPERIENCE' stands starkly unadorned while below two children weep over their dead parents against a bare rectilinear wall. Similarly in the frontispiece (also not exhibited) the piper has abandoned his pipe and holds the putto captive (see the illustrations to *The Book of Job*, Nos.191 and 196, where the taking down and playing of the musical instruments demonstrates Job's salvation through creative inspiration).

The illustrations to 'The Clod and the Pebble' echo the bitter irony of the poem in which the meek Clod of Clay, trodden underfoot by cattle, proclaims that 'Love seeketh not itself to please', only to be answered by the hard Pebble,

> *Love seeketh only Self to please,*
> *To bind another to Its delight:*
> *Joys in another's loss of ease,*
> *And builds a Hell in Heaven's despite.*

The passive acceptance of the sheep and cattle at the top of the page is contrasted with the lively 'delight' of the aquatic life below, the sameness of selfless harmony with the energy of individual self-seeking.

The verses of 'The Chimney Sweeper' reveal Blake's scorn of established religion: the young sweep's parents have left him to go to church,

> *And are gone to praise God & Priest & King*
> *Who made up a heaven of our misery.*

The illustration, much more rectilinear in composition than those in *Songs of Innocence*, stresses the child's woe.

55

56

57

58

'The Tyger' sets out in a different form the paradox of the Lion and the Ox (see No.40):

Did he who made the Lamb make thee

Blake stresses this paradox with a picture of the tiger that is more or less comical according to which copy of the book one looks at.

'The Human Abstract' sets out much of the essence of Blake's philosophy. Starting with the paradox,

Pity would be no more
If we did not make somebody Poor:
And Mercy no more could be
If all were as happy as we;

it goes on to describe how Cruelty engenders Humility with his tears and weaves a tree of Mystery and Deceit; the Gods of Nature then seek this tree of oppressive religion,

But this search was all in vain:
There grows one in the Human Brain.

Below Blake has drawn one of his characteristic images of negative authority, the crouching old man entangled in his own net. The old-man type and the significance of this figure aligns it with Urizen, one of the leading protagonists in Blake's own self-made mythology from *Visions of the Daughters of Albion* and *America* of 1793 on.

Like 'The Clod and the Pebble', 'A Little Boy Lost' is another paradoxical overturning of the normal criteria of good and evil, echoing the irony of *The Marriage of Heaven and Hell*, completed the previous year. The boy who holds that 'Naught loves another as itself' and cannot love his father and brothers any differently from

. . . the little bird
That picks up crumbs around the door,

is less to be condemned than the priest who has him burnt for such views. At the foot of the page Blake shows the parents weeping in vain that 'such things are done on Albion's shore'.

This last page is a good example of Blake's colour printing before he went over it to give the forms greater definition with watercolour and pen. All the pages of this copy of *Songs of Experience* show how apt his new technique, developed in this year, was to his growing pessimism.

'America' 1793/c.1800

59   Opening of Preludium: plate 1
60   Plate 7
61   Plate 10
62   Plate 11
Relief etchings finished in watercolour, approx. $9\frac{1}{2} \times 6\frac{3}{4}$ (26 × 17) on paper $14\frac{3}{4} \times 10\frac{1}{2}$ (37.5 × 26.8).
Mr and Mrs Paul Mellon

America is dated '1793' on the title-page. These pages, from Copy M, are on paper watermarked '1799', which may be the approximate date of the colouring. Coloured copies of *America* are relatively rare, even though it was often bound together with coloured copies of *Europe* (Blake's two later 'Continental' myths, 'Africa' and 'Asia', were issued together as the much shorter *Song of Los*, 1795). The early history of this copy is not known. It was acquired in the mid-nineteenth century by Richard Monckton Milnes and later formed part of the largest ever private American Blake collection, that of W. A. White.

America was the first book Blake subtitled 'a Prophecy' and it is the closest, in its concentration on a short period of actual history, to *The French Revolution*, which was to have been published by Joseph Johnson in ordinary letterpress in 1791, but never progressed beyond a final proof. It covers the years from the outbreak of the American War of Independence to the stirrings of revolution in Europe, but unlike *The French Revolution*, which used the names of real contemporary figures, the story is cloaked in mythical terms as the story of the emergence of Orc, the embodiment of energy, from the captivity to which he had been submitted by his parents Los and Enitharmon.

Blake did not publish the full story of that captivity until the following year, in *Urizen* (see No.83), but he illustrated it in the headpiece to the Preludium. Orc is chained to the ground, while Los and Enitharmon stand by in horror. In the text, however, Blake does not yet seem to have reached the final version of the event; instead he writes of how 'The Shadowy Daughter of Urthona stood before red Orc', describing her as 'The nameless female', fourteen years old, and, by implication, Orc's sister. There is also an earlier watercolour, *c.*1791–2 (Tate Gallery), which shows, in reverse, the chained Orc with his father Los or Urthona alone and which presumably formed the basis for this illustration, an interesting case of the idea apparently first occurring to Blake in visual form rather than in his writings. Blake later, *c.*1802–3, elaborated the story in his unfinished manuscript of *Vala or the Four Zoas*, accompanying it with a rough drawing based on this design, and returned to the subject again in a small relief etching of 1812.

The idyllic illustration to plate 7 accompanies a description of the confrontation of Albion's wrathful angel with the 'serpent-form'd' Orc, 'Lover of wild rebellion'. The sleeping ram and children presumably represent the passive indifference of the unenlightened to the impending revolution, typified by the awakening Orc on the facing plate 6. On plate 10 Orc reappears amidst the flames of revolution, while again the facing plate 11 is strangely idyllic, though here the presence of Orc is reflected in the serpent, tamed by the children who ride it, and perhaps also in the swan.

59

60

61

62

63

64

65

'Europe' 1794/c.1795–6

63 **Title-Page**
Inscr. 'Lambeth Printed by Will: Blake: 1794'.

64 **Opening of Preludium: plate 1**

65 **'Mildews Blighting Ears of Corn': plate 9**
Relief etchings, partly colour-printed and finished in watercolour, approx. $9\frac{1}{2} \times 6\frac{3}{4}$ (24 × 17) on paper $14\frac{3}{4} \times 10\frac{5}{8}$ (37.5 × 27).
Glasgow University Library

These pages are from Copy B of *Europe*, probably coloured *c.*1795–6 at the height of Blake's interest in colour-printing (see pp.48–9). This copy belonged to P. A. Hanrott, being sold with his Library in 1833. It was later in the Cunliffe collection.

Europe treats of the problem of Christ's birth and why it was not followed by immediate salvation. Enitharmon, the Female Will and representative of the arts in their debased form, hides her revolutionary child Orc and establishes the oppressive Church of King and Priest. Finally the awakening of Orc leads to the American and French Revolutions. For the famous frontispiece known as 'The Ancient of Days', which shows the creation of the material world by Jehovah in the guise of Urizen, the embodiment of unimaginative reason, see Nos.66–8.

The rampant serpent on the title-page represents Orc, 'serpent-form'd' as he is described in *America*, 1793. For Blake's later reworkings of this design see Nos.69–71.

The illustrations to the preludium are not directly related to the text but show the dangers awaiting the 'Mental Traveller' in the Fallen World. On page 1 an assassin lies in wait. The composition was later adapted by Blake for his watercolour of 'Malevolence', No.141. In one copy of *Europe*, Copy D, George Cunningham added titles to the plates, in this case 'The Assassin'.

Plate 9 Cunningham entitled 'Mildews blighting ears of Corn'. This is one of the plagues that occur while 'Enitharmon slept Eighteen hundred years' in 'The night of Nature'. *Europe* also includes full-page designs of 'Famine' and 'Pestilence' and concludes with a depiction of 'Fire'. ('Pestilence' is actually based on the series of watercolours of 'Pestilence' (see Nos.21–5) and all this group of illustrations reflect Blake's obsession with such afflictions from *c.*1779–80 up to 1805.) 'Mildews blighting Ears of Corn' is one of Blake's most striking curvilinear designs, figures and text being swept up together in one great 'S' curve.

66 *God Creating the Universe ('The Ancient of Days')* c.1794

Relief etching finished in watercolour, $9\frac{1}{2} \times 6\frac{11}{16}$ (24.1 × 17).
Private collection, England

Printed from the first state of the plate, which differs slightly in size and details from that used in the book *Europe*, 1794, where the design appears as the frontispiece. It may therefore have been conceived as a separate print before the book was issued as a whole.

It was J. T. Smith who first called the design 'The Ancient of Days', relating it to Proverbs 8:27. He also says that Blake was inspired 'by a vision which he declared hovered over his head at the top of the staircase'. However, Blake's meaning must be seen in the context of his own writings. A sketch for the composition, on page 96 of Blake's Notebook, is entitled, 'who shall bind the Infinite', which is part of a passage in the preludium to *Europe*,

> And who shall bind the infinite with an eternal band?
> To compass it with swaddling bands? . . .

In *Urizen*, 1794, the protagonist, whom Blake saw as Jehovah, the Creator,

> . . . formed golden compasses
> And began to explore the Abyss.

66

This design is therefore Blake's depiction of the Creation of the World, to be seen in the same negative light as the Creation of Man in the large colour print of 1795, No.85. Another of the colour prints, 'Newton' (No.92), uses the compasses in the same sense as a symbol of a defining, limiting creation by the reason unenlightened by the imagination. The connection in Blake's mind was brought full circle by the fact that the composition of 'The Ancient of Days' is based on the frontispiece to the de luxe 1729 edition of Motte's translation of Newton's *Principia*: Blake parodies the frontispiece to Newton's unenlightened display of reason in his own frontispiece to *Europe*, his imaginative prophecy of the overthrow of all Newton stood for.

67 *God Creating the Universe ('The Ancient of Days')* c.1794

Relief etching finished in pen and watercolour, $9\frac{5}{16} \times 6\frac{11}{16}$ (23.7 × 17).
Private collection, England

This copy of the print was possibly printed from the same early state of the plate as No.66, but certain slight differences, such as the fact that the compasses are here open at an angle of slightly over 90°, suggest that this could have been made from a third, hitherto unrecorded state.

68 *God Creating the Universe ('The Ancient of Days')* c.1794/1824 or 7 (?)

Relief etching finished in gold, gouache and watercolour, $9\frac{3}{16} \times 6\frac{5}{8}$ (23.4 × 16.8).
Signed 'Blake 1824 [?, or a clumsy 'inv'; the end of the inscription is smudged]'.
Whitworth Art Gallery, University of Manchester

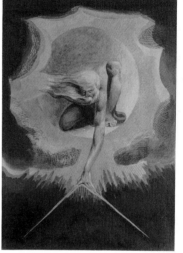

67

This copy of the print is generally identified as that which, according to J. T. Smith and Frederick Tatham, Blake coloured for Tatham on his deathbed. It is however exceedingly difficult to read the last digit of the date, if indeed it is a date, as a seven. The print is nevertheless typical of Blake's late rich elaborate colouring, including the use of gold. It seems to be from the later state of the engraving, that actually used in copies of *Europe*.

69 *'Europe': touched proof of title-page* 1794/c.1815–20

Relief etching finished in watercolour with additions in pencil and pen, $9\frac{3}{8} \times 6\frac{13}{16}$ (23.8 × 17.3) on paper approx. $10\frac{1}{8} \times 8$ (26.5 × 20.5).
Inscr.'LAMBETH Printed by Will: Blake: 1794' and, not by Blake, 'W. Blake for Blairs Grave'.
Private collection, England

This is one of four reworked proofs of the title-page to *Europe*, 1794, all with proofs of plates from *Jerusalem* on the back, in this case plate 24. At least some of the *Jerusalem* plates concerned were probably printed c.1815–20, which is presumably also the date on which Blake worked over the *Europe* title-pages.

In this reworking Blake has added a young man who struggles with the serpent. If the serpent is Orc (see Nos.59–63) the young man is presumably Los, attempting to direct his revolutionary ardour.

This page comes from the collection of John Linnell. For two of the other reworked *Europe* title-pages see Nos.70 and 71. The fourth, formerly in the collection of Kerrison Preston, is now in the National Gallery of Australia, Canberra.

68

69

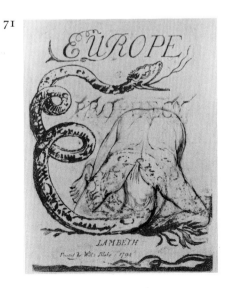

70

71

70   *'Europe': touched proof of title-page*   1794/c.1815–20
Relief etching with additions in pencil, ink and grey wash, $8\frac{7}{8} \times 6\frac{3}{4}$
(22.6×17) on paper, irregular, $9\frac{3}{8} \times 6\frac{13}{16}$ (23.8×17.6).
Inscr. 'LAMBETH printed by Will: Blake: 1794'.
Pierpont Morgan Library, New York

See No.69. On the back is a proof of plate 74 of *Jerusalem*.

In this version the serpent has been transformed into Leviathan (see the similar head in No.205). Reclining on the head of the monster is an old man with plumed pen and double tablets, Moses, representing the oppressive code of the Old Testament; he looks up apprehensively at three diving figures. Moses is portrayed in the guise Blake gave to his own character Urizen, the rational, ordering principle, and is presumably shown here having transformed the revolutionary ardour of the serpent Orc into the repressive negative energy of War.

71   *'Europe': touched proof of title-page*   1794/c.1815–20
Relief etching with additions in pencil, ink and grey wash, approx.
$9 \times 6\frac{3}{4}$ (23×17) on paper $13 \times 9\frac{5}{8}$ (33.1×24.4).
Inscr. 'LAMBETH printed by Will: Blake: 1794'.
Pierpont Morgan Library, New York

See No.69. This page, only recently rediscovered, is on the back of plate 70 of *Jerusalem*.

In this version Blake has altered his design so that the serpent emerges from the neck of a human figure who crouches bowed over. This is perhaps a representation of the birth of the serpent Orc, the embodiment of revolution, from the head of Los, the poetic genius, though in most of Blake's versions of the story of the birth of Orc he was, though the child of Los, actually born of Enitharmon.

72   *A Serpent*   c.1790–95
Watercolour, approx. $2\frac{5}{8} \times 4\frac{5}{8}$ (6.5×11.5).
Inscr. on mount, not by Blake, 'by William Blake'.
Mr Malcolm Frazier

Serpents appear repeatedly in Blake's illustrations to his illuminated books; see especially *The Marriage of Heaven and Hell*, 1790–93, *America*, 1793 (see No.62), and *Europe*, 1794 (see No.63). None however exactly corresponds to this finished watercolour.

'Urizen'   1794/c.1794–5

73   **Urizen and his Book of Brass: plate 5**
74   **Urizen as Skeleton: plate 8**
Colour-printed relief etchings finished in watercolour, approx.
$6\frac{1}{4} \times 4\frac{1}{4}$ (16×11) on paper $15\frac{1}{8} \times 10\frac{3}{4}$ (38.5×27.2).
Pierpont Morgan Library, New York

Dated '1794' on the title-page, the full title of this book is *The First Book of Urizen*. No further books followed, though *The Book of Ahania*, 1795, follows on and *The Book of Los* gives an alternative viewpoint of the same Creation myth; in two copies, including the only one to have been done after *c.*1795, Copy G, watermarked 1815, Blake erased the word 'First'. These pages are from Copy B, watermarked '1794' and probably coloured in that year or the next. *Urizen* was colour-printed from the beginning, only the later Copy G being coloured in watercolour alone.

The rich, heavy colouring is an integral part of the idea of the book as a whole, abetting as it does the mood of this, the most sombre and oppressive of all Blake's writings. *Urizen* is Blake's starkest account of how the Fall of Man and the Creation are inextricably bound up with each other. Urizen, the 'primeval Priest', is spurned by the Eternals and falls into chaos. Los, the poetic principle, gives Urizen form so that eventually he may be overthrown, but this leads to Los' own fall into division, first the division of the sexes with the creation of Enitharmon, then the birth of the first child, the revolutionary Orc. Later, in a would-be synthesis of his earlier prophetic writings, Blake began the long manuscript *Vala or the Four Zoas*, worked on over the years *c.*1796–1807; into this he gradually introduced the idea of redemption through Christ, but the manuscript was finally abandoned unfinished.

For the title-page, which characterises Urizen, see No.75, one of the designs reissued on their own in the so-called 'Small' and 'Large Book of Designs'; see also Nos.76–83. Plate 5, like the title-page, shows Urizen with his 'Book of Brass' in which are written:

> . . . the secrets of wisdom,
> *The secrets of dark contemplation,*

which treat of the

> *Seven deadly Sins of the soul.*

For plate 8 see No.79, a separately issued copy of this design without the text.

75 *'Urizen': title-page* 1794/1796

> Reissued as title-page of the 'Small Book of Designs'.
> Colour-printed relief etching finished in pen and watercolour,
> $3\frac{5}{16} \times 4\frac{1}{16}$ (8.4 × 10.3) on paper $10\frac{3}{8} \times 7\frac{1}{4}$ (26.5 × 18.5).
> Inscr. 'LAMBETH. Printed by Will Blake 1796' and, below design,
> '"Which is the Way"/"The Right or the Left",' and, on the back by
> Frederick Tatham, 'This coloured Print by Wm Blake was given me
> by his Widow Frederick Tatham Sculptor'.
> *Private collection, England*

From Copy B of the 'Small Book of Designs', now dispersed. As now traced, eight designs are the same as in Copy A (which contains twenty-three designs) while three are different. There are also other separate colour-printed designs, apparently never bound up into a book. This is the lower half of the original title-page to *Urizen*. Blake also used this design as the title-page to Copy A, in the British Museum, but left the original date of '1794', as in *The Book of Urizen* itself.

The design is the archetypal image of Urizen, for Blake the embodiment of unenlightened reason and consequently of intellectual oppression. Here he crouches over his 'Book of Brass', writing 'the secrets of wisdom',

> *Laws of peace, of love, of unity,*
> *Of pity, compassion, forgiveness;*
> . . .
>
> *One command, one joy, one desire,*
> *One curse, one weight, one measure,*
> *One King, one God, one Law.*

Behind are the Mosaic tables of the Law, representing the oppressive moral code of the Old Testament. The setting is the roots and trunk of the Tree of Mystery (this is clearer in the full-page design in the book itself).

In Copy B of the 'Small Book of Designs' Blake added legends below each design. This one seems to stress Urizen's lack of direction, hemmed in between the differing codes of books and tables by which he is surrounded.

76 *'Urizen': plate 3* 1794

> Reissued as plate 9 of the 'Small Book of Designs'.
> Colour-printed relief etching finished in pen and watercolour,
> $2\frac{3}{8} \times 3\frac{7}{8}$ (6.1 × 9.8) on paper $10\frac{3}{16} \times 7\frac{7}{16}$ (25.9 × 18.9).
> *Trustees of the British Museum, London*

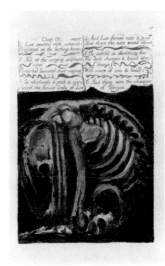

From Copy A of the 'Small Book of Designs', sold to Ozias Humphry, the miniature painter (1742–1810), presumably before he went blind in 1797. It contains twenty-three designs in all.

In *Urizen* this design appears as the head-piece to Chapter I, and probably

shows Los in the flames of inspiration. On the version of the same design from Copy B of the 'Small Book of Designs', Blake seems to have written 'Oh! Flames of Furious Desires' (private collection, England). In another context the youthful figure would be more likely to represent Orc amidst the flames of revolution, but in *Urizen* he only plays a small, passive role. Later Blake was to adapt this figure to represent Satan before the Throne of God in one of his illustrations to the Book of Job, No.192.

77 *'Urizen': plate 5* 1794

Reissued as plate 21 of the 'Small Book of Designs'.
Colour-printed relief etching finished in pen and watercolour,
$3 \times 4\frac{3}{16}$ (7.6 × 10.6) on paper $10\frac{3}{16} \times 7\frac{7}{16}$ (26 × 18.9)
Trustees of the British Museum, London
From Copy A of the 'Small Book of Designs', Urizen with his Book of Brass; see No.73. On the version of this design from Copy B of the 'Small Book of Designs' Blake wrote '"The Book of my Remembrance"' (Beinecke Library, Yale University).

This is a particularly good example of the richness of effect Blake could produce with his colour-printing technique.

78 *'Urizen': plate 7* 1794

Reissued as plate 18 of the 'Small Book of Designs'.
Colour-printed relief etching finished in pen and watercolour,
$4\frac{11}{16} \times 4\frac{3}{16}$ (11.8 × 10.6) on paper $10\frac{1}{4} \times 7\frac{7}{16}$ (26 × 19).
Trustees of the British Museum, London
From Copy A of the 'Small Book of Designs'. In *Urizen* the design takes up most of the page, with a few lines of text above.

Urizen has been rent from Los' side as part of his creation as a separate material entity: 'Los howld in a dismal stupor.'

79 *'Urizen': plate 8* 1794

Reissued as plate 13 of the 'Small Book of Designs'.
Colour-printed relief etching finished in pen and watercolour,
$4\frac{3}{16} \times 4$ (10.6 × 10.1) on paper $10\frac{1}{8} \times 7\frac{1}{2}$ (25.7 × 19).
Trustees of the British Museum, London
From Copy A of the 'Small Book of Designs'. In *Urizen* the design fills most of the page, with a few lines of text above.

This design shows the beginning of Los' creation of Urizen in material form. He starts with the skeleton, shown by Blake in a foetal position, a marvellous visual paradox.

80 *'Urizen': plate 17* 1794

Reissued as plate 3 of the 'Small Book of Designs'.
Colour-printed relief etching finished in pen and watercolour,
$5\frac{13}{16} \times 3\frac{9}{16}$ (14.8 × 9) on paper $10\frac{1}{4} \times 7\frac{3}{16}$ (26 × 18.2).
Watermarked '1794 JWhatman'.
Trustees of the British Museum, London
From Copy A of the 'Small Book of Designs'. This full-page design shows the moment at which Los begins to feel pity for the horrific Urizen that he has created. But for Blake pity was a negative virtue (see No.95), associated with the failure of inspiration and a further dividing of the unified Man:

> . . . & *Pity began,*
> *In anguish dividing & dividing,*
> *For pity divides the soul*
> *In pangs, eternity on eternity,*
> *Life in cataracts pourd down his cliffs.*
> *The void shrunk the lymph into Nerves*
> *Wandring wide on the bosom of night*

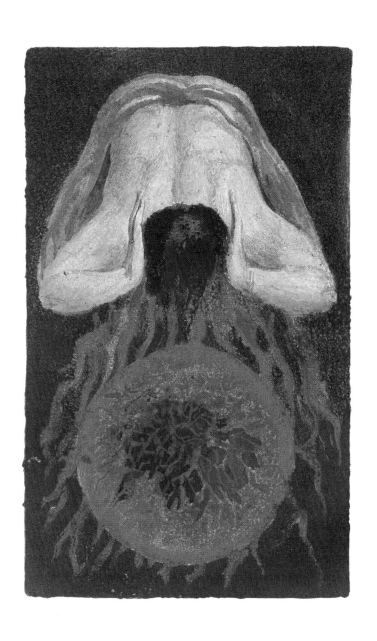

80 *'Urizen': plate 17, 1794* (entry on p.56)

85 *Elohim Creating Adam,* 1795 (entry on p.59)

78

And left a round globe of blood
Trembling upon the Void.
Thus the Eternal Prophet was divided.
The globe of blood trembled
Branching out into roots,
Fibrous, writhing upon the winds,
Fibres of blood, milk and tears.

The result is Los' female emanation Enitharmon, and the scene, both in Blake's verses and in this extraordinary illustration, is Blake's horrific retelling of the Creation of Eve:

Eternity shudderd when they saw
Man begetting his likeness
On his own divided image.

81 *'Urizen': plate 19* 1794
    Reissued as plate 14 of the 'Small Book of Designs'.
    Colour-printed relief etching finished in pen and watercolour,
    $2\frac{13}{16} \times 4\frac{1}{8}$ (7.2 × 10.4) on paper $10\frac{3}{16} \times 7\frac{7}{16}$ (25.9 × 18.9).
    Trustees of the British Museum, London
From Copy A of the 'Small Book of Designs', originally a headpiece to the page of text that it illustrates, showing Los crouching before the newly created Enitharmon, who shrinks from his embrace.

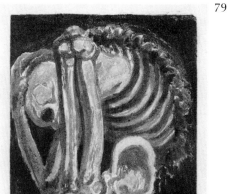

79

82 *'Urizen': plate 27* 1794
    Reissued as plate 11 of the 'Small Book of Designs'.
    Colour-printed relief etching finished in pen and watercolour,
    $6 \times 4\frac{1}{16}$ (15.3 × 10.3) on paper $10\frac{1}{4} \times 7\frac{1}{2}$ (26 × 19).
    Trustees of the British Museum, London
From Copy A of the 'Small Book of Designs'. This full-page design varies in its position in the different copies of *The Book of Urizen*, showing the independence of some of Blake's designs from any specific lines of text. Urizen progresses through the darkened void, but his precise activity depends on where the plate is placed in the book. As an independent design it stands on its own intrinsic visual qualities.

    This page was one of those printed from a reworked fragment of the copper plate of 'The Approach of Doom', No. 35. The bold lines of the top left-hand quarter of No. 35 can be seen underlying the colour-print, and, of course, are even clearer in Copy G of *Urizen* which was coloured by hand (Rosenwald Collection). The reverse of the plate seems already to have been used for page 12 of *The Marriage of Heaven and Hell*, 1790–93.

80

81

82

83

83 'Urizen': plate 21 1794/c.1795

Reissued as plate 3 of the 'Large Book of Designs'.
Colour-printed relief etching finished in pen and watercolour,
6¼ × 4 (16.5 × 10.2) on paper 13⅝ × 9⅝ (34.6 × 24.5).
Trustees of the British Museum, London

From the so-called 'Large Book of Designs', sold with Copy A of the 'Small Book' to Ozias Humphry before 1797. The book consists of eight designs, five from the prophetic books, three from independent engravings; see also No.10.

This full-page design from *Urizen* shows Los' jealousy of Orc, his child by Enitharmon, which results in a tightening girdle round his chest; every time he bursts it by his sobbing it renews itself, the previous bands forming an iron chain. Later in the story, though already illustrated by Blake in *America* (see No.59), Los chains Orc to a rock on the top of a mountain.

The composition recalls the common Renaissance subject of 'Venus, Vulcan and Cupid at the Forge'. This was almost certainly a deliberate allusion to Vulcan's jealousy of Venus for her love not so much of Cupid as of Mars.

84 *Lucifer and the Pope in Hell: 'The Lord hath Broken the Staff of the Wicked'* c.1795

Line engraving, 7³⁄₁₆ × 9¹¹⁄₁₆ (18.3 × 24.6).
Trustees of the British Museum, London

Until this monochrome print turned up in 1966 it was only known in the colour-printed version of *c.*1795 in the Huntington Library, San Marino; the colour print is slightly larger, 7¹⁵⁄₁₆ × 10¾ (20.1 × 27.3), the colours having also been applied to the unengraved margin of the plate. The engraving is based on a pen and wash drawing of the early 1780s (Royal Library, Windsor) but probably also dates from the mid 1790s.

The subject comes from Isaiah 14:9–12, in which however it is the King of Babylon who is in Hell, as in Blake's earlier drawing. In the engraving Blake follows the Protestant tradition that substituted the Pope for the King of Babylon, thus equating the Catholic Church with Babylonian materialism; a similar identification was often made between the Church and the Whore of Babylon (see Nos.115 and 190).

The Large Colour Prints of 1795

The large colour prints of 1795 represent the culmination of Blake's colour-printing technique, first deployed in his books and in the 'Small' and 'Large Book of Designs'. The technique seems to be pure colour printing with no previous printed outlines, in the manner of the illustrations to *The Book of Ahania* and *The Book of Los*. The experimental half-size print of *Pity* (No.98) shows the technique particularly clearly.

The large prints illustrate subjects from a number of different sources: the Bible, Milton and Shakespeare, as well as Blake's own earlier writings, but they are unified in that each one represents some aspect of Blake's philosophy. All can be paralleled in his writings, but for Blake, and indeed for the receptive viewer, texts are no longer necessary to appreciate the power of these designs, even if some of the subtleties of meaning have to be sensed rather than intellectually understood. This is, indeed, the point at which Blake the artist finally breaks free of Blake the writer. And in these, the first of Blake's completely personal designs, we feel all the excitement of this new liberation.

---

85 Elohim Creating Adam 1795

Colour print finished in pen and watercolour, $17 \times 21\frac{1}{8}$ (43.1 × 53.6).
Signed '1795 W B inv [as monogram]', and inscr. 'Elohim creating Adam' below design (covered by mount).
Tate Gallery, London

85

Sold to Thomas Butts on 7 September 1805 for one guinea. Butts had examples of eleven if not all twelve of the large colour prints; those in the Tate came from the collection of W. Graham Robertson. This is the only copy of the print known to-day but one other must have existed in 1818 when Blake offered a complete set of the twelve designs to Dawson Turner, this time for five guineas each. There is a pencil sketch for the design in Blake's Notebook.

Elohim is one of the Hebrew names for God and would have been associated by Blake with the repressive God of the Old Testament. However, the Creator also fulfilled a positive function by defining error in material form, without which it could not be overthrown. In *Vala or The Four Zoas*, on which Blake was working c.1796–1807, Elohim appears as one of the seven Eyes of God, sent by the Eternals to lead Man out of the error of selfhood: 'They sent Elohim who created Adam to die for Satan'. Here the material element of the Creation is stressed by the worm that entwines Adam's leg. The expressions of Elohim and Adam, and the oppressive forms of the composition, further stress Blake's negative view of the Creation as a stage in Man's Fall.

86 Satan Exulting over Eve 1795

Colour print finished in pencil, pen and watercolour, $16\frac{11}{16} \times 20\frac{15}{16}$ (42.5 × 53.2).
Signed 'W Blake 1795'.
Bateson Collection

86

This copy of the print seems to have remained in Blake's possession. Later it may have been 'the Satan and Eve' offered c.1843 by the dealer Joseph Hogarth, through George Richmond, to John Ruskin. Another copy was sold to Thomas Butts, though it is not recorded in any surviving accounts; this seems to be the print now in the collection of John Craxton.

The subject, though recalling Milton's *Paradise Lost*, does not seem to be an illustration to any particular passage. In composition it appears to be a companion to 'Elohim creating Adam', No.85, and it probably represents the second stage of the Fall, the division into the two sexes. In Blake's parallel Creation myth, *Urizen*, the creation of Urizen in material form is followed by that of Enitharmon (see No.80).

87

Fig. 12 George Stubbs, *The Fall of Phaeton*, 1775
(Private collection)

87 *God Judging Adam* 1795

Colour print finished in pen and watercolour, $17 \times 21\frac{1}{8}$
(43.2×53.5).
Signed 'WB inv [as monogram] 1795' and inscr. 'God speaking[?]
to Adam' below design (concealed by mount).
Tate Gallery, London

One of the prints listed in Blake's accounts with Butts as having been sold to him on 5 July 1805. For two other copies of the print and an earlier watercolour see Nos.88–90.

For many years this subject was untraced, the large colour prints being thought since the early 1860s to show Elijah in the fiery chariot, handing on the mantle of inspiration to Elisha (2 Kings 2:11–13). However, the discovery of the faintly pencilled inscription below this copy of the design led to its being identified with the lost print from the Butts collection. The mood is certainly pessimistic as opposed to the optimism of the Elijah story, and it is reinforced by the geometrical design which stresses the way in which God the Father imposes his law on the stooping figure of Adam, aged in Jehovah's own Urizen-like image.

There are indeed close parallels in Blake's *Book of Urizen* of the previous year, 1794. Urizen, striving to give form to the primaeval chaos, writes in his 'Book of Brass' the 'Laws of peace', etc. (see No.75). In other words he imposes all the rigour of conformity. As a result,

All the seven deadly sins of the soul
In living creations appear'd
In the flames of eternal fury.

It is these flames that dominate the composition, not the flames of inspiration handed on from Elijah to Elisha. A few lines further on Blake writes of the flames,

But no light from the fires. all was darkness
In the flames of Eternal fury,

a darkness found in the last of the three known copies of the print, No.89.

For close visual parallels among the illustrations to *Urizen*, particularly Urizen with his 'Book of Brass' and his association with 'the flames of eternal fury', see Nos.73 and 75.

There is an extraordinary but possibly unwitting parallel with the composition of George Stubbs' 'Fall of Phaeton' (fig.12). A version of this may well have been known to Blake and the subject could have been interpreted by him as representing the consequences of Phaeton (who corresponds to Blake's own character Orc) letting his energies run away with him. Here in contrast Blake shows the reverse: everything is static and dead.

88 *God Judging Adam* 1795

Colour print finished in pen and watercolour, $16\frac{3}{4} \times 20\frac{11}{16}$
(42.6×52.6).
Signed 'Fresco. WBlake inv.'
Metropolitan Museum of Art, New York (Rogers Fund, 1916)

Probably the first pull to be taken of this design: the printing is heavier than in Nos.87 and 89, giving greater definition to the forms and leaving less to be completed in watercolour and pen. Among the flames on the lower right-hand side are what appear to be capital letters, seen upside down and at a diagonal, suggesting that an engraved plate bearing such letters was deliberately or accidentally involved in the printing of the design.

This version, which was taken to the United States by Mrs Alexander Gilchrist, may earlier have been among the group of Blakes offered to John Ruskin by the dealer Joseph Hogarth, with George Richmond acting as intermediary.

88

89 *God Judging Adam* 1795
    Colour print finished in pen and watercolour, approx. $16\frac{11}{16} \times 20\frac{3}{8}$ (42.3 × 51.7).
    Philadelphia Museum of Art: Gift of Mrs William T. Tonner

89

The last pull of this design, with the background painted much darker than in Nos.87 and 88 as if to illustrate the related passage from *Urizen*,
    But no light from the fires. all was darkness
    In the flames of Eternal fury.
This copy of the design belonged successively to Frederick Tatham, Col. Gould Weston and Mrs William T. Tonner, the donor to the Philadelphia Museum of a considerable group of works by Blake.

90 *God Judging Adam* c.1790–3
    Pen and watercolour, approx. $7\frac{3}{4} \times 11\frac{1}{2}$ (19.5 × 29.5).
    Signed 'WBlake'.
    Private collection, England

90

This is an earlier version of the large colour print now recognised as showing 'God judging Adam' though previously, like this watercolour, known as 'Elijah and Elisha'; for the change in title see No.87. It has been suggested that nevertheless the watercolour does show Elijah handing on the mantle of divine inspiration to Elisha (2 Kings 2:11–13), and that when Blake came to do the colour print he changed the subject. However, although in the watercolour the seated figure does not impose his will on the other with a rod but merely gazes sternly at him, the oppressive mood is the same as in the print. Moreover, the very fact that there is no chariot of flames, only a billowing mass of grey clouds illumined by a red glow overhead, removes the subject still further from 'Elijah mounted in the Fiery Chariot', the title mistakenly applied to the print by William Rossetti in 1863.

    This watercolour is one of four anticipations of the large colour prints, executed in pen and watercolour or monochrome in the early 1790s. The others are 'The Good and Evil Angels' in the Cecil Higgins Museum, Bedford, 'The House of Death' in the Tate Gallery, and 'Los and Orc', also related to 'The Good and Evil Angels', in the Tate Gallery. A fifth watercolour, similar in style, of 'Three falling Figures' in the Fogg Museum is related in theme to plate 2 of *Europe*, 1794. This group, though not completely consistent in style and technique, suggests that Blake may have intended to do a series of independent watercolour designs similar to the large colour prints, but that the development of colour printing in his illuminated books led him to adopt this technique instead.

91 *Nebuchadnezzar* 1795
    Colour print finished in pen and watercolour, irregular, $17\frac{5}{8} \times 24\frac{3}{4}$ (44.6 × 62).
    Signed '1795 WB inv [as monogram]', and inscr. 'Nebuchadnezzar' below design (covered by mount).
    Tate Gallery, London

91

One of the prints sold to Butts on 7 September 1805 for a guinea. There are two other versions, in the Minneapolis Institute of Arts and the Boston Museum.

    Blake had already used this figure on a smaller scale as one of his illustrations to *The Marriage of Heaven and Hell*, 1790–93, where it illustrates the line, 'One Law for the Lion and Ox is Oppression'. The print shows one aspect of Man in his divided state after the Fall, the bestial, and is paralleled by the aspect shown in 'Newton', the rational (No.92).

92

93

94

95

92 *Newton* 1795

Colour print finished in pen and watercolour, $18\frac{1}{8} \times 23\frac{5}{8}$
(46 × 60).
Signed '1795 WB inv [as monogram]', and inscr. 'Newton' below design (covered by mount).
Tate Gallery, London

One of the prints sold to Butts on 7 September 1805 for a guinea. There is another copy of the print in the possession of the Lutheran Church in America, Philadelphia (on loan to the Philadelphia Museum). A drawing in reverse is in an English private collection.

The figure of Newton is developed from Abias, one of Michelangelo's frescoes of the Ancestors of Christ on the ceiling of the Sistine Chapel, which Blake had copied from Ghisi's engraving (see No.14). The design is also a development of one of the plates in *There is No Natural Religion*, 1788, which shows an old man kneeling and drawing on the ground with a pair of compasses to illustrate the text, 'Application. He who sees the Infinite in all things sees God. He who sees the Ratio only sees himself only'. Newton is thus the self-obsessed rational man. However, in Blake's myth Newton had a part to play in giving a tangible form to error: in *Europe*, 1794, he blows the trumpet that awakens Enitharmon and leads to the French Revolution. For Blake's use of the compasses as a symbol of material creation see also Nos.66–8.

93 *Lamech and his Two Wives* 1795

Colour print finished in pen and watercolour, the corners cut across, $17 \times 23\frac{15}{16}$ (43.1 × 60.8).
Signed 'WB inv [as monogram] 1795', and inscr. 'Lamech and his two Wives' below design (covered by mount).
Tate Gallery, London

One of the prints delivered to Butts on 5 July 1805 for a guinea. There is another version in the collection of Mr Robert N. Essick.

This was probably printed as a pair to the version of 'Naomi entreating Ruth' in the Victoria and Albert Museum which also has its corners cut across; see No.94. In this obscure subject from Genesis 4:23–4, Lamech, Cain's great-great-grandson, is telling his wives that he has slain a man: 'If Cain shall be avenged sevenfold, truly Lamech seventy and sevenfold'. There was a tradition, partly derived from the text of Genesis 4:15 and 23, and more fully developed in the Apocrypha, that Lamech had in fact killed Cain. Why Blake should choose this obscure subject rather than the story of Cain and Abel to epitomise murder and vengeance is difficult to understand, though it has been pointed out that Lamech's sons by his two wives, Jubal and Tubalcain, could be seen as representatives of music and the plastic arts in the Fallen World (Jubal had his lyre and Tubalcain was 'an instructor of every artifice in brass and iron').

94 *Naomi Entreating Ruth and Orpah to Return to the Land of Moab* c.1795

Colour print finished in pen, gold and Chinese white, the corners cut across, sight $16\frac{7}{8} \times 22\frac{7}{8}$ (42.8 × 58).
Signed 'Fresco WBlake'.
Victoria and Albert Museum, London

The early history of the print is not known. There is another copy of the print in an English private collection and a version in watercolour of 1803, painted for Butts, No.168.

As well as the cutting across of the corners both the general composition and the colouring, sombre and dominated by a slate-blue, suggest that Blake intended this print as a pendant to 'Lamech', No.93. It is however difficult to see any connection between the two subjects except that they both deal with family relationships, Lamech with his two wives and Naomi with her two Moabite daughters-in-law. In the text Ruth insists on accompanying her mother-in-law to her own town of Bethlehem while Orpah turns back to Moab (Ruth 1 : 11–17).

Blake's use of the word 'Fresco' for this work suggests that the medium of the colour prints was basically the same as that of his tempera paintings of a few years later (see p.75).

95 *Pity* c.1795

Colour print finished in pen and watercolour, irregular, $16\frac{3}{4} \times 21\frac{1}{4}$ (42.5 × 53.9).
Signed 'Blake'.
Tate Gallery, London

From the collection of Thomas Butts though, unlike eight of the series, not actually documented in the surviving accounts between Butts and Blake. There are two other copies of this print, in the Metropolitan Museum, New York, and in the Yale Center for British Art (Paul Mellon Collection). There are also two pencil sketches and a small scale colour-printed try-out (see Nos.96–8). Unlike other drawings related to the large prints, the earliest for 'Pity' is an upright composition, which, together with the small scale try-out suggests that 'Pity' was the first of the designs to be planned.

This print is a marvellously literal depiction of the famous lines from Shakespeare's *Macbeth*, Act 1, Scene 7:

> And pity, like a naked new-born babe,
> Striding the blast, or heaven's cherubin, hors'd
> Upon the sightless couriers of the air,
> Shall blow the horrid deed in every eye,
> That tears shall drown the wind . . .'

But in *Urizen* Pity is seen as a divisive and therefore negative force, 'For pity divides the soul' and, as in Shakespeare's simile of the new-born babe, is associated with the act of procreation (see No.80).

96

96 *First sketch for 'Pity'* c.1795

Pencil, approx. $12 \times 11\frac{1}{8}$ (30.5 × 28.3).
Inscr. by Frederick Tatham, 'Shakespeares Pity. And Pity like a newborn Babe &c &c F. Tatham –.'
Trustees of the British Museum, London

The first separate drawing for the large colour print, No.95; there is also a very rough sketch on page 106 of Blake's Notebook which may be connected. The drawing shows an upright composition and is considerably more dramatic than the final print: the horses rise at a steeper angle while the mother twists and turns as she gives birth, her legs apart and her fingers expressively spread out. Large grasses or rushes are drawn at an angle across the mother's body, and rain falls in the opposite direction.

On the back there is a rough drawing seemingly of two figures surprised by an apparition.

97

97 *Second sketch for 'Pity'* c.1795

Pencil, $10\frac{3}{4} \times 16\frac{5}{8}$ (27.2 × 42.2).
Trustees of the British Museum, London

The format is now the oblong one of the final print and details such as the pose of the mother are now closer to the small trial print, No.98.

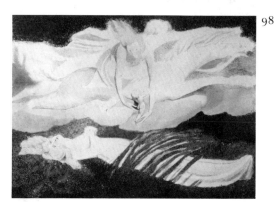

98

98 *'Pity': trial print* c.1795

Colour print touched with pen and watercolour, $7\frac{3}{4} \times 10\frac{13}{16}$ (19.7 × 27.5) on paper $10\frac{15}{16} \times 14\frac{1}{4}$ (27.7 × 36.2).
Trustees of the British Museum, London

An unfinished try-out for the large colour print, No.95. It is in the same direction as the final print, reversing that of the drawings, Nos.96 and 97.

The effect of long grasses sweeping across the figure of the mother is retained from the drawings but there is now no suggestion of falling rain. The mother is clothed and lies passively with clasped hands as in the final print. The group above is also close to the final print though the whole composition is condensed, with less room between the mother and the horses.

99 *Hecate* c.1795

Colour print finished in pen and watercolour, $17\frac{1}{4} \times 22\frac{7}{8}$ (43.9 × 58.1).
Signed 'Blake'.
Watermarked '1794 JWHATMAN'.
Tate Gallery, London

One of the prints from the Butts Collection, though not listed in any of the surviving accounts. Two other copies are known, in the National Gallery of Scotland, Edinburgh, and in the Huntington Library, San Marino. For a pencil sketch in reverse see No.100.

This seems to have been intended as a pair to 'Pity', No.95. The form of the signature, actually incised into the pigment, is the same, the colouring is similar, and there again seems to be a reference to Shakespeare, either to *Macbeth*, in which Hecate appears, or to Puck's closing speech in *A Midsummer Night's Dream*. Both seem to show aspects of the divisive properties of the female will in the Fallen World. In 'Hecate' there is a particular stress on material and vegetative nature. Later, in his *Descriptive Catalogue*, 1809, Blake wrote, 'Shakespeare's Fairies also are the rulers of the vegetable world', and in his description of his lost picture of 'The Last Judgment', 1810 (see p.104) he described two rather similar beings who, 'each with three heads . . . Represent Vegetative Existence'. Hecate is shown with her hand on a book very similar in appearance to Urizen's 'Book of Brass' (see Nos.73 and 75), another sign of the Fallen World.

100 *Sketch for 'Hecate'* c.1795

Pencil and wash, $9\frac{1}{2} \times 10\frac{15}{16}$ (24.2 × 27.8).
Inscr. by Frederick Tatham, 'drawn by . William Blake.'
Private collection, England

A drawing, in reverse, for No.99.

101 *The House of Death* 1795

Colour print finished in pen and watercolour, $19\frac{1}{8} \times 24$ (48.5 × 61).
Signed 'WB 1795', and inscr. 'The House of Death Milton' below design (covered by mount).
Tate Gallery, London

One of the prints delivered to Butts on 5 July 1805 for a guinea. There are two other copies, in the British Museum and in the Fitzwilliam Museum, and a drawing from the early 1790s in the Tate Gallery (see under No.90). This last is particularly close to Fuseli, who did a large painting of the subject for his Milton Gallery in 1793.

An illustration to *Paradise Lost*, xi, 477–93, also known as 'The Lazar House'. Death is shown as much the same Urizenic old man as the God of the Old Testament in the companion prints of 'Elohim creating Adam' and 'God judging Adam', Nos.85 and 87. He is blasting the figures below with thunderbolts from the ends of a scroll that may represent the Mosaic Law. The figures of the dead and dying recall those in Blake's various watercolours of 'A Breach in a City' or 'War' of c.1784 and later (see under Nos.20 and 22–5).

102 *The Good and Evil Angels Struggling for Possession of a Child* 1795

Colour print finished in pen and watercolour, $17\frac{1}{2} \times 23\frac{3}{8}$ (44.5 × 59.4).
Signed 'WB inv [as monogram] 1795', and inscr. 'The Good and Evil Angels' below design (covered by mount).
Tate Gallery, London

One of the prints delivered to Butts on 5 July 1805 for a guinea. There is another copy of the print in the collection of Mr and Mrs John Hay Whitney and a watercolour, in reverse, of two or three years earlier in the Cecil Higgins Museum, Bedford (see under No.90).

All derive from a small design in *The Marriage of Heaven and Hell*, 1790–93, which seems to illustrate 'the following Errors. 1. That Man has two real existing principles Viz: a Body & a Soul. 2. That Energy, called Evil, is alone from the Body, & that Reason, calld Good, is alone from the Soul. 3. That God will torment Man in Eternity for following his Energies.' Blake goes on to assert that the 'following Contraries . . . are True. 1. Man has no body distinct from his Soul . . . 2. Energy is the only life and is from the Body and Reason is the bound or outward circumference of Energy. 3. Energy is Eternal Delight.' The design is thus an attack on the error of dividing Man into his different elements.

Blake had developed and refined this idea in his prophetic books, identifying the different aspects into which Man had become divided by various personifications. Here the fettered figure can be identified as Orc, the son of Los and Enitharmon and Blake's symbol of energy and revolt. His chaining by Los had been described in *Urizen*, 1794; see No.83, and also the plate from *America*, 1793, No.59. Here he is older and (in this version of the composition only) blind. The other figure is Los, the imaginative force of Man but equally liable to fall into a negative state, as in his chaining of Orc, the result of jealousy. The child is not paralleled in Blake's writings (Blake had now reached the stage where his myth could evolve independently in either medium) but may represent the lost innocence of undivided Man, now torn between the two angels.

102

103 *Christ Appearing to the Apostles after the Resurrection* c.1795.

Colour print finished in pen and watercolour, varnished, $17 \times 22\frac{1}{2}$ (43 × 57.3).
Signed 'WB inv' as monogram and possibly with traces of a date.
Yale University Art Gallery, New Haven, Connecticut

Despite its different later history, this is one of the prints delivered to Thomas Butts on 7 September 1805 for one guinea, being listed in his account with Blake as 'Christ appearing'. In 1863 it belonged to J. C. Strange, and later to Charles Eliot Norton.

An illustration to Luke 24:36–40: the Apostles 'terrified and affrighted' at Christ's appearance. After the condemnatory nature of the rest of the large colour prints it is difficult to see this merely as the happy end of the story. Blake contrasts the young Apostle who gazes up at Christ with the rest who bow in adoration. Perhaps he is the only one to see Him truly, while the others worship Him as an idol, a state even worse than that under the dispensation of the Old Testament. Alternatively the young Apostle may be Doubting Thomas; there is a parallel illustration of that subject on page 265 of the *Night Thoughts* designs of 1795–7.

103

The Great Book Illustrations, c.1795–8

At the same time as Blake's development of his illustrations to his own writings reached its paradoxical climax in the independent colour prints of 1795 he was beginning his greatest and most ambitious series of book illustrations to the text of another writer, the 537 illustrations to Edward Young's *Night Thoughts*. Prodigious in number and large in format, they also show a revolutionary reversal of the roles of text and illustration. Here the illustration literally surrounds the text. The pages of an earlier edition of the book were set off-centre into large sheets of Whatman paper on which Blake drew and coloured his designs. His use of this at first sight awkward format is amazingly varied; he skilfully handles the available irregular areas of paper, wider at the bottom and on one side, suggesting actions or giant figures continuing behind the text panel; Blake even placed little figures sitting on the top of the text panel as if it were a solid object. In the projected engravings the effect was retained although, of course, the actual physical separation of text page from drawing paper was not. Unfortunately, as so often in Blake's career, the projected four-volume publication ran out of steam after the first volume, and this itself, as indeed was probably envisaged from the beginning, used only forty-three of the 156 designs for that section of the text. As with so many other ambitious artistic schemes of the 1790s, such as Boydell's Shakespeare Gallery and Fuseli's Milton Gallery, the war with France caused an economic setback that cut at the roots of artistic patronage.

The text of Young's *Night Thoughts* was one of many eighteenth-century texts moralising over death and salvation, three of which were treated by Blake; as well as the *Night Thoughts* he was later to illustrate Robert Blair's *The Grave* (see Nos.152–8) and, in the form of a single elaborate watercolour, James Hervey's *Meditations Among the Tombs* (No.314). Typically, the text, as well as giving Blake ample opportunity to illustrate a theme broadly congenial to him, was subjected to a certain amount of re-interpretation and even criticism, not overt but through subtleties of emphasis and detail.

Similar in format, but more varied in subject and treatment, are the illustrations to Gray's *Poems* commissioned by Blake's friend the sculptor John Flaxman for his wife Nancy. Here ladies in contemporary dress mingle with figures from ancient mythology and humanoid cats, a diversity unified by Blake's fresh treatment of the text, sometimes almost cheekily literal, sometimes again critical or interpretative.

104

Illustrations to Young's 'Night Thoughts' c.1795–7

Pen and watercolour over pencil, each approx. $16\frac{1}{2} \times 12\frac{7}{8}$
(42 × 32.5), enclosing inlaid text page approx. 9 × 6 (23 × 15).
Trustees of the British Museum, London

These designs were commissioned, probably in 1795, by the bookseller Richard Edwards for a new edition of Edward Young's *The Complaint, and the Consolation; or, Night Thoughts*, first published in 1742–5. Four volumes were planned, for which Blake was to engrave a selection from his own designs. The project was one of many such *de luxe* editions published in the eighteenth century, particularly towards the end; at this time the idea of illustrating the literary classics also spilled over into the even more ambitious displays of the paintings from which the illustrations were to be engraved, such as Boydell's Shakespeare Gallery and Fuseli's Milton Gallery. However, only the first volume containing forty-three plates, engraved in 1796 and 1797, was ever published owing to the economic recession caused by war with France. Blake was paid twenty guineas for his designs.

As Edwards stated in his introduction, 'the narrative is short', dealing with the death abroad of Young's fictitious daughter Narcissa and the refusal of the local Catholic priests to bury her; 'the morality arising from it forms the bulk of the poem'. The poem is divided into nine 'Nights'; their subtitles, given below, give some idea of the nature of the text.

Blake did his drawings on large sheets of Whatman paper (some watermarked 1794) into which were set pages from the 1742–5 edition of the book. Edwards seems to have suggested certain lines for illustration, usually by marking them in ink. The pencilled stars or crosses, which usually correspond with what actually was illustrated, seem to be by Blake himself.

The watercolours remained with the Edwards family until 1874. In 1905 they were bought by the American collector Marsden J. Perry, who sold them in 1908 to W. A. White. They were given to the British Museum twenty years later by White's daughter, Mrs Frances Emerson.

This fantastic number of illustrations, 537 in all, represents about a quarter of Blake's total surviving output. On the whole Blake seems to have been content to let the text stand without too much criticism or reinterpretation in the illustrations, though he was always quick to add visual metaphors for Young's somewhat pedantic verses. The lack of much narrative continuity in the text made it difficult for Blake to build up any sustained visual commentary, though he does seem to have consistently strengthened the Christian allusions; see Nos.122 and 124.

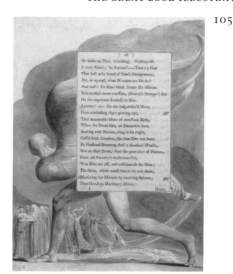

105

104 Night I: page 15
Illustrations to *Night Thoughts* no.20.
An illustration to line 203 of 'Night the First, on Life, Death and Immortality': 'Death! Great Proprietor of all!', treading down Empire and quenching the stars. This design was one of those that were engraved, on page 8 of the 1797 edition.

105 Night II: page 16
Illustrations to *Night Thoughts* no.49.
An illustration to line 204 of 'Night the Second, on Time, Death and Friendship': 'Time's Omnipotence', in which Time is shown mowing down people of all ages with his scythe. This design was also engraved, on page 26 of the 1797 edition.

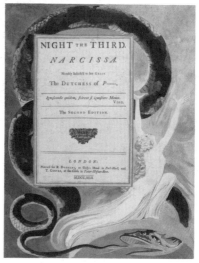

106

106 Night III: title-page
Illustrations to *Night Thoughts* no.78.
Partly based on lines 81–2 of 'Night the Third, Narcissa': Narcissa, compared to Cynthia, the 'patroness of song' with her crescent, escapes from the serpent, sweeping upwards in a glory of light. Narcissa is shown as the 'woman clothed in the sun' of Revelation 12:1, transcending the serpent which, with its tail in its mouth closing the circle, here symbolised for Blake the endless revolutions of time rather than those of eternity. This design was engraved on page 43 of the 1797 edition.

107 Night III: page 12
Illustrations to *Night Thoughts* no.87.
Blake starred line 127 but illustrated the whole passage, lines 120–30: the sun has failed to give Narcissa 'his wonted succour', while,

> Queen Lilies! and ye painted populace!
> Who lived in fields . . .
> . . . drink the sun, which gives your cheeks to glow.

The design was engraved on page 49 of the 1797 edition.

107

108 Night III: page 28
Illustrations to *Night Thoughts* no.103.
An illustration to lines 430–2, in which this life is compared to the Moon:
> Dark in herself . . . but Rich
> In borrow'd Lustre from a higher Sphere.

109 Night III: page 32
Illustrations to *Night Thoughts* no.107.
An illustration to line 496, showing 'Age and Disease', notable for its most beautiful overall colour wash.

108

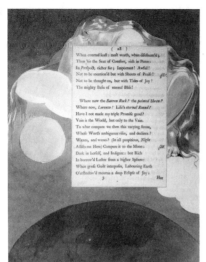

111

109

112

110

113

110 **Night IV: page 5**
Illustrations to *Night Thoughts* no.114.
An illustration to lines 44–6 of 'Night the Fourth, The Christian Triumph':
When, on their Exit, Souls are bid invoke
Toss Fortune back her Tinsel, and her Plume,
And drop this Mask of Flesh behind the Scene.

111 **Night V: page 46**
Illustrations to *Night Thoughts* no.201.
An illustration to line 785 of 'Night the Fifth, the Relapse': Death 'sweeps his Rubbish to the Grave'.

112 **Night VI: page 37**
Illustrations to *Night Thoughts* no.258.
An illustration to lines 721–2 of 'Night the Sixth, the Infidel Reclaim'd . . . Containing the Nature, Proof, and Importance of Immortality': 'Here, dormant Matter, waits a call to Life; Half-life, half-death join There'. Dormant matter, or a state of half-death, is typified by Blake as the roots and branches of a tree, symbolising vegetative existence.

113 **Night VII: page viii**
Illustrations to *Night Thoughts* no.272.
This page is the list of contents for 'Night the Seventh, being the Second Part of the Infidel Reclaimed'. A woman crouches in a red blossom with a butterfly, symbol of the return of the soul to the body after the temporary sleep of death. She apparently holds a cocoon, another symbol of rebirth.

114 **Night VII: page 52**
Illustrations to *Night Thoughts* no.324.
An illustration to lines 1042–3; Christ in Hell where,
. . . astonisht at his Guest,
For one short Moment Lucifer ador'd.

115 **Night VIII: title-page**
Illustrations to *Night Thoughts* no.345.
The title-page to 'Night the Eighth, Virtue's Apology; or, the Man of the World Answer'd, in which are Considered, the Love of This Life; the Ambition and Pleasure, with the Wit and Wisdom of the World'. Blake typifies this by the Whore of Babylon, her forehead inscribed 'MYSTERY' and with two deliberately illegible lines of writing (Revelation 17:3–4). She rides the Beast with Seven Heads, differentiated by Blake to represent various officers of Church and State; these are (beginning on the right) a judge, a warrior, a war lord crowned and with ram's horns, a Pope with tiara and goat's horns, a king, a mitred bishop and a priest.

116 **Night VIII: page 7**
Illustrations to *Night Thoughts* no.353.
An illustration to lines 113–4, showing Time's daughters 'as they spin our Hours on Fortune's Wheel', watched over by Time as he appears throughout these illustrations, with bald patch and top-knot.

117 **Night VIII: page 10**
Illustrations to *Night Thoughts* no.356.
An illustration to lines 182–3, of the young who launch out into the world, 'And fondly dream each Wind, and Star, our Friend'; the facing page shows three shipwrecked figures. Blake gets a wonderful sense of movement into the oarsman on the prow.

114

115

116

117

120

118

121

119

122

118 Night VIII: page 63
Illustrations to *Night Thoughts* no.409.
An illustration to line 1179, etc., 'A Dance of Spirits, a mere Froth of Joy . . .'.
The text panel is surmounted by a monstrous bat, a harbinger of the dismal
aftermath shown on the following page (not shown here).

119 Night IX: page 7
Illustrations to *Night Thoughts* no.425.
An illustration to lines 111–13, etc., of Night the Ninth, 'The Consolation',
When down thy Vale, . . .
O Death! I stretch my View; what Visions rise?
What Triumphs! Toils imperial! Arts divine!
In wither'd Laurels, glide before my sight?
Death is shown as a huge bowman, his eye starting out from behind the
text panel.

120 Night IX: page 28
Illustrations to *Night Thoughts* no.446.
An illustration to lines 558–61, a personification of Night:
A starry Crown thy Raven-Brow adorns,
An azure Zone, thy Waist; Clouds, in Heav'n's Loom
Wrought thro' Varieties of Shape and Shade,
In ample Folds of Drapery divine,
Thy flowing Mantle form . . .
The cross-reference by the text to the personification of Darkness in
'Night III' is presumably in Edwards' hand.

123

121 Night IX: page 34
Illustrations to *Night Thoughts* no.452.
An illustration to lines 664–5,
When Giant-Angels met,
To controvert the Sceptre of the Skies . . .
This composition was developed in a series of drawings beginning in the
1780s, when the subject was seen as a direct illustration to Milton's
Paradise Lost; see No.12.

122 Night IX: page 70
Illustrations to *Night Thoughts* no.488.
An illustration to lines 1430–1,
As in a golden Net of Providence,
How art thou caught? Sure captive of Belief.
Blake gives this a specifically Christian imagery by showing two Apostles
fishing for souls with Christ above.

124

123 Night IX: page 82
Illustrations to *Night Thoughts* no.500.
An illustration to lines 1678–80, '. . . the Queen of Heaven, Walking in
Brightness', shown as Diana with a crescent-moon on her forehead.

124 Night IX: page 94
Illustrations to *Night Thoughts* no.512.
An illustration to lines 1945–6, '"In One agglomerated Cluster, hung,
Great Vine! on Thee . . ."' Another case in which Blake gives Young's text a
more specific Christian reference, showing Christ as the centre of a vine in
which cluster various souls including an embracing couple and a mother
with two children (Cf. John 15: 1: 'I am the true vine').

125

126

127

Illustrations to Gray's 'Poems' c.1797–8

Pen and watercolour over pencil on paper, each approx. $16\frac{1}{2} \times 12\frac{7}{8}$ (42 × 32.5), enclosing inlaid text page approx. $6\frac{1}{4} \times 3\frac{5}{8}$ (16 × 9).
Mr and Mrs Paul Mellon

Presumably after seeing some of the *Night Thoughts* illustrations, Blake's friend John Flaxman commissioned a series of illustrations to the collected poems of Thomas Gray for ten guineas. Blake completed 116 illustrations. There does not seem to have been any idea of engraving the series.

As in the case of the *Night Thoughts* illustrations, pages from an earlier edition of Gray's poems, that of 1790, were inlaid into the same '1794 JWHATMAN' paper. Blake marked the lines he intended to illustrate in the margin, listing these, poem by poem, on the blank backs of text pages. He numbered each poem's illustrations separately whereas the numbering on the inlaid text pages runs consecutively starting at Page 43 (the pages up to 42 containing the preliminary matter of the 1790 edition were omitted). The continuous numbering used here follows the order in which the illustrations were formerly bound, with a drawing of Blake by Flaxman inserted as a frontispiece.

Following the Flaxman sale of 1828 the illustrations were acquired by William Beckford of Fonthill fame. His daughter married the 10th Duke of Hamilton, in whose descendants' possession they remained until 1966 when they were sold to Mr and Mrs Paul Mellon.

Unlike the *Night Thoughts* Gray's poems, as arranged in the 1790 edition, gave Blake much greater scope for sustained critical commentary through his illustrations, the poems very generally mapping out a course from birth to death. A series of depictions of the poet at intervals throughout the book shows him becoming progressively less and less inspired; see no.125.

125 'Ode on the Spring': page 2

Illustrations to Gray no.2.

Blake has used the blank reverse of the title-page to write his list of illustrations to the first poem; this design is '2 Gray writing his Poems'. At the foot of the list he has added the couplet,

> *Around the Springs of Gray my wild root weaves*
> *Traveller repose & dream among my leaves.*
> *–Will. Blake*

This serves as warning that the interpretation embodied in his illustrations may be rather 'wild'. The imagery of the root weaving around Gray's 'Springs' is taken up in the next illustration, No.126. Here the poet is shown illuminated by a giant sun of inspiration. Later, at the beginning of 'The Progress of Poesy', he is shown being inspired indirectly by a six-winged cherub through the medium of a muse writing on a scroll. Later still, at the opening of 'Elegy in a Country Church-Yard', he is crouching over his writing, hooded by his deep collar, in a Gothic interior without any shafts of light to indicate inspiration.

126 'Ode on the Spring': page 3

Illustrations to Gray no.3.

Entitled in the list on page 2, '3 The Purple Year awakening from the Roots of Nature, & the Hours suckling their Flowery Infants', a paraphrase of the opening lines of the poem,

> *Lo! where the rosy-bosom'd hours,*
> *Fair Venus' train, appear,*
> *Disclose the long-expected flowers,*
> *And wake the purple year!*

Blake also shows the 'Attic warbler' of line 5 in the form of a girl with a Greek lyre, and the 'Cool Zephyrs' in 'the clear blue sky' of line 9. The poet, from the facing page 2, here starts up at the signs of spring.

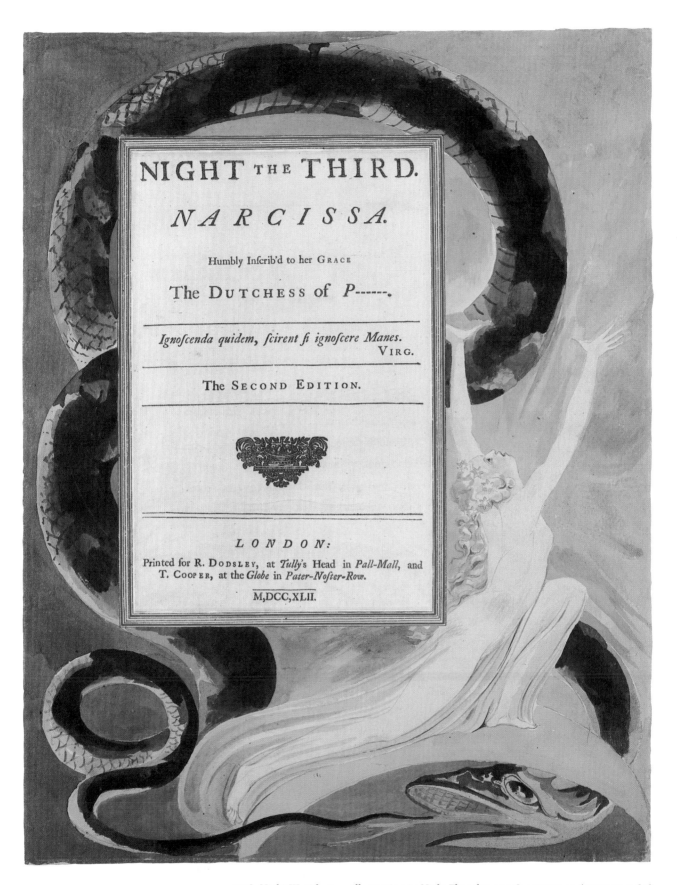

NIGHT THE THIRD.

NARCISSA.

Humbly Infcrib'd to her GRACE

The DUTCHESS of P——.

Ignofcenda quidem, fcirent fi ignofcere Manes.
VIRG.

The SECOND EDITION.

LONDON:

Printed for R. DODSLEY, at *Tully's* Head in *Pall-Mall*, and
T. COOPER, at the *Globe* in *Pater-Nofter-Row*.

M,DCC,XLII.

138 *Our Lady with the Infant Jesus Riding on a Lamb, with St. John,* 1800 (entry on p.76)

127 'Ode on the Death of a Favourite Cat': page 3
> Illustrations to Gray no.9.

Entitled in the list of illustrations to this poem on the previous page,

> *3 'The Pensive Selima*
> *Her Ears of Jet & Emerald Eyes*
> *She saw & purr'd applause.'*

This is a condensation of the opening of the poem on this page. Blake obviously delighted in the story of the sad fate of Horace Walpole's cat Selima, drowned while trying to fish goldfish out of their bowl, which Gray treated as a cautionary tale for the females of all species. Blake makes much of the ambiguity between Selima as cat and as woman, and extends this ambiguity to the fish. The ambiguity is further extended in the case of Selima: her 'conscious tail' which declares her joy is detached and placed above the text box, and her cat-like ears do not appear in her reflection.

128 'A Long Story': page 8
> Illustrations to Gray no.30.

Entitled in the list of illustrations to this poem, 'Out of the window whisk they flew'. Gray's poem is a fanciful account of the visit to his house of two ladies while he was out, and gave Blake a marvellous opportunity to apply his imagination to figures in contemporary dress.

129 'The Progress of Poesy': page 6
> Illustrations to Gray no.46.

Entitled by Blake, '6. "Hyperions march they spy & glittering shafts of war"'; the same line is marked in the margin. Blake follows Gray's metaphor of Hyperion as Dawn driving out the forces of Night to illustrate how poetry can overcome the ills of everyday life. The youthful god in a blaze of light resembles Blake's depictions of his own personification of imaginative energy, Orc. For a preliminary drawing see No.132. Blake later developed the compositions in 'The Rout of the Rebel Angels', one of his illustrations to Milton's *Paradise Lost*, No.222.

130 'The Fatal Sisters, An Ode': page 6
> Illustrations to Gray no.72.

The poem ('from the Norse tongue', Gray adds in brackets) is the song of twelve giant women, the valkyrie, as they decide the fates of those about to be involved in a battle in eleventh-century Ireland; they accompany the song by weaving a web on a loom. Blake shows the fatal sisters as only three in number, presumably an allusion to the three Fates. This illustration shows them at their work. Blake marked the first line on this page, 'See the grisly texture grow!' and quotes lines 5 and 6 in his list of illustrations to this poem,

> *6. 'Shafts for shuttle dipd in gore,*
> *Shoot the trembling cords along'.*

He illustrates the whole grisly business, how 'glitt'ring lances are the loom' (on the previous page), how shafts 'dipt in gore' act as the shuttles, how each weight is 'a gasping warrior's head', and how the web is 'of human entrails made', and produces one of his amazingly original designs sheerly by using the images in the text.

131 'The Descent of Odin, an Ode': page 10
> Illustrations to Gray no.86.

This page, though bearing the list of titles for 'The Triumphs of Owen', is in fact illustrated with the last design to 'The Descent of Odin, an Ode', another work 'from the Norse tongue'. It is entitled, '10. The Serpent and the Wolvish Dog, two terrors in the Northern Mythology,' and is remarkable for the power of one of Blake's most simple symmetrical designs.

132 *Hyperion ('The Bowman'), Study for Gray's 'Poems':*
page 46 c.1797 8
Pencil, sight $7\frac{11}{16} \times 8\frac{7}{16}$ (19.5 × 21.4).
Private collection, England

In the illustrations to Gray, No.129, Blake omitted the angry figure who seems to spur Hyperion on, presumably Jove whose laws and gift of 'the heav'nly Muse' are fulfilled when Hyperion drives away the Night.

133 Not exhibited

131

132

Blake's First Works for Thomas Butts:
Tempera Paintings of Biblical Subjects, c.1799–1800

Blake never achieved commercial success. Although he continued to exhibit at the Royal Academy at irregular intervals until 1808 he seems to have sold nothing there after the Joseph watercolours in 1785, if indeed he sold those. The *de luxe* edition of Young's *Night Thoughts* had foundered because of the economic climate. The most hopeful source of income, ordinary commercial engraving, was a fitful one and Blake's rather old-fashioned technique meant that most of his commissions came through friends and that only spasmodically. However, what really kept him alive was the long-lasting patronage of two people. The first was Thomas Butts, a clerk in the office of the Commissary General of Musters who seems to have paid him a more or less regular wage in return for the bulk of his output from 1799 until at least 1816 and probably considerably later. Second was the young artist John Linnell whom Blake met in 1818 and who seems to have kept Blake going in much the same way for the last years of his life (see p.133).

On 26 August 1799 Blake wrote to his friend George Cumberland, 'As to Myself, about whom you are so kindly Interested, I live by Miracle. I am Painting small Pictures from the Bible . . . . My Work pleases my employer, & I have an order for Fifty small Pictures at One Guinea each, which is Something better than mere copying after another artist.' The new employer was Thomas Butts and the fifty small pictures are the small works in tempera some of which are dated 1799 or 1800; one had been exhibited at the Royal Academy earlier in 1799 and another was shown there in 1800. Although some are lost a total of about fifty titles can be accounted for. The medium of these paintings, and their relatively dark and rich colouring, is similar to that of the large colour prints of 1795. Although Blake claimed that his process was that described in the Renaissance treatise of Cennini, in fact, possibly through a mistake in translation, he used carpenters' glue instead of the usual size or egg medium. This has often caused his temperas to crack and darken, though late in his life he radically altered his process (see p.142). Later, in the *Descriptive Catalogue* to his own exhibition of 1809–10, he describes his technique as 'Fresco' in deliberate allusion to Renaissance practice, though he does not seem to have realised that Renaissance wall paintings in fresco differed in technique from paintings on panel in tempera.

These tempera paintings are mainly the same size (though a few are uprights). There is also a smaller group from the same series somewhat larger in size. From 1800 onwards Blake seems to have switched to watercolour for the Biblical subjects he painted for Butts; examples of these are treated in a later section; see Nos.159–90.

134

134 *Moses Indignant at the Golden Calf* c.1799–1800

    Tempera on canvas, $15 \times 10\frac{1}{2}$ (38×26.6).
    Signed 'WB [inv]'; the signature is damaged but was probably Blake's usual monogram.
    Private collection, England

Exodus 32:19. Moses protests at the Israelites' idolatrous worship of the Golden Calf, set up by Aaron during his absence. Blake contrasts the magnificent angular figure of the indignant Moses with the graceful dancers on the left, behind whom stands Aaron. The Tables of the Law lie broken at Moses' feet.

From the Butts and W. Graham Robertson collections. This is one of the few upright compositions in the series of biblical subjects painted in tempera. The only other known examples are of the four Evangelists though there may have been others among those now missing.

135 *Bathsheba at the Bath* c.1799–1800

    Tempera on canvas, $10\frac{3}{8} \times 14\frac{13}{16}$ (26.3×37.6), cut down from approx. $10\frac{1}{4} \times 15$ (26.5×38).
    Signed 'WB inv' as monogram.
    Tate Gallery, London

2 Samuel 11:2. King David spies on the naked Bathsheba. Blake adds the two children, who are absent from the biblical text. This is one of the most sensuous of Blake's works, contrasting strongly with the harshness of Nos.134 and 139. In strong contrast to Blake's later aesthetic principles he seems here to have been influenced by Correggio or Parmigianino.

135

136

137

138

136 *The Flight into Egypt* 1799

Tempera on canvas, $10\frac{11}{16} \times 15\frac{1}{16}$ (27.2 × 38.3).
Signed 'WB inv [as monogram] 179[9]'.
Private collection, England

Matthew 2:13–14. Blake adds the guardian angels, the outspread wings of those on the right extending protectively over the Virgin and Child on the donkey. Unfortunately the next tempera in the series, 'The Repose in Egypt', is now lost, but William Rossetti's description suggests that it would have been a worthy companion to this wonderfully imaginative picture: 'The Holy Family are within a tent; an angel at its entrance; the donkey outside'.

From the Butts and W. Graham Robertson collections.

137 *The Christ Child Asleep on the Cross* c.1799–1800

Tempera on canvas, $10\frac{5}{8} \times 15\frac{1}{4}$ (27 × 38.7).
Victoria and Albert Museum, London

Blake painted two if not three versions of this rare, non-biblical subject. The other known example in an English private collection shows St. Joseph standing on the right holding a pair of compasses, with a set-square lying on the ground beside the cross; it has an open landscape setting, not the timber scaffolding of this version. Here the compasses rest against the scaffolding on the right and, with the heavy rectangular wooden forms, represent the law of reason, perhaps to signify the forces by which Christ was to suffer, or to imply that these forces were to be reconciled with those of love and imagination as part of Man's Redemption through Christ.

From the Butts and Stirling Maxwell collections.

138 *Our Lady with the Infant Jesus Riding on a Lamb, with St. John* 1800

Pen and tempera on canvas, $10\frac{3}{4} \times 15\frac{1}{4}$ (27.3 × 38.7).
Signed 'WB inv [as monogram] 1800'.
Victoria and Albert Museum, London

Like the other paintings of the infancy of Christ this is not based on a biblical text, but the subject is a traditional one. Blake follows precedent in including St. John, the bridge between the dispensations of the Old and New Testaments, and in using the symbolism of the lamb, a prefiguration of Christ's sacrifice.

139 *The Agony in the Garden* c.1799–1800

Tempera on copper, $10\frac{5}{8} \times 15$ (27 × 38), cut off diagonally at each corner.
Signed 'WB inv' as monogram.
Tate Gallery, London

Luke 22:41–4. Blake depicts the details of Christ's sweat, 'as it were great drops of blood falling down to the ground', and, unusually, shows the angel actually physically supporting the swooning Christ. The main source of light is the angel and the glory from which he emerges, which falls full upon the figure of Christ and flickers over the trees and sleeping Apostles in the background.

From the Butts and W. Graham Robertson collections.

140 *The Body of Christ Borne to the Tomb* c.1799–1800

Tempera on canvas, $10\frac{1}{2} \times 14\frac{7}{8}$ (26.7 × 37.8).
Signed 'WB inv' as monogram.
Tate Gallery, London

The procession from Calvary is not actually described in the Gospels. Joseph of Arimathea, shown in this picture with staff and jar of unguents (and also in the following scene of 'The Entombment' at Pollok House, Glasgow),

may have been given prominence here on account of his being both the archetype of the artist and, in legend, the first of Christ's followers to come to England.

The strongly Neo-Classical composition of this painting is in marked contrast to others of the series and anticipates Blake's biblical watercolours of some five years later. The influence of such a work as Flaxman's 'Elektra leading a Procession to Agamemnon's Tomb', from the *Choëphoroe*, 1795, has been demonstrated.

From the collections of Thomas Butts and F. T. Palgrave of *Golden Treasury* fame.

The Hazards of Patronage:
William Hayley and 'The Grave', c.1799–1806

The same letter to George Cumberland of 26 August 1799 that mentions Blake's commission to paint biblical subjects for Thomas Butts also includes Blake's account of the conclusion of another, but unsuccessful, attempt to secure patronage, in this case from the Rev. Dr John Trusler, who had asked for a pair of watercolours on the subject of 'Benevolence' and 'Malevolence'. Although the one surviving watercolour (No.141) is not perhaps among Blake's greatest works, the affair provoked Blake into a fascinating declaration of artistic principles, one at marked variance from what he was to say ten years or so later (see p.104).

A more long-lasting but equally negative patronage was that of William Hayley, the poet, biographer and man of letters, to whom Blake had been recommended by John Flaxman. Hayley persuaded Blake to leave London for the only time in his life to live near Chichester, at Felpham, where Hayley had his own house 'The Turret', with the well-meaning but ultimately disastrous idea of getting Blake to help him with various artistic projects. Unfortunately Hayley, though the patron and biographer of such imaginative spirits as the painter George Romney and the poet William Cowper, tried to divert Blake from his own creative work to such more commercially viable but uninspired projects as the decoration of his library (see No.145), the painting of miniature portraits, and the illustration of Hayley's poems and biographies (see Nos.146–8). After three years Blake had had enough and returned to London, though Hayley continued to befriend him, including paying for a lawyer to defend him from a charge of sedition that arose out of an incident when Blake threw a drunken soldier out of his cottage garden.

The years at Felpham were not wasted, however. Not only did Blake continue with his biblical illustrations for Thomas Butts but the period also saw the gestation of his two last prophetic books, *Milton* and *Jerusalem*. Blake referred to these years both as 'my three years slumber on the banks of the Ocean' (in his address 'To the Public' at the beginning of *Jerusalem*) and as 'my three years' rest from perturbation' (in a letter to Hayley of 23 October 1804). In the same letter to Hayley he remarked how 'Suddenly, on the day after visiting the Truchsessian Gallery of pictures', a collection, albeit largely of copies, which introduced Blake in particular to Flemish and German primitive art, 'I was again enlightened with the light I enjoyed in my youth, and which has for exactly twenty years been closed from me as by a door and by window-shutters'. The result can be seen in the change of style discernable over the years 1800–05 and particularly within the series of water-colour illustrations to the Bible painted for Thomas Butts, Nos.159–90.

Blake suffered a more direct form of betrayal in yet another at first sight providential invitation, that of the engraver and publisher Robert Hartley Cromek to do a series of illustrations to Robert Blair's *The Grave*. This was another example of 'grave-yard poetry' like Young's *Night Thoughts* and had first been published in 1743. In 1805 Cromek invited Blake to design and engrave twenty illustrations but, at least in part behind Blake's back, he cut the number of illustrations to twelve and switched the remunerative job of engraving them from Blake to the fashionable Luigi Schiavonetti. The probable reason for the switch can be demonstrated by comparing Blake's trial engraving of 'Death's Door' with that by Schiavonetti (Nos.152 and 153). Relations between Blake and Cromek were not improved by the latter's rejection of an extra design Blake had done to accompany his dedication to the Queen (see No.158). In turn this dispute led to a further row over 'Chaucer's Canterbury Pilgrims'; see No.210.

Paradoxically, these illustrations, engraved by another, were probably the works of Blake that received the widest attention during his lifetime. The publication secured him the fullest press-coverage of his life though two of the three reviews that have been traced were extremely critical. Nevertheless the book was issued by Cromek in both folio and quarto in 1808 and again by Ackermann in 1813, and the plates were reused in 1826 for Jose Joaquin de Mora's *Meditaciones Poeticas*, for which the Spanish poet had specially written the verses that illustrate the designs of 'Guillermo Black'.

The book was published with a frontispiece engraved after Thomas Phillips' portrait of Blake (now in the National Portrait Gallery), an appreciation by Fuseli, and an unsigned description of the plates almost certainly by Blake's friend Benjamin Heath Malkin. Cromek's advertisement included a testimonial to the excellence of the drawings signed by eleven members of the Royal Academy, headed by the president Benjamin West and including not only friends of Blake like Flaxman and Stothard but also Lawrence, Beechey and Nollekens.

Even for Thomas Butts, Blake executed certain tasks that must have been uncongenial to him. Miniature portraits of Butts (No.150), his wife and his son presumably reflect the influence of William Hayley. He also gave both son and father lessons in engraving. Even Mrs Butts was not left out. A needlewoman of great accomplishment, at least one of her panels seems to have been designed by Blake (No.151).

141 *Malevolence* 1799

Pen and watercolour, $11\frac{7}{8} \times 8\frac{7}{8}$ (30 × 22.5).
Signed 'W B inv' as monogram.
Philadelphia Museum of Art: Gift of Mrs William T. Tonner

141

This was painted for the Rev. Dr John Trusler of Englefield Green, near Egham, Surrey as the result of an introduction from George Cumberland. Trusler's dissatisfaction with the result provoked two letters from Blake which are particularly interesting in that they contain Blake's views on art at the time.

Trusler had asked for a pair of watercolours showing 'Malevolence' and 'Benevolence' and had apparently specified more or less exactly how the subjects were to be treated. On 16 August 1799 Blake wrote to Trusler enclosing 'Malevolence'. 'I find more and more that my Style of Designing is a Species by itself, & in this which I send you have been compelled by my Genius or Angel to follow where he led . . . . I attempted every morning for a fortnight together to follow your Dictate, but when I found my attempts were in vain, resolved to shew an independence which I know will please an Author [Trusler was the author, among other things, of *Luxury not Political Evil* and *The Way to be Rich and Respectable*] better than slavishly following the track of another . . . .

'If you approve of my Manner, & it is agreeable to you, I would rather Paint Pictures in oil [sic!] of the same dimensions than make Drawings, & on the same terms; by this means you will have a number of Cabinet pictures, which I flatter myself will not be unworthy of a Scholar of Rembrandt and Teniers, whom I have Studied no less than Rafael & Michael angelo'.

Trusler rejected the watercolour saying, according to Blake's report in a letter to Cumberland of 26 August 1799, that, '"*Your Fancy*, from what I have seen of it, & I have seen variety at Mr Cumberland's, seems to be in the other world, or the World of Spirits, which accords not with my Intentions, which, whilst living in This World, Wish to follow *the Nature of it*."'

Blake added, 'I could not help smiling at the difference between the doctrines of Dr Trusler & those of Christ', and could not refrain from teasing Trusler, in his reply to him of 23 August, by being really sorry that he had 'fallen out with the Spiritual World . . . . I had hoped that your plan comprehended All Species of this Art, & Expecially that you would not regret that Species which give Existence to Every other, namely, Visions of Eternity. You say I want somebody to Elucidate my Ideas. But you ought to know that What is Grand is necessarily obscure to Weak men. That which can be made Explicit to the Idiot is not worth my care'. Later in the letter Blake accuses him of having an eye 'perverted by Caricature Prints'; in his letter to Cumberland Blake regretted that Trusler 'should be so enamoured of Rowlandson's caricatures as to call them copies from life & manners, of fit Things for a Clergyman to write upon'.

Blake's second letter to Trusler continued, 'And I know that this World is a World of imagination & Vision. I see Every thing that I paint In This World, but Every body does not see alike . . . . The tree which moves some to tears of joy is in the Eyes of others only a green thing that stands in the way . . . . But to the Eyes of the Man of Imagination, Nature is Imagination itself.' The greatest art and literature 'are addressed to the Imagination, which is Spiritual Sensations, & but mediately to the Understanding or Reason'.

142

Blake described 'Malevolence' as follows: 'A Father, taking leave of his Wife and Child, is watched by Two Fiends incarnate, with intention that when his back is turned they will murder the mother and her infant. If this is not Malevolence with a vengeance, I have never seen it on Earth . . . .' The composition is a development of the illustration to the Preludium of *Europe*, 1794, in which a solitary assassin crouches in wait for an approaching traveller; see No.64.

142 *Churchyard Spectres Frightening a Schoolboy*

c.1795–1800

Pen and watercolour over pencil, 7 × 4½ (17.5 × 11.5).
Private collection, England

A somewhat similar scene occurs in Robert Blair's *The Grave*, for which Blake was to do a series of illustrations in 1805, but there is no justification in the text for the figure on the right, who looks like a schoolmaster holding a birch, nor for the fact that the boy is clutching a doll rather than his satchel. Moreover, in so far as one can judge from an unfinished watercolour, the style suggests a date in the later 1790s, perhaps contemporary with 'Malevolence', No.141.

Although the early history of this watercolour is not known it belonged to Mrs Alexander Gilchrist, the widow of Blake's biographer, and later to William Rossetti, who helped his brother Dante Gabriel Rossetti to edit Gilchrist's *Life* and was responsible for the list-catalogue that appears in the second volume.

143

143 *Moore and Co's Advertisement* 1797–8

Line engraving, 10⁷⁄₁₆ × 9⁷⁄₁₆ (26.5 × 24); platemark 14 × 10¾ (35.5 × 27.3).
Signed 'Blake d. & sc:'; for further inscriptions see below.
Trustees of the British Museum, London

An advertisement for 'MOORE & CO'S MANUFACTORY & WAREHOUSE of Carpeting and Hosiery, Chiswell Street, MOOR-FIELDS', datable 1797–8 as these were the only years when the firm was known under this particular title. Above are the royal arms. Below, Blake has shown three of the firm's machines at work, labelling them 'Common Carpet Loom', 'Persian and Turkey Carpet Loom' and 'Stocking Frame'; they are manned by charming Stothard-like figures. Underneath is an adaptation of Martial's Epigram 150 from Book 14, translatable as follows: 'The district of London offers you these services: the needle of Babylon is already surpassed by the loom of Britain'. As Geoffrey Keynes remarks, 'He must have been an unusual manufacturer who employed Blake to design his advertisement and spiced it with a quotation from Martial's epigrams.'

There is a sketch for this engraving in the Fondazione Horne, Florence, on the back of an earlier drawing, perhaps for a subject from English history, c.1779–80.

144

144 *Landscape near Felpham* c.1800

Pencil and watercolour, 9⅜ × 13½ (23.7 × 34.3) on paper, irregular, 11¹³⁄₁₆ × 16³⁄₁₆ (30 × 41.2).
Inscr. by Frederick Tatham, 'William Blake vouched by Frederick Tatham. subject not known, perhaps near Felpham'.
Tate Gallery, London

'Heaven opens here on all sides her Golden Gates; her windows are not obstructed by vapours; voices of Celestial inhabitants are more distinctly heard, & their forms more distinctly seen, & my Cottage is also a Shadow of their houses.' So wrote Blake to John Flaxman on 21 September 1800, three days after his arrival at Felpham.

Despite Tatham's inscription the landscape can be precisely identified. The church of St. Mary is on the left, beyond the windmill, and William Hayley's house 'The Turret' is in the centre. Blake's own cottage is on the right, illumined by the beam of sunlight breaking through the clouds.

145

145 *Voltaire* c.1800–03

Pen and tempera on canvas, 16½ × 27¾ (41.9 × 70.6).
City of Manchester Art Galleries

146

One of the eighteen heads of poets painted for the library of William Hayley's house 'The Turret' at Felpham. Blake was already working on some of the heads by November 1800 but the series was probably not finished until 1803. The choice of subjects was Hayley's, hence the inclusion of Voltaire, hardly likely to be a favourite with Blake though he was later the subject of one of Blake's Visionary Heads (private collection, England); Hayley owned Voltaire's complete works. The other portraits included in the scheme are of Homer, Demosthenes, Cicero, Dante, Chaucer, Camoëns, Ercilla, Tasso, Spenser, Shakespeare, Milton, Dryden, Otway, Pope, Klopstock, Cowper and Thomas Alphonso Hayley, usually known as Tom, William Hayley's illegitimate son whose early death in May 1800 at the age of nineteen may have inspired the whole scheme.

The head of Voltaire (1694–1778) is based on the portrait by Maurice Quentin de Latour, painted in England c.1731 and engraved by B. Guelard in the reverse direction to Blake's picture. As in the other pictures of the series, the head is surrounded by a wreath, in this case made up of honeysuckle, convolvulus and pimpernel, and there are flanking figures referring to the subject's writings, here Joan of Arc and a group of soldiers from Voltaire's *La Pucelle*. The choice is an odd one even for Hayley, who condemned Voltaire's poem as 'the wittiest levity of wanton France'; perhaps, seen in juxtaposition with the convoluted forms of the wreath, the scene should be regarded ironically.

Three Engravings from Hayley's 'Ballads' 1805

146 **The Dog**
Line engraving, $4\frac{7}{16} \times 2\frac{13}{16}$ (11.3 × 7.1).
Signed 'Blake inv & s' and inscr. 'The Dog.' and 'Pub^d
June.18.1805. by R Phillips N6. Bridge Street. Black Friers'.
Private collection, England

147 **The Eagle**
Line engraving, $4\frac{1}{4} \times 2\frac{3}{4}$ (10.8 × 7).
Signed 'Blake inv & s' and inscr. 'The Eagle.' and 'Pub^d
June.18.1805. by R. Phillips. N⁰ 6 Bridge Street Black Friers'.
Private collection, England

148 **The Horse**
Line engraving, $4\frac{3}{16} \times 2\frac{13}{16}$ (10.7 × 7.2).
Signed 'Blake inv & sc.' and inscr. 'The Horse' and 'Pub^d
June.18.1805. by R. Phillips N⁰ 6. Bridge Street Black Friers'.
Private collection, England

147

Three of the five plates from the second, 1805 edition of *Ballads, by William Hayley, Esq. Founded on Anecdotes relating to Animals, with Prints, Designed and Engraved by William Blake*. The first edition had been issued in separate parts, a ballad at a time, in 1802, but had petered out after four instalments (spare pages were subsequently used by Blake for scrap paper; see Nos.149 and 154). The 1805 edition was less ambitious, with only one illustration per ballad rather than three. Hayley wrote the Ballads, as he stated rather patronisingly in his preface to the first edition, to provide 'such literary relaxation as might relieve my own mind, and still more amuse a friendly fellow-labourer, whose assiduous occupation gives him a better claim to such indulgence:– I mean my friend, Mr. Blake, the Artist.'

'The Dog' tells of the heroic deed of the pet of a youth who was determined to swim in crocodile-infested waters. Detecting the crocodile below, the dog forestalled his master and sacrificed himself by plunging into the beast's welcoming jaws. 'The Eagle' shows the happy discovery by a mother of her child in an eagle's eyrie, to which he had been carried in the eagle's talons. Both engravings are variants of the designs engraved for the 1802 edition. 'The Horse' only appears in the 1805 edition and was in fact

148

149

150

nearly omitted. Blake succeeded in having it included as he considered the design to be one of his best. It shows a mother defending her young daughter by outfacing a runaway horse, 'Fiercest of Arabia's race'. There is a version in tempera in the Mellon Collection.

149 *Portrait Drawing of Mrs Blake* c.1805 (?)

Pencil, $11\frac{1}{4} \times 8\frac{11}{16}$ (28.6 × 22.1).
Inscr., probably by John Varley, 'Catherine Blake' and 'Mrs Blake drawn by Blake'.
Watermarked '1802'.
Tate Gallery, London

Blake drew this portrait of his wife on the back of page 9 of the quarto edition of William Hayley's *Ballads*, published in 1802. There are many cases of Blake using spare pages from this edition, presumably beginning in 1805, when it was decided to reissue the *Ballads* in a less fully illustrated edition (see Nos.146–8).

This is a fine example of Blake's qualities as a draughtsman. Although usually dated c.1805 the drawing is just possibly that done by Blake on his deathbed. 'Three days before his death', according to Allan Cunningham, after colouring a copy of 'The Ancient of Days' (see No.68), 'He saw his wife in tears – she felt this was to be the last of his works – "Stay, Kate! (cried Blake) keep just as you are – I will draw your portrait – for you have ever been an angel to me" – she obeyed, and the dying man made a fine likeness.' However, there exists a drawing of Catherine Blake by Frederick Tatham in which she appears considerably older than in the Tate Gallery drawing so it is more likely that the latter was done some time before Blake's death.

From the collections of Mrs Alexander Gilchrist and Miss Alice G. E. Carthew.

150 *Miniature Portrait of Thomas Butts* 1801(?)

Watercolour on ivory, oval, $3\frac{5}{16} \times 2\frac{1}{2}$ (8.4 × 6.3).
Trustees of the British Museum, London

For Thomas Butts (1757–1845), Blake's chief patron from 1799 to c.1816 or later, see p.75. Blake was set to painting portrait miniatures by William Hayley, who wrote condescendingly of Blake to David Parker Coke on 13 May 1801, enclosing a miniature of Mrs Hayley: 'I have recently formed a new artist for this purpose by teaching a worthy creature (by profession an Engraver) who lives in a little Cottage very near me to paint in miniature.' Blake himself wrote to Butts on 10 May 1801 that 'Miniature is become a Goddess in my Eyes, & my Friends in Sussex say I excel in the pursuit. I have a great many orders, & they Multiply', and on 11 September he sent Butts 'an attempt at your likeness', probably this work. In 1801 Blake also did miniatures for Hayley of George Romney and William Cowper, and in 1802 he did one of the Rev. John Johnson ('Johnnie of Norfolk') while Johnson was visiting Hayley. Later this sort of work became irksome to Blake, though in 1809 he did two further miniatures, of Mrs Butts and their son Thomas, also now in the British Museum.

MRS BUTTS after BLAKE

151 *Hares* c.1800–05

Needlework, $19\frac{3}{4} \times 22\frac{7}{8}$ (50 × 58).
Private collection, England

The attribution of the design to Blake is suggested by a comparison with the conventional design of a needlework panel of ducks from the same source. There are also parallels with the colouring of hand-tinted engravings attributed to Blake such as No.210. The panel was sold by the Butts family in 1932.

151

152 *Death's Door* 1805

> Relief engraving, $7\frac{5}{16} \times 4\frac{5}{8}$ (18.5 × 11.8).
> Inscr. 'DEATHS DOOR'.
> *Mrs Charles J. Rosenbloom*

152

This is the only engraving Blake did himself for Blair's *Grave* before the remunerative task of doing the engravings after Blake's designs was transferred to Luigi Schiavonetti. The first version of Robert Cromek's Prospectus for his new edition, dated November 1805, announced that 'The original Drawings, and a Specimin of the Stile of Engraving, may be seen at the Proprietor's'; this was presumably the print displayed. However, according to the son of Thomas Stothard, who was doing his version of 'The Canterbury Pilgrims' at this time (see No.210), 'Cromek found, and explained to my father, that he [Blake] had etched one of the subjects, but so indifferently and so carelessly . . . that he employed Schrovenetti [*sic*] to engrave them'.

A comparison with Schiavonetti's print (No.153) perhaps explains Cromek's reluctance to let Blake continue with the engravings, but it also shows up the timidity of his taste. Besides the much more powerful forms, the highly dramatic lighting expresses the content of the design in contrasting the old man entering death's door with the rejuvenated, resurrected soul starting up above. This effect of light is produced by Blake's process of printing in relief, from the raised parts of the plate; normally the plate is wiped so that the ink only remains in the engraved or etched lines and the printing, under much greater pressure, is from those lines rather than from the raised areas. It is also interesting that Schiavonetti chose the easy way out and, unlike Blake, seems to have reversed Blake's design.

The design itself is a combination of two of Blake's earlier images, both figures having appeared separately as illustrations to plates 6 and 12 of *America*, 1793. The old man entering death's door on plate 12 also appears on plate 17 of *The Gates of Paradise*, also of 1793, while the young man starting up from the ground on plate 6 also appears on plate 21 of *The Marriage of Heaven and Hell*, 1790–93. In these earlier versions the young man represents the revolutionary energy of the young Orc.

This is the only known copy of Blake's print, and was formerly in the collection of Samuel Palmer.

> Engraved by SCHIAVONÉTTI

153 *Death's Door* 1806

> Plate 11 of Robert Blair's *The Grave*.
> Line engraving, $11\frac{3}{16} \times 6\frac{7}{8}$ (29.7 × 17.5).
> Inscr. 'Drawn by W. Blake', 'Etched by L. Schiavonetti' and
> 'London, Published May 1st 1808, by Cadell & Davies, Strand.'
> *Private collection, England*

153

See No.152. An early proof by Schiavonetti is dated 12 February 1806 (Robert N. Essick Collection).

154 *The Death of the Strong Wicked Man* 1805

> Sketch for plate 5 of Robert Blair's *The Grave*.
> Pencil on paper, irregular, $5\frac{7}{8} \times 10\frac{15}{16}$ (14.3 × 27.8).
> *Victoria and Albert Museum, London*

154

John Flaxman, writing to William Hayley on 18 October 1805, in the first surviving reference to Blake's commission to illustrate *The Grave*, mentions among 'the most striking' compositions he has seen, the 'Wicked Strong man dying'; this may have been this drawing or a more finished version, perhaps in the style of No.155. The contrast between this sketch and No.155 is striking. This has all the power and vigour of Blake's own engraving of 'Death's Door', No.152, whereas the other is much more exquisitely drawn.

155

156

157

The drawing is on a piece of paper salvaged by Blake from the first, 1802 edition of Hayley's *Ballads* (see Nos.146–8); the erased catchword 'Run' from page 24 can be seen. On the back is a drawing of a figure soaring upwards with arms outstretched towards a Gothic arch, perhaps for the Dedication, No.158.

155 *The Soul Hovering over the Body Reluctantly Parting with Life* 1805

Sketch for plate 6 of Robert Blair's *The Grave*.
Pencil, $10\frac{3}{4} \times 17\frac{7}{8}$ (27.2 × 45.6).
Tate Gallery, London

An illustration of the death of a voluptuary:
> . . . *How wishfully she looks*
> *On all she's leaving, now no longer her's!*

In Schiavonetti's engraving the dying man is shown on his back, without the lyre and wreath of the voluptuary. An earlier drawing, untraced since it belonged to F. T. Palgrave in 1863, showed his soul as 'a female figure expressive of coarse passions' contemplating him 'with repulsion', according to William Rossetti.

A comparison with No.154 shows the range of Blake's drawing style at this time.

156 *The Resurrection of the Dead* 1806

Alternative design for title-page to Robert Blair's *The Grave*.
Pen, wash and blue watercolour, irregular, $16\frac{3}{4} \times 12\frac{3}{16}$ (42.5 × 31) on thin card $17\frac{7}{8} \times 13\frac{5}{8}$ (45.4 × 33.8).
Signed '1806 W Blake inv'.
Trustees of the British Museum, London

The published title-page to *The Grave*, engraved by Schiavonetti, is a variation of one of Blake's illustrations to Young's *Night Thoughts*, plate 12, showing a diving angel with a trumpet reanimating a skeleton. This finished watercolour shows the Resurrection of the Dead and is based on two pencil sketches, the first in an American private collection, the second No.157.

The early history of this watercolour is unknown. It was sold by the dealer Evans to the British Museum in 1856.

157 *The Resurrection of the Dead* c.1805–06

Sketch for the alternative design for title-page to Robert Blair's *The Grave*.
Pencil, $15 \times 11\frac{1}{2}$ (38.1 × 29.3).
Bateson Collection

A sketch for No.156. There is an earlier sketch in an American private collection. On the back is a very rough, unidentified sketch, the top of the composition having been trimmed away.

158 *Design for Dedication to the Queen* 1807

For Robert Blair's *The Grave*.
Pen and watercolour over pencil, irregular, $11\frac{7}{8} \times 9\frac{3}{8}$ (30.2 × 23.8).
Inscr. by Blake 'To the Queen' and with traces of his dedicatory verses (see below).
Trustees of the British Museum, London

Blake, having received permission in April 1807 to dedicate Cromek's new edition of *The Grave* to Queen Charlotte, asked Cromek for four guineas for this extra design, which he painted between 17 and 20 April. However, it was rejected by Cromek in May in an abusive letter: 'I have returned the drawing w^h this note, and I will briefly state my reasons for so doing. In the first place I do not think it merits the price you affix to it, *under any circumstances*. In the next place I never had the remotest suspicion that you c^d for a moment entertain the idea of writing *me* to supply money to create an honour in w^h I cannot possibly participate' (this did not stop Cromek from printing Blake's dedicatory verses, which obviously served to increase the sales of the book!); and so on, including an implication that he would have paid Schiavonetti *ten* guineas for engraving Blake's design. Blake's verses read:

> *The Door of Death is made of Gold,*
> *That Mortal Eyes cannot behold;*
> *But, when the Mortal Eyes are clos'd,*
> *And cold and pale the Limbs repos'd,*
> *The Soul awakes; and, wond'ring, sees*
> *In her mild Hand the golden Keys*
> *The Grave is Heaven's golden Gate,*
> *And rich and poor around it wait;*
> *O Shepherdess of England's Fold,*
> *Behold this gate of Pearl and Gold!*
>
> *To dedicate to England's Queen*
> *The Visions that my Soul has seen,*
> *And, by Her kind permission, bring*
> *What I have borne on solemn Wing*
> *From the vast regions of the Grave,*
> *Before Her Throne my Wings I wave;*
> *Bowing before my Sov'reign's Feet,*
> *'The Grave produc'd these Blossoms sweet*
> *'In mild repose from Earthly strife;*
> *'The Blossoms of Eternal Life!'*

158

Watercolour Illustrations to the Bible for Thomas Butts, c.1800–09

The small tempera paintings of biblical subjects of 1799 and 1800 (see Nos. 134–40) were followed by an even greater number of biblical subjects painted in watercolour, also painted for Butts, numbering over eighty in all. Some are dated 1800 while others are dated or documented to 1803 and 1805; a few further examples, dated 1806 and 1809, seem to be afterthoughts, signed in a different form (with 'W Blake' written out instead of the characteristic 'WB inv' written as a monogram) and in a slightly different style. Two examples were shown at the Royal Academy in 1808 and four in Blake's own exhibition of 1809.

The series shows a considerable development in style. The works datable to 1800 are handled in a bold, rather impressionistic style which still recalls the forcefulness of the large colour prints of 1795 and of the best of the *Night Thoughts* and Gray illustrations. The works of 1803 have brighter colouring, stippled technique and often symmetrical compositions and lead to the more linear, flatly coloured watercolours of 1805, in which Blake returns anew to the Neo-Classicism of the 1780s but in a much more personal way. Some of the variations within the series are, of course, the result of the different expressive needs of the various subjects, and one cannot be too

rigorous in trying to assign a date to each example, but the overall development is quite striking if one compares the extremes of 1800 with the extremes of 1805.

Within this large group of biblical watercolours certain sub-groups can be isolated, united not only by being devoted to one particular part of the Bible story but also by size and treatment. Nos. 177–83 and 186–9 are examples of such sub-groups.

Blake's new concentration on biblical subjects may have been in part merely the result of Butts' commission but it also accompanied a change in his writing. The extreme pessimism of the mid 1790s was replaced by a growing stress on the role of Christ in man's salvation, though this is still sharply differentiated from the repressive, petrified religion of Jehovah and the Old Testament.

It seems that originally every watercolour from the series had its biblical reference inscribed just below the lower right-hand corner. In addition the title was given above and the actual text below, in a distinctive copperplate hand, written by Blake, his wife or one of the Butts family. In many cases these have now vanished as the result of the watercolours being trimmed or remounted.

159

159 *The Angel of the Divine Presence Bringing Eve to Adam* c.1803

Pen and watercolour, $16\frac{7}{16} \times 13\frac{3}{16}$ (41.8 × 33.5).
Signed 'WB inv' as monogram.
Metropolitan Museum of Art, New York (Rogers Fund, 1906)

Genesis 2:22. A few years later Blake, in the draft of his description of a picture of the Last Judgment, c.1810, equated 'That Angel of the Divine Presence mentioned in Exodus XIV c 19v & in other Places' with 'Jehovah Elohim, The I Am of the Oaks of Albion'. The Creation of Eve is shown, therefore, as negative, a stage in the division of man imposed by the Urizen-like God of the Old Testament, similar to that of Adam himself (see No.85) and paralleling the creation of Enitharmon in Blake's own myth (see No.80).

Bought at one of the Butts sales by Richard Monckton-Milnes, later first Lord Houghton.

160 *Jacob's Dream* c.1805

Pen and watercolour, irregular, $14\frac{9}{16} \times 11\frac{1}{2}$ (37 × 29.2) on paper $15\frac{11}{16} \times 12\frac{9}{16}$ (39.8 × 30.6).
Signed 'WB inv' as monogram and inscr. 'Genesis XXVIII c. 12v.'
Trustees of the British Museum, London

Genesis 28:12. Jacob's vision of the ladder extending from earth to heaven on which he sees the angels of God ascending and descending, including figures bearing scrolls, food and drink, and even the compasses that Blake normally associated with the unimaginative limit-setting of reason; here all the diverse attributes of the complete man are seen unified in the heavenly vision.

The affinity of the spiral composition and elongated figures to certain Mannerist works is probably less the result of a specific borrowing (the most likely source was not engraved and could only have been known to Blake through reports by friends returning from Italy) than of common artistic principles and models. These characteristics are found developed further in 'An Epitome of James Hervey's "Meditations among the Tombs"', No. 314.

Exhibited at the Royal Academy in 1808 and in Blake's own exhibition of 1809–10, where it was described as one of 'four drawings the Artist wishes were in Fresco on an enlarged scale to ornament the altars of churches, and to make England, like Italy, respected by respectable men of other countries on account of Art. It is not the want of Genius that can hereafter be laid to our charge; the Artist who has done these pictures and Drawings will take care of that; let those who govern the Nation take care of the other. The times require that every one should speak out boldly; England expects that every man should do his duty, in Arts, as well as in Arms, or in the Senate.' The watercolour probably already belonged to Butts when Blake exhibited it, and was later in the Monckton-Milnes and W. Graham Robertson collections.

161 *The Finding of Moses: The Compassion of Pharoah's Daughter* c.1805

Pen and watercolour over pencil, $12\frac{3}{4} \times 12\frac{5}{8}$ (32.3 × 32).
Signed 'WB inv' as monogram and inscr. on mount 'Exod: ch: 2ⁿᵈ v. 7ᵗʰ & 8ᵗʰ'.
Victoria and Albert Museum, London

Exodus 2:5–9. The infant Moses, hidden in an ark of bulrushes to save him from the Egyptian edict that all male Jewish babies should be killed, is found by Pharoah's daughter. The subject was traditionally seen as a forerunner of the Infant Jesus' preservation in Egypt following the Massacre of the Innocents, and the pelican feeding her young from her own breast is a symbol of the Resurrection. For Blake the scene would also have represented a birth into materialistic bondage, represented by the oppressive pyramids in the background, from which Moses was to deliver the people of Israel. Moreover, the exultant leap of the infant represents his role in ensuring the survival of the inspiration of true religion, and is found again in some of Blake's representations of the infant Christ.

The watercolour is one of the most exquisite examples of Blake's gentler vein in this series of biblical subjects. It comes from the Butts and W. Graham Robertson collections.

162 *Moses at the Burning Bush* c.1800–03

Pen and watercolour over pencil, irregular, $15\frac{1}{2} \times 12$ (39.3 × 30.4).
Signed 'WB inv' as monogram.
Victoria and Albert Museum, London

Exodus 3:1–2. The angel of the Lord appears to Moses in the midst of a bush that burns in a flame of fire but is not consumed. When Moses turns aside at this the Lord himself appears and tells Moses that he is to deliver his people from Egypt. It has been suggested that Blake has deliberately shown Moses ignoring the scroll of inspiration in his hand. The oak tree behind him would also stand as a symbol of error, of the Druidical oppression of the Old Dispensation.

The figure of Moses is one of the most imposing among the biblical watercolours, recalling the monumentality of such a work as 'Moses indignant at the Golden Calf' from the slightly earlier tempera series, No. 134. This and the rich, relatively free application of watercolour suggest a date of c.1800–03.

From the Butts and Dilke collections.

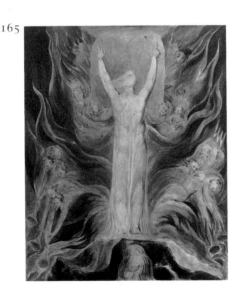

163 *Pestilence: The Death of the First-Born* c.1805

Pen and watercolour over pencil, $12 \times 13\frac{1}{2}$ (30.4 × 34.2).
Signed 'WB inv' as monogram.
Museum of Fine Arts, Boston

Exodus 12:21–3, 29–30. Although this watercolour has often been grouped with the watercolours of about the same date of 'Fire', 'Plague' and 'Famine', those seem to be part of a distinct group of non-biblical subjects; see Nos.25 and 26. Unlike No.25, which developed out of a watercolour of the Great Plague of London, this watercolour shows the Mosaic Plague of Egypt. The angel standing in the doorway in the background (which is shown much larger in the preliminary drawing, last recorded in the W. Graham Robertson sale, Christie's 22 July 1949, lot 79) presumably refers to Moses' promise of protection to the Jews who marked their door-lintels and sideposts with the blood of the Passover lamb. The same verses, 21–3, refer to the Lord's 'destroyer', here personified by Blake as a huge scaly figure. The heavy geometric forms of buildings and pyramids are typical Blakean representations of the materialism and despotic oppression of Pharaonic Egypt.

This is one of the thirty-three watercolours by Blake that were acquired in 1890 by the Boston Museum, long before any comparable group of Blake's finished works entered any British public collection.

164 *The Blasphemer* c.1800

Pen and watercolour, $15 \times 13\frac{3}{8}$ (38.4 × 34).
Signed 'WB inv' as monogram and inscr. in a copperplate hand on the old mount, now removed, 'The Blasphemer' and with the text from Leviticus 24:23.
Tate Gallery, London

Leviticus 24:23: the execution at Moses' order of the Israelite woman's son for blaspheming the name of the Lord. Blake has added the flames, presumably to emphasise the horror of the incident which he would have condemned, coming as it does immediately after the Lord has dictated to Moses the law of an eye for an eye and a tooth for a tooth (Leviticus 24:13–22).

The Michelangelesque central figure can probably be traced back, perhaps by way of Flaxman, to an Antique 'Fallen Warrior'. It recurs in Nos.264 and 276.

Bought by Sir Charles Wentworth Dilke, Bart, at the Butts sale of 1852.

165 *God Writing upon the Tables of the Covenant* c.1805

Pen and watercolour over pencil, $16\frac{1}{2} \times 13\frac{3}{4}$ (41.9 × 34.9).
Signed 'WB inv' as monogram and inscr. with traces of a reference to Deuteronomy 9:10 on mount (now covered).
National Gallery of Scotland, Edinburgh

Deuteronomy 9:10 (also Exodus 31:18). Moses bows in abject submission before Jehovah as he inscribes the rigid Law of the Ten Commandments, a restrictive moral code of the kind abhorrent to Blake.

The symmetrical composition, tight handling and firm, sculptural modelling producing a Neo-Classical effect of form, very different from the treatment of 'Moses at the Burning Bush', No.162, are typical of Blake's drastic stylistic development between 1803 and 1805. The exaggerated contrast of scale between Moses and Jehovah is found stressed even more in 'The Angel of the Revelation', No.185.

166 *Samson Breaking his Bonds* c.1800(?)

Pencil, pen and watercolour, approx. $15\frac{1}{2} \times 14\frac{1}{16}$ (39.4 × 35.7).
Signed 'WB inv' as monogram.
Pierpont Morgan Library, New York: Bequest of Mrs Landon K. Thorne

174 *The Woman Taken in Adultery*, c.1805 (entry on p.92)

189 *The Number of the Beast is 666, c.*1805 (entry on p.97)

Judges 16:10–12. Delilah stands by astonished as Samson breaks his bonds and the soldiers flee. For a companion see No.167.

The two watercolours were apparently delivered to Thomas Butts on 12 May 1805 (for a guinea each) but the bold Michelangelesque figure of Samson and the strong-featured, Fuseli-like Delilah recall the strength of Blake's large colour prints of 1795 and suggest a date of c.1800. For a possible example of Fuseli finding Blake 'Damned good to steal from' see Fuseli's drawing 'Kriemhild, Accompanied by Two Hun Servants, shows the Imprisoned Hagen the Ring of the Nibelungen', dated 1807 (fig.13).

Sold from the Butts Collection in 1853, this watercolour later belonged to George A. Smith and the Pre-Raphaelite follower William Bell Scott; it was bequeathed to the Pierpont Morgan Library with the rest of the Blake collection of Mrs Landon K. Thorne.

167 *Samson Subdued* c.1800(?)

Pencil, pen and watercolour, $15\frac{3}{8} \times 13\frac{7}{8}$ (39.1 × 35.3).
Signed 'WB inv' as monogram and inscr. on back 'Judg Ch. 16 v. 19'.
Philadelphia Museum of Art: Gift of Mrs William T. Tonner

Judges 16:15–20. Blake shows Delilah with a pair of scissors with which she herself has cut off most of Samson's hair, whereas in the Bible she gets a man to shave Samson's head. Samson's strength having gone with his hair, the soldiers timidly return at Delilah's imperious command. It has to be confessed that this watercolour demonstrates both the uneven quality of Blake's work and his lack of self-criticism; the effect, particularly in contrast to the companion No.166, is almost comic.

For the date of this watercolour see No.166. It passed from the Butts Collection to that of W. Graham Robertson and was later presented to the Philadelphia Museum as part of the Blake collection of Mrs William T. Tonner.

168 *Ruth the Dutiful Daughter-in-Law* 1803

Pencil and watercolour, $13\frac{5}{8} \times 12\frac{11}{16}$ (34.7 × 32.3).
Signed 'WB inv [as monogram]1803' and inscr. on mount 'Ruth ch. 1ˢᵗ v. 16ᵗʰ' and in copperplate hand with the title 'The dutiful Daughter in law' and the text (now covered); also on back, 'Ruth I Ch 16 v'.
Southampton Art Gallery

Ruth 1:11–17: for the subject see No.94. Blake mentioned this watercolour as being 'now on the stocks' in a letter to Thomas Butts of 6 July 1803 and probably sent it to him on 16 August. It is typical of the rather loose handling that distinguishes the 1803 watercolours, while the elongated Neo-Classical figures already anticipate the watercolours of 1805.

Blake included this watercolour in his 1809–10 exhibition as one of the compositions he would like to paint on a large scale in 'Fresco'; see No.160. Presumably lent by Thomas Butts, it was later in the W. Graham Robertson Collection.

Fig.13 Henry Fuseli
Kriemhild, Accompanied by Two Hun Servants, Shows the Imprisoned Hagen the Ring of the Nibelungen, 1807
(Zurich, Kunsthaus)

169 *The Ghost of Samuel Appearing to Saul* c.1800

Pen and watercolour, $12\frac{9}{16} \times 13\frac{9}{16}$ (32 × 34.4) on paper $21\frac{1}{4} \times 17\frac{1}{4}$ (54 × 44).
Signed 'WB inv' as monogram and inscr. on the mount '1ˢᵗ Samuel 28ᵗʰ ch: v. 12ᵗʰ to 21.' and with the text in the copperplate hand (now covered).
National Gallery of Art, Washington (Rosenwald Collection)

1 Samuel 28:8, 11, 15–19. For an earlier treatment of the same subject, completely different in composition, see No.27. The design is now much more compact with all the figures virtually on one plane, while the earlier

168

169

170

drawing, though representative of one of the peaks of Neo-Classical influence on Blake's work, implies a considerable amount of space and recession; the Neo-Classical element in Blake's art is now completely absorbed into his own personal style.

Sold by Thomas Butts' son in 1853, this was later in the important American Blake collection of A. E. Newton, from which it passed in 1941 to the even larger Blake collection of Lessing J. Rosenwald.

170 *Ezekiel's Wheels* c.1803–5

Black chalk, pen and watercolour over pencil, $15\frac{9}{16} \times 11\frac{5}{8}$ (39.5 × 29.5).
Signed 'WB inv' as monogram.
Museum of Fine Arts, Boston

Ezekiel 1:4–28. Ezekiel looks up at the vision, which emerges from the midst of the whirlwind, of the likenesses of four living creatures, each with four faces and four wings, surrounded by rings or wheels full of eyes and with the Lord enthroned above. The four cherubim prefigure the four Beasts of the Apocalypse, which were paralleled in Blake's own mythology by the four Zoas, the four aspects of Man in his divided state. The vision completely dwarfs the tiny figure of Ezekiel who lies by, or apparently partly submerged in, the River Chebar, thus symbolising inspiration emerging from the waters of materialism.

This watercolour was delivered to Thomas Butts on 12 May 1805 for one guinea, but the loose hatching of the central figure and elsewhere recalls the watercolours known to date from 1803, e.g. No.168, so it may have been begun about that time.

171 *Christ in the Carpenter's Shop* c.1805(?)

Pen and watercolour over pencil, $12\frac{1}{2} \times 13\frac{1}{2}$ (32 × 34.5).
Signed 'WB inv' as monogram and inscr. on the mount 'Luke ch: 2nd v. 51st' and in copperplate hand with the title 'The Humility of the Saviour' and the text.
Walsall Museum and Art Gallery, Garman-Ryan Collection

The passage in Luke 2:51 merely states that Christ went down to Nazareth with his parents; the stories of Christ in his father's carpenter's shop derive from later legends. The pair of compasses held by the young Christ are related in symbolism to their appearance in 'The Ancient of Days', the colour print 'Newton', and 'The Christ Child asleep on the Cross' (see Nos.66–8, 92 and 137). They may represent the synthesis of reason and imagination under the new dispensation of Christ, though it has been suggested that, as 'dividers' rather than compasses, they may reflect Blake's statement in *The Marriage of Heaven and Hell* that 'Jesus Christ did not wish to unite but to seperate [*sic*] them [the Prolific and the Devouring], as in the Parable of sheep and goats! & he says I came not to send Peace but a Sword'; however, *The Marriage of Heaven and Hell*, an ironic work of the early 1790s, is at a considerable remove from Blake's views on the role of Christ ten years later.

From the Butts and Monckton-Milnes collections, this watercolour later belonged to Sir Jacob Epstein and was presented to the Walsall Art Gallery by his widow. There is a copy in the Tate Gallery.

172 *The Parable of the Wise and Foolish Virgins* c.1805

Pen and watercolour over pencil, $14\frac{1}{8} \times 13\frac{1}{16}$ (35.9 × 33.1).
Signed 'WB inv' as monogram and inscr. on the back 'Matt. 25 ch. v. 9'.
Metropolitan Museum of Art, New York (Rogers Fund, 1914)

Matthew 25:1–13: the kingdom of heaven is likened to ten virgins who go to meet a bridegroom, five with their lamps filled, five with their lamps empty so that they arrive late and are refused admission: 'Watch therefore, for ye know neither the day nor the hour wherein the Son of man cometh.'

This is the first version of a much repeated composition (see No. 173) and was delivered to Thomas Butts on 12 May 1805 for one guinea. It later belonged to B. G. Windus and then to his daughter Mrs J. K. de Putron.

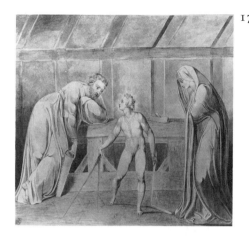

171

173 *The Parable of the Wise and Foolish Virgins* c.1822–5

Pen and watercolour, $16\frac{5}{8} \times 13\frac{7}{8}$ (42.3 × 35.3) on paper
$17\frac{11}{16} \times 14\frac{3}{16}$ (45 × 36).
Signed 'W Blake inv'.
Yale Center for British Art (Paul Mellon Collection), New Haven, Connecticut

Developed by Blake himself from the second version of the subject, painted *c.*1822 for John Linnell (Fitzwilliam Museum, Cambridge). As compared with the first version of *c.*1805 (No.172) the figures are more or less the same but the handling is more fluid and the modelling softer yet at the same time more three-dimensional. A still later version of the composition belongs to Philip Hofer. According to Gilchrist that version and the later version of 'The Vision of Queen Katherine' now in the Rosenwald Collection (see No.253) were commissioned by Sir Thomas Lawrence for fifteen guineas each and were among Blake's last works (Joseph Hogarth gives the price as twenty-five guineas but is unreliable in other respects). It marks a further development beyond the Mellon watercolour: the pose of the foremost of the Wise Virgins has been made still more graceful, as has that of the central kneeling figure. There is a copy of this version, perhaps by Linnell or his circle, in the Tate Gallery (fig.14).

This watercolour was painted for William Haines of Chichester (1778–1848), who like Blake had done engravings for William Hayley's *Life of George Romney*, 1809. It was later in the A. E. Newton Collection. A copy of the Linnell version, probably by Linnell or one of his family or pupils, is in the Santa Barbara Museum.

172

173

Fig.14 John Linnell or his studio,
after William Blake
*The Parable of the Wise
and Foolish Virgins*
(Tate Gallery)

174

174 *The Woman Taken in Adultery* c.1805

Pen and watercolour over pencil, 14 × 14⅛ (35.5 × 35.7).
Signed 'W B inv' as monogram.
Museum of Fine Arts, Boston

John 8 : 3–9: Christ chides the Scribes and the Pharisees with the words 'He that is without sin among you, let him first cast a stone at her', whereupon, 'being convicted by their own conscience', they go out one by one 'beginning at the eldest, even unto the last'. The design is remarkably expressive in its simplicity, the elegantly stooping figure of Christ, writing on the ground, standing out against the backs of the retiring Scribes and Pharisees and in contrast to the still, erect figure of the woman.

175 *The Hymn of Christ and the Apostles* c.1805

Pen and watercolour over pencil, 14⅖ × 12¹¹⁄₁₆ (37.9 × 32.2).
Signed 'W B inv' as monogram and inscr. 'Mark XIV c26 v'.
Private collection, USA

Mark 14 : 26: following the Last Supper, 'And when they had sung an hymn, they went out into the mount of Olives'. The smoothly finished, elongated figures and their relatively firm modelling point towards Blake's development leading up to the *Paradise Lost* watercolours of 1808, Nos.216–27.

From the Butts and W. Graham Robertson collections.

175

176 *The Soldiers Casting Lots for Christ's Garments* 1800

Pen and watercolour over pencil, 16½ × 12⅜ (42 × 31.4) on paper, irregular, 17⅞ × 13³⁄₁₆ (44 × 33.5).
Signed 'W B inv [as monogram] 1800' and inscr. 'John XIX c.23 & 24 v.'
Syndics of the Fitzwilliam Museum, Cambridge

John 19 : 23–4: the soldiers, having divided the rest of Christ's garments, cast lots for his seamless coat. This dramatic scene with its atmospheric, flickering lighting and strongly modelled, Fuseli-like faces is in strong contrast to the series of sombre, restrained watercolours of subjects from the Passion here dated c.1805; see Nos.177–83. The contrast demonstrates Blake's radical change of style in the first five years of the nineteenth century. The depiction of the three crosses from behind may reflect the influence of Nicolas Poussin's 'Crucifixion' (Wadsworth Atheneum, Hartford, Conn.): this was in the Sir Laurence Dundas sale in London in 1794 and could also have been known to Blake from engravings.

This watercolour was included in Blake's exhibition of 1809–10 as one of the 'four drawings the Artist wishes were in Fresco on an enlarged scale' (see No.160). Presumably lent by Thomas Butts, it was later in the Monckton-Milnes and W. Graham Robertson collections.

176

177 *The Raising of Lazarus* c.1805

Pen and watercolour over pencil, 16⁹⁄₁₆ × 11¹³⁄₁₆ (42 × 30).
Signed 'W B inv' as monogram.
Aberdeen Art Gallery and Museums

John 11 : 43–4. The miracle of the raising of the dead Lazarus is often seen as a prefiguration of Christ's Resurrection and this may have been intended as one of the series of sombre upright compositions illustrating Christ's Passion; see No.178.

From the Butts and Monckton-Milnes collections. There is a copy in the Tate Gallery.

178 *The Crucifixion: 'Behold thy Mother'* c.1805

> Pen and watercolour, $16\frac{1}{4} \times 11\frac{13}{16}$ (41.3 × 30).
> Signed 'WB inv' as monogram.
> *Tate Gallery, London*

John 19:26–7. Christ commends the Virgin to the care of his favourite disciple, St. John. The title given this watercolour by William Rossetti, 'Christ taking leave of His Mother', is misleading in that this usually refers to the incident when Christ first leaves home.

This watercolour is one of a distinct sub-group within the series of watercolours of biblical subjects painted for Thomas Butts. Similar in size and upright format, near-symmetrical composition and dark near-monochromatic colouring, they are all of subjects associated with the Crucifixion and the Resurrection; see also Nos.177 and 179–83. They also reflect a return to Neo-Classical principles, though now in a completely personal form, and can all be dated *c.*1805; they contrast strongly with 'The Soldiers casting Lots for Christ's Garments' of 1800, No.176.

From the Butts and W. Graham Robertson collections.

177

179 *The Entombment* c.1805

> Pen and watercolour, $16\frac{7}{16} \times 12\frac{3}{16}$ (41.7 × 31).
> Signed 'WB inv' as monogram and inscr. on the mount 'Luke ch: 23rd v. 53rd' and, in the copperplate hand, with the title 'Joseph burying Jesus' and the text (now covered).
> *Tate Gallery, London*

Luke 23:53–5. As well as the actual Entombment, with Joseph of Arimathea kneeling on the left, Blake shows the arrival of the three Marys. This is one of the sub-group of watercolours treating the Crucifixion and Resurrection; see No.178. Blake had already painted a tempera picture of the Entombment for Thomas Butts, *c.*1799–1800, but that shows a slightly different episode, the arrival of Nicodemus with myrrh and aloes, John 19:39 (Pollok House, Glasgow).

From the Butts and W. Graham Robertson collections.

178

180 *Christ in the Sepulchre, Guarded by Angels* c.1805

> Pencil, pen and watercolour, irregular, $16\frac{1}{2} \times 11\frac{7}{8}$ (42 × 30.2) on paper $17 \times 12\frac{1}{2}$ (43.2 × 31.7).
> Signed 'WB inv' as monogram and inscr. 'Exod: c xxv. v20'.
> *Victoria and Albert Museum, London*

The reference written below the drawing, to Exodus 25:20, the cherubim covering the mercy seat with their wings, is to the Old Testament prefiguration of this incident, which does not actually occur in the Gospels, though the Magdalene, looking into the sepulchre after the Resurrection, sees 'two angels in white sitting, the one at the head, and the other at the feet, where the body of Jesus had been' (John 20:12).

The placing of the angels and the line of their wings recall Blake's apprenticeship copying tombs in Westminster Abbey; see No.3. There is a parallel in Blake's own writings, Night VIII of *Vala or the Four Zoas*, where 'The Fallen Man', Albion, lies 'stretchd like a corse';

> . . . hovring high over his head
> *Two winged immortal shapes, one standing at his feet*
> *Towards the East, one standing at his head towards the west,*
> *Their wings joind in the Zenith over head . . .*

This watercolour was exhibited at the Royal Academy in 1808 and, as one of four watercolours Blake would have liked to have done on a large scale (see No.160), at his own exhibition in 1809–10. Presumably lent by Thomas Butts, it was later in the Morse Collection.

179

180

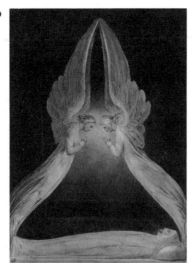

181 *The Angel Rolling the Stone away from the Sepulchre* c.1805

Pen and watercolour, $16\frac{3}{8} \times 12\frac{1}{4}$ (41.5 × 31.1).
Signed 'W B inv' as monogram and inscr. 'Mat^W ch: 28th v. 2nd'
and, in the copperplate hand, with text (now covered).
Victoria and Albert Museum, London

Matthew 28:2. Another in the sequence of near-monochrome depictions of the Passion and Resurrection; see No.178. Blake denies any feeling of spatial recession by his placing of the angel, whose feet show him to be beyond the archway while his outspread wings remain on this side, framing the composition at the top. The next in the series, showing the Resurrection itself (No.182), balances this work in composition.

From the Butts and Morse collections.

182 *Photograph of 'The Resurrection'* c.1805

Pen and watercolour over pencil, $16\frac{1}{2} \times 11\frac{15}{16}$ (42 × 30.3).
Signed 'W B inv' as monogram and inscr. on the matt '1st Corinth:
ch : 15th : v.4th' and in the copperplate hand with the title 'The
Resurrection' and part of the text (now covered and omitted from
this photograph).
Fogg Art Museum, Harvard University, Cambridge, Mass.

1 Corinthians 15:4 (see also Matthew 28:6). This is a companion to No.181. Christ, rising effortlessly in the centre with outspread arms, balances the angel in the previous scene.

183 *The Magdalene at the Sepulchre* c.1805

Pen, ink and watercolour, $16\frac{13}{16} \times 12\frac{1}{4}$ (42.7 × 31.1).
Signed 'W B inv' as monogram.
*Yale Center for British Art (Paul Mellon Collection), New Haven,
Connecticut*

John 20:11–16. This is an alternative story to the account of the three Marys coming to the empty tomb in the other Gospels, which was the subject of one of the earlier Butts watercolours (1800–03; Fitzwilliam Museum, Cambridge). However, Blake makes no attempt to show the Risen Christ as a gardener, which the Magdalene at first thinks Him to be.

From the Butts and F. T. Palgrave collections.

181

182

183

184 *Death on a Pale Horse* c.1800

Pen and watercolour over pencil, $15\frac{1}{2} \times 12\frac{1}{4}$ (39.5 × 35.1).
Signed 'W B inv' as monogram.
Syndics of the Fitzwilliam Museum, Cambridge

Revelation 6:8: 'And I looked, and behold a pale horse: and his name that sat on him was Death, and Hell followed with him'. This was a relatively common subject for late eighteenth-century British artists, there being examples, among others, by Benjamin West (1802; Philadelphia Museum), John Hamilton Mortimer (an engraving of 1784) and P. J. de Loutherbourg (1798, for Macklin's *Bible*; Tate Gallery). However, these are all relatively naturalistic, the figures being shown as three-dimensional corporeal realities in a definable space, whereas Blake has produced a flat, emblematic composition, all the more convincing for its lack of naturalistic elements. This sublime, allegorical treatment recalls the great colour prints of 1795 and is in strong contrast to the equally powerful, but very different, series of Apocalyptic watercolours of c.1805, Nos.185–9, hence a dating of c.1800.

From the Butts and Alfred Aspland collections.

184

185 *The Angel of the Revelation* c.1805

Pen and watercolour over pencil, $15\frac{7}{16} \times 10\frac{5}{16}$ (39.3 × 26.2).
Signed 'W B inv' as monogram.
Metropolitan Museum of Art, New York (Rogers Fund, 1914)

Revelation 10:1–6: 'And the angel which I saw lifted up his hand to heaven, And swore . . . that there should be time no longer'. St. John the Divine sits writing the Book of Revelation on the Island of Patmos, looking up at the enormous figure of the angel, 'his face . . . as it were the sun, and his feet as pillars of fire', with the 'seven thunders' riding across the sky behind.

Unlike No.184, the figures are seen as tangible realities in an actual setting. The extraordinary contrasts in scale, which are however justified by the text, recall Dürer's magnificent Apocalypse woodcuts which must have been known to Blake (see fig.15).

From the Butts and B. G. Windus collections.

185

186 *The Great Red Dragon and the Woman Clothed with the Sun* c.1803–5

Pen, black chalk and watercolour, approx. $17\frac{1}{8} \times 13\frac{1}{2}$
(43.5 × 34.5) on paper $21\frac{1}{2} \times 16\frac{15}{16}$ (54.5 × 43).
Signed 'W B inv' as monogram and inscr. 'Rev^{ns} ch: 12th v 4th';
there are traces of the usual copperplate text below.
Brooklyn Museum, New York: Gift of William Augustus White

Revelation 12:1–4. The Red Dragon with seven heads and eleven horns waits to devour the child expected of 'the woman clothed with the sun, and the moon under her feet': 'And his tail drew the third part of the stars of heaven, and did cast them to the earth'. In the Book of Revelation the Woman stands for Israel, about to give birth to a male child to rule all the nations from a throne in heaven, and for the Church.

This is the first of a sub-group within the biblical watercolours, devoted to the great allegorical monsters of the Book of Revelation; see also Nos.187–9. The Great Red Dragon appears in all four watercolours. In no other case does Blake devote so many illustrations to a mere two chapters of the Bible. In the Book of Revelation, and particularly in the account of the appearance of the various monsters, Blake found imagery close to that of his own prophetic writings, and he was later to use this imagery in the long titles and descriptions given to his pictures of 'The Spiritual Form of Nelson', 'The Spiritual Form of Pitt' and 'The Last Judgment', Nos.205–6 and 211–13. The relatively loose handling of the back of the Dragon resembles that of watercolours of 1803, e.g. No.168, but is less marked in

Fig.15 Albrecht Dürer, *St. John devouring the Book* from the Apocalypse, 1498 (British Museum)

186

the rest of the group.

Bought in an untraced sale of works from the Butts Collection for the famous Turner collector H.A.J. Munro of Novar, this watercolour later belonged to the great American Blake collections of Marsden J. Perry and W. A. White.

187 *The Great Red Dragon and the Woman Clothed with the Sun: 'The Devil is Come Down'* c.1805

Pen and watercolour, $16\frac{1}{16} \times 13\frac{1}{4}$ (40.8 × 33.7).
Signed 'WB inv' as monogram and inscr on the mount 'Rev^{ns} ch[. . .]th [. . .]th' (damaged) and in the copperplate hand with the title 'The Devil is Come Down' and part of the text (now covered).
National Gallery of Art, Washington (Rosenwald Collection)

Revelation 12:12–17: 'Woe . . . ! for the devil is come down unto you, having great wrath'. A slightly later moment than that shown in the Brooklyn watercolour, No.186: the Woman, having brought forth the child, flees from the Dragon and is given wings, while the earth swallows up the flood spewed out by the Dragon. Lightning from the Dragon smites 'the remnant of her seed, which keep the commandments of God, and have the testimony of Jesus Christ'.

Though also from the Butts Collection, this has a different later provenance than Nos.186, 188 and 189: it was in the Butts sale of 26 March 1852 and it was later in the collection of A. E. Newton before being acquired by Lessing J. Rosenwald.

187

188 *The Great Red Dragon and the Beast from the Sea* c.1805

Pen and watercolour, $15\frac{13}{16} \times 14$ (40.1 × 35.6).
Signed 'WB inv' as monogram and inscr. on the mount 'Rev^{ns} Ch: 13th v. 1: & 2:', and in the copperplate hand with the title 'And Power was given him over all Kindreds, and Tongues, and Nations' and text.
National Gallery of Art, Washington (Rosenwald Collection)

Revelation 13:1–2, 7: a new Beast rises up from the sea with seven heads and ten horns and the Dragon gives him his power 'over all kindreds, and tongues, and nations'.

Like No.186 this is from the Butts, Munro, Perry and White collections.

189

188

189 *The Number of the Beast is 666* c.1805

Pen and watercolour, $16\frac{3}{16} \times 13\frac{3}{16}$ (41.2 × 33.5).
Signed 'WB inv' as monogram and inscr. on the mount 'Rev^{ns} ch:
13th v. 11th & 12th' and, in the copperplate hand, with the title and
text (now covered).
Philip H. and A. S. W. Rosenbach Foundation, Philadelphia

Revelation 13:11–12, 18. The Red Dragon and the Beast from the Sea, as
in No.188, are joined by 'another beast coming up out of the earth: and he
had two horns like a lamb, and he spake as a dragon'. He 'causeth the earth
and all them which dwell therein to worship the first beast' and 'maketh
fire come down from heaven', apparently onto the upraised head of the
Dragon. 'Here is wisdom. Let him that hath understanding count the
number of the beast: for it is the number of a man; and his number is Six
hundred three-score and six.'

This watercolour shares the same provenance as Nos.186 and 188,
from the Butts, Munro, Perry and White collections.

190 *The Whore of Babylon* 1809

Pen and watercolour, $10\frac{1}{2} \times 8\frac{13}{16}$ (26.6 × 22.3) on thin card
$10\frac{5}{8} \times 9$ (27 × 22.8).
Signed 'WBlake inv & del 1809'.
Trustees of the British Museum, London

190

Revelation 17:1–4. Blake had already painted the Whore of Babylon as
one of his illustrations to Young's *Night Thoughts*, No.115. Here the heads
of the monster on which she rides are shown devouring the peoples of the
earth, and the whole design is an allegory of the interconnection of
material existence in all its aspects, particularly the sensuous, represented
by the Whore as the Female Will, and war.

Although this watercolour apparently belonged to Thomas Butts (the
only evidence for this is in William Rossetti's list catalogue of 1863) it was
bought by the British Museum from the dealer Evans as early as 1847 and
is completely distinct in style and treatment from the other Apocalyptic
watercolours. The form of signature, written out instead of the usual 'WB
inv' monogram, reflects a change in Blake's practice that seems to have
occurred in 1806, and this watercolour is thus further distinguished from
all but a few other stragglers in the biblical series as a whole.

Illustrations to the Book of Job, c.1805–25

Blake painted two series of watercolours illustrating the Book of Job, the first for Butts, the second for John Linnell who also commissioned a series of engravings from them. Linnell's set was painted by Blake in 1821 over tracings made by Linnell from the Butts set. The engravings, commissioned two years later, are dated 1825 but were probably not actually published until the following year. To help him in the reduction in scale, Blake also did a series of drawings in a small sketchbook now in the Fitzwilliam Museum, Cambridge. A number of further sketches in pencil and watercolour are of subjects apparently either first painted as part of the Linnell set (see No.198) or as try-outs for alternative compositions; they date from c.1821–5.

The watercolours painted for Thomas Butts have until recently been thought to date from shortly before the Linnell set, but in fact stylistically they are much closer to the biblical watercolours of circa 1805; indeed, it is difficult to see why Blake would have needed to have had the outlines traced when he painted the second set had there not been a considerable lapse of time between them. A further reason for dating the Butts set to about 1805 is that some of the watercolours are signed with the 'WB inv' monogram, a form of signature that Blake seems to have abandoned in 1806 (though see Nos.215 and 217). The idea of doing a set of illustrations to the Book of Job would of course have followed on logically from the other Bible illustrations. There is however no documentary evidence for this early dating (nor for the probability that two of the designs, not included in this exhibition, were added to the Butts series after the subjects had been first painted for John Linnell; these are 'The Vision of Christ' and 'Job and his Daughters'; see No.203).

Blake re-interpreted the biblical story of Job to give a less arbitrary reason for Job's sufferings. For Blake these were justified as a result of Job's concentration on the observance rather than the inspiration of religion. The contrasted details of the first and last designs, which are stressed by the otherwise similar compositions, clearly express this; in the first design musical instruments hang unplayed on the tree as the sun sets behind a large church, representing established religion, while in the final design Job and his family stand playing the musical instruments as the sun rises.

In the last stage of the evolution of the designs, in some cases literally as they were being engraved, Blake added the marginal designs with their texts which stress and add further subtleties to his own personal interpretation. The prints show Blake's engraving technique at its height with a technical subtlety that matches the richer and more sophisticated finish of his late paintings in tempera and watercolour. Earlier there had been a striking contrast between Blake's commercial engravings, in which he showed a technical accomplishment matching that of many of his more successful rivals but rather lacking in character, and the much more rugged technique of the engravings after his own designs such as 'Death's Door' (see No.152). Now he achieved a high degree of technical finesse without sacrificing anything of the power of his drawings.

Illustrations to The Book of Job c.1805–6

191 Job and his Family
Illustrations to The Book of Job, no.1.
Pen and watercolour, $8\frac{7}{8} \times 10\frac{13}{16}$ (22.5 × 27.4).
Inscr. 'Our Father which art in Heavn Hallowed be thy Name thy Will be' in arc of setting sun.
Pierpont Morgan Library, New York

Job 1:1–3. Job 'the greatest of all the men of the east' with his family, the counterpart of the last design of the series, No.196. In his own interpretation of the text, Blake shows the family as observing the forms alone of religion: they kneel, take it all from books, and leave their musical instruments unplayed on the tree. The Lord's Prayer, the opening of which is inscribed within the setting sun, is contrasted with the unqualified praise of the passage from Revelation 15:3, inscribed within the rising sun of the other design.

The Lord's Prayer, and the presence of a Gothic cathedral in the background, recall the mediaeval tradition that Job foreshadowed Christ, a tradition elevated by the Swedenborgians to the belief that Job was a Christian priest in Old Testament times. However, if he is a priest, he is, at this stage, only the priest of a negative religion.

192   Satan Before the Throne of God

Illustrations to The Book of Job, no.2.
Pen and watercolour over pencil, $11\frac{11}{16} \times 8\frac{15}{16}$ (29.6 × 22.8).
Pierpont Morgan Library, New York

192

Job 1:6–12. The Lord boasts of Job's righteousness, whereupon Satan says that he has been specially protected and challenges the Lord to test him by letting him come to harm. The Lord puts all that Job has, but not Job himself, in Satan's power. Below can be seen Job and his family, with two guardian angels.

Blake shows the Lord in Job's image, though even more passive on his throne with a large book open on his knees. Satan by contrast is a young, physically ideal, energetic figure, recalling Blake's representations of his own spirit of revolutionary energy, Orc, in particular plate 3 of *Urizen*, 1794 (see No.76).

The compartmentalisation of the composition, characteristic of several of the best of the Job designs, is typical of Blake's conceptual attitude to narrative by this date. Also characteristic is the fact that the lower part of the composition is developed in reverse from a large watercolour of *c.*1780 of 'Enoch walked with God' (?) now in the Cincinnati Museum of Art.

193   Satan Smiting Job with Sore Boils

Illustrations to The Book of Job, no.6.
Pen and watercolour, $9\frac{3}{16} \times 11$ (23.4 × 28).
Pierpont Morgan Library, New York

193

Job 2:7. Satan, having failed to provoke Job by attacking his goods and family, obtains the Lord's permission to harm Job himself, provided that his life is saved. Satan then smites Job with sore boils. In the Bible Job remains steadfast, but his affliction has been related to a passage on plate 21 of *Jerusalem* in which Blake sees boils as the symptom of shame:

The disease of Shame covers me from head to feet: I have no hope
Every boil upon my body is a separate & deadly Sin,
Doubt first assaild me, then Shame took possession of me
Shame divides Families . . .

Blake here shows Job's wife absorbed in her own grief, separated from her husband by his shame.

For a late painting developed from this design, see No.313.

194   Job's Evil Dreams

Illustrations to The Book of Job, no.11.
Pen and watercolour over pencil, $9\frac{5}{16} \times 11\frac{5}{16}$ (23.7 × 28.8).
Signed 'WB inv' as monogram, and with inscription in Hebrew on the Tables of the Law.
Pierpont Morgan Library, New York

194

Job 7:13–15. In the text the nature of Job's dreams is not stated but Blake took some of his imagery from elsewhere in the Book of Job (e.g. Job 30:17 and 30, from which Blake quotes in the margins of the engraving of this design). Traditionally Job's dreams were identified with a vision of Hell, but Blake adds his personal idea that such concepts as Hell are the evil products of authoritarian religion, typified by the Mosaic Tables of the Law to which the Lord points. The Lord himself is now shown as thoroughly evil, with cloven hoof and entwined by a serpent; Job's God has become Satan.

This dream is the turning point in the story. It marks Job's lowest point but also the point at which he recognises that it is his conception of God that is wrong.

195

195 When the Morning Stars Sang Together

Illustrations to The Book of Job, no.14.
Pen and watercolour, $11\frac{1}{16} \times 7\frac{1}{4}$ (28 × 18.4).
Pierpont Morgan Library, New York

Job 38:4–7. God, having appeared to Job in a whirlwind, describes the Creation, after which the morning stars had sung together and all the sons of God had shouted for joy. Job, his wife and his friends kneel in a distinct, cave-like Earth below. The two halves of the composition are linked by the figure of the Lord with outstretched arms, under which appear the sun-god Helios and moon-goddess Selene, representing day and night.

These Greek gods were probably taken from Antique gems, which Blake later described, on his Laocoön print, No.315, as 'The Gems of Aaron's Breast Plate'. He thus, as in other cases, related them to an original biblical source, now lost, rather than to the debased art of the Greeks and Romans.

196 Job and his Family Restored to Prosperity

Illustrations to The Book of Job, no.21.
Pen and watercolour, $9\frac{3}{16} \times 10\frac{7}{8}$ (23.4 × 27.6).
Inscr. 'Great & Marvellous are thy Works Lord God Alm[ighty]
Just & tru[e]' in arc of rising sun.
Pierpont Morgan Library, New York

Job 42:12–13. Blake, as in the previous design of 'Job and his Daughters', draws on the apocryphal *Testament of Job*, in which Job tells his daughters to honour God with music and song. Traditionally music was linked with prophecy. The contrast with the opening design of the series is stressed by their basic similarity; see No.191.

The figures of Job and his wife are close to two of the figures playing musical instruments in 'The Hymn of Christ and the Apostles' of *c*.1805, No.175. The figure of Job also recalls the Ancient Bard on the last plate of *Songs of Experience*.

196

197 *Job and his Family Restored to Prosperity* 1821

Illustrations to The Book of Job, no.21.
Pen and watercolour, $9\frac{3}{16} \times 11$ (23.4 × 28).
Inscr. 'Great & Marvellous are thy Works Lord' in arc of rising sun.
National Gallery of Art, Washington (Rosenwald Collection)

Job 42:12–13. This is one of the replicas of the Butts series (see No.196) painted by Blake in 1821 for John Linnell over tracings made by Linnell. The figures and other details correspond closely with those in the Butts version, though the more sensuous modelling and expressions of some of the figures, for instance the daughter in the centre, are typical of Blake's later style. The colours are slightly richer than in the Butts watercolour and have been redistributed among the figures.

All but two of the Linnell series are now in the Fogg Art Museum. This watercolour was once in the W. A. White Collection. The second of the series, 'Satan before the Throne of God', is said to be in a private American collection in Paris.

197

198 *Job and his Daughters* c.1821–5

Pencil, pen, ink and watercolour on paper, $7\frac{7}{8} \times 10$ (20 × 25.4).
Dr R. E. Hemphill

For the subject and the complicated history of this composition see No.203. This watercolour sketch is similar in style and technique to two others, of 'Job's Sacrifice' and 'Every Man also gave Job a Piece of Money' (City Art Gallery, Leeds, and P. & D. Colnaghi & Co. Ltd, respectively); in addition all share the same early history from Blake's widow and Frederick Tatham. The sketch of 'Job's Sacrifice' is on paper watermarked 1820, and so cannot be a sketch for the much earlier watercolour from the series painted for

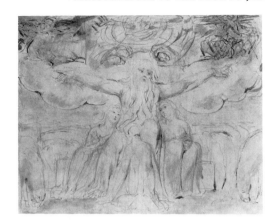

198

Thomas Butts. In fact all three watercolours are either of compositions which Blake varied considerably as between the Butts and Linnell versions or, in the case of 'Every Man also gave Job a Piece of Money', of an alternative project for an upright composition. This watercolour is therefore either a preliminary sketch for the watercolour in the Linnell series of 1821, or possibly, in view of the probability that in this case the Butts version was painted later (see No.203), an intermediate stage between the two.

In any case, this watercolour is a fine example of Blake's late free style, similar to the less finished among the Dante series such as No.336.

Engraved Illustrations to The Book of Job 1823–6

The engravings were commissioned by Linnell on 25 March 1823 with an advance payment of £100, to which Linnell later added about £50 more. Despite the date '1825' the engravings do not seem to have been printed as a set until March 1826, when both 'Proof' and ordinary sets were published. The plates remained in the possession of John Linnell who had further copies printed in 1874, probably including the Tate Gallery's set which was sold from the Linnell collection in 1918. The plates were acquired by the British Museum in 1919.

199

199 Title-page

Line engraving, $7\frac{1}{2} \times 5\frac{3}{4}$ (19.1 × 14.7).
Signed 'Invented & Engraved by William Blake 1825' and inscr.
'London Published as the Act directs March 8:1825. by William Blake Nº 3 Fountain Court Strand'.
Tate Gallery, London

The title-page was added to the series for the engravings and does not figure in either of the sets of watercolours. There is a pencil, pen and ink sketch in the Rosenwald Collection.

200 The Lord Answering Job out of the Whirlwind

Illustrations to The Book of Job, no.13.
Line engraving, $7\frac{3}{4} \times 5\frac{7}{8}$ (19.8 × 15.1).
Signed 'WBlake invenit & sculp' and inscr. 'London Published as the Act directs March 8: 1825 by William Blake Nº 3 Fountain Court Strand', and with the texts referred to below.
Tate Gallery, London

Job 38: 1. The Lord appears out of the whirlwind to answer Job, and says, as is quoted above the design, 'Who is this that darkeneth counsel by words without knowledge' (Job 38:2). He continues with rhetorical questions such as that quoted below, 'Hath the Rain a Father & who hath begotten the Drops of the Dew' (Job 38:28); the other question is from Psalm 104:3. The whirlwind is shown, in the distinct world of the marginal design outside the main picture, to be made up from images of God. Below, trees are pressed to the ground, echoing the figures of Job's friends, but they remain unbroken just as Job has remained unbroken under adversity.

In one state of the engraving Blake showed the whirlwind bursting out of the central design into the margin above, but did away with this to preserve the usual distinct frame, considerably to the loss of dramatic effect.

200

201 When the Morning Stars Sang Together

Illustrations to The Book of Job, no.14.
Line engraving, $7\frac{1}{2} \times 5\frac{7}{8}$ (19.1 × 15).
Signed 'W Blake Invenit & Sc' and inscr. 'London. Published as the Act directs March 8: 1825 by Willm Blake N3 Fountain Court Strand', and with the texts referred to below.
Tate Gallery, London

201

The main composition, though closely based, with minor differences in the angles of the heads, on the earlier watercolours (see No.195), differs in that Blake has added further arms of angels cut off by the frame, as if the line of angels continued to infinity. In the margins Blake has shown the six acts of Creation, each with its text from Genesis, adding at the bottom the great sea-monster Leviathan from Job 41. However, although the next design shows Leviathan with his counterpart Behemoth, here Blake shows a great headless worm, entwined around a featureless piece of mere matter, recalling the negative symbolism of the worm in the large colour print of 1795 of 'Elohim creating Adam', No.85.

Below the main design Blake has added the text from Job 38:7 as a title. Above is a quotation from Job 38:31: 'Canst thou bind the sweet influences of Pleiades or loose the bands of Orion'; the two constellations are represented by the angels accompanying the stars in the upper corners. St. Gregory, commenting on this passage, had equated the Pleiades with the Gospel and Orion with the Law. Blake is therefore asking if one can bind the Gospels, as Job had attempted by following the rigid tenets of orthodox religion, or loose the Mosaic Law, as Jesus did to achieve Man's salvation.

202 Behemoth and Leviathan

Illustrations to The Book of Job, no.15.
Line engraving, $7\frac{7}{8} \times 5\frac{15}{16}$ (20.1 × 15.1).
Signed 'W Blake invenit & sculpt' and inscr. 'London Published as the Act directs March 8: 1825 by Willm Blake N 3 Fountain Court Strand', and with the texts referred to below.
Tate Gallery, London

202

Job 40:15–Job 41:34. The Lord humbles Job by enumerating the extent and power of His creation: 'Behold now Behemoth, which I made with thee' (quoted below the design). In the right-hand margin Blake introduced the descriptions of the two monsters from Job 40:19 and 41:34 with his own words, 'Of Behemoth [or 'Of Leviathan'] he saith . . .'. Leviathan is described in various places in the Bible as a sea-monster, while the representation of Behemoth as a hippopotamus is the traditional one, marvellously stylised in a way that parallels Dürer's famous print. Blake shows them inhabiting two distinct areas of the globe, the land and the sea. The other two texts, from Job 36:29 (above) and 37:11–12 (on the left), relate them to such natural phenomena as clouds and thunder ('the noise of his Tabernacle').

203 Job and his Daughters

Illustrations to The Book of Job, no.20.
Line engraving, $7\frac{7}{8} \times 5\frac{15}{16}$ (20 × 15.1).
Signed 'WBlake invenit & Sc' and inscr. 'London. Published as the Act directs March 8: 1825 by William Blake Nº3 Fountain Court Strand', and with the texts referred to below.
Tate Gallery, London

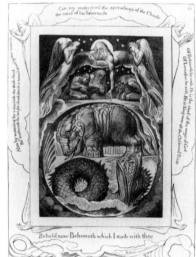

203

Job 42:13–15. The text contains no more than the statement that, after the Lord had 'blessed the latter end of Job more than his beginning', he had seven sons and three daughters, adding the daughters' names and concluding with the verse quoted below the design. Blake has drawn on the apocryphal *Testament of Job* in which Job, shortly before his death, tells his daughters the story of his afflictions and his salvation. These are shown pictured on the wall. On the left is the destruction of Job's servants (Job 1:17), on the right the destruction of his ploughmen (Job 1:15), and in the centre the Lord answering Job out of the whirlwind, the subject of the thirteenth design in the series (Job 38:1; see No.200: here Job's wife bows to the ground, unseeing, like Job's friends, whereas in No.200 she shares the vision). The two semi-circles below contain representations of Job's wife in despair.

The texts at the top and bottom of the plate are from Psalms 139 and 8 respectively, reflecting two aspects of the knowledge that Job has gained through his experiences. The marginal designs contain angels, vines representing family love, and the musical instruments that Job and his family are to take up and play in the next, final scene of the story.

Blake had a lot of trouble with this design. The watercolour in the Butts set (Pierpont Morgan Library) seems to have been added to the set at a late date, showing all the marks of Blake's late style and in addition evidence of having been completed by another hand. The watercolour from the Linnell set (Fogg Museum) was therefore the first to be completed, though it may have been preceded by the watercolour sketch, No.198. The sketch, like the Butts watercolour, shows the scene taking place out of doors, the scenes from Job's past appearing amidst clouds. The Linnell watercolour, and a further sketch in pencil in the Rosenwald Collection, show a strange mixture of indoors and outdoors. Finally, in the engraving, Blake returned to a composition of some twenty-five years earlier, the small tempera painting of c.1799–1800, one of the biblical series painted for Thomas Butts (Rosenwald Collection).

204 Job and his Family Restored to Prosperity

Illustrations to The Book of Job, no.21.
Line engraving, $7\frac{11}{16} \times 5\frac{13}{16}$ (19.6 × 14.8).
Signed 'WBlake inv & sculp' and inscr. 'London Published as the Act directs March 8: 1825 by William Blake Fountain Court Strand', and with the texts referred to below.
Tate Gallery, London

204

The final stage of the composition of Nos.196 and 197, with the usual additional marginal texts and designs. The title below the main design comes from Job 42:12, while the concluding lines of the book, Job 42:16 and 17, occupy the two lower corners. The upper corners contain the full text (from the Song of Moses in Revelation 15:3) of which abbreviated fragments had appeared in the rising sun in the two watercolours:

Great and Marvellous are thy Works Lord God Almighty
Just and True are thy Ways O thou King of Saints.

Below in the middle appears an altar, as in the very similar border to the first design; the flanking ram and ox have been reversed. Whereas the altar on the first design is inscribed 'The Letter Killeth The Spirit giveth Life [2 Corinthians 3:6] It is Spiritually Discerned [1 Corinthians 2:14]', here the altar is inscribed 'In burnt offerings for Sin thou hast no Pleasure' from Hebrews 10:6; between the two they spell out Blake's abhorrence of the material observances of the Old Testament, the adherence to which had been Job's downfall.

Blake's Exhibition, 'The Last Judgment' and other works, c.1800–1810

Undeterred by his repeated failure to achieve commercial success, Blake made one final attempt to appeal to the public, this time avoiding a dependence on patrons, publishers and other middlemen, by holding his own exhibition at his brother's house, 28 Broad Street, Golden Square, Soho. The comparative success of his independent pictures, those illustrating the Bible and Milton, may have suggested this means rather than another appeal through book illustrations. The exhibition opened in the middle of May and was planned to close at the end of September. In fact it was still open well into 1810, Crabb Robinson visiting it in April and taking Charles Lamb and his sister there in June. Alas, the prolongation of the exhibition does not seem to have been the result of any 'public demand', but rather an act of inertia and despair. Only one review appeared, and that was hostile.

Admission to the exhibition was by means of Blake's *Descriptive Catalogue*, sold for 2s.6d. This was an ambitious publication, giving long descriptions of the pictures, discussing their significance and defending Blake's tempera technique, here called 'fresco', against the 'blurring demons' that attacked paintings in oil. The core of the exhibition was the group of nine tempera paintings, of which four are now lost (but see No.254), to which were added seven 'Drawings' or rather watercolours, including a version of 'The Penance of Jane Shore' (see Nos.16 and 17) to show 'that the productions of our youth and of our maturer age are equal in all essential points'; also included were Nos.160, 168, 176, 180, a version of No.312, and 'The Brahmins', now lost. In his preface Blake attacked 'the eye that can prefer the Colouring of Titian and Rubens to that of Michael Angelo and Rafael', and Venetian painting to Florentine. 'Till we get rid of Titian and Correggio, Rubens and Rembrandt, we never shall equal Rafael and Albert Durer, Michael Angelo, and Julio Romano'. This represents a marked change from the views Blake expressed in his letter to the Rev. Trusler in 1799 (see No.141) but one well in tune with his stylistic development over the intervening ten years.

In 1810 Blake may have been considering adding another painting to his exhibition, for there is a long draft account of a painting of 'The Last Judgment', headed 'For the Year 1810 Additions to Blakes Catalogue of Pictures &c.' According to J. T. Smith, at the time of his death Blake was working on a large picture of this subject 'said to be over 7 ft. high' which he was to have exhibited at the Royal Academy in 1828. Blake was reported as working on a 'large drawing in Water Colours' of the same subject in 1815; this may have been the same work as that on which he was working in 1810 and even, allowing for a mix-up over the medium, as that on which he was working at his death. No such picture is now known though the composition probably followed a drawing that still survives in the Rosenwald Collection; this is a development of two surviving watercolours of 1806 and 1808 (Nos.211 and 213), themselves a development of the composition of one of the illustrations to *The Grave*.

What seems to have been Blake's largest picture, a small token of his desire to paint pictures in which 'the figures were one hundred feet in height', was another work in his exhibition, 'The Ancient Britons', which apparently measured ten by fourteen feet. As it is, the largest known surviving picture by Blake is 'The Spiritual Condition of Man' in the Fitzwilliam Museum, which is about five feet high. This is one of a group of tempera paintings on which Blake, undeterred by the failure of his exhibition, seems to have been working in about 1810 and which also included 'Adam naming the Beasts', its companion 'Eve naming the Birds', 'The Virgin and Child in Egypt' and 'Christ Blessing' (see No.214). These paintings, unusually for Blake, were half lengths concentrating on the head, possibly under the inspiration of Renaissance Madonnas; 'The Virgin and Child in Egypt' in particular recalls Bellini.

---

205 *The Spiritual Form of Nelson Guiding Leviathan* c.1809

Tempera on canvas, $30 \times 24\frac{5}{8}$ (76.2 × 62.5).
Tate Gallery, London

The first work in Blake's exhibition. In his catalogue the title continues, 'in whose wreathings are infolded the Nations of the Earth.' The significance of this work and its companion 'The Spiritual Form of Pitt' is discussed under No.206.

Nelson had died at the Battle of Trafalgar in 1805 and Blake may have been in part inspired (or provoked) by John Flaxman's monument in St. Paul's, begun in 1808 though not completed until 1811, and Benjamin West's 'Apotheosis of Nelson', exhibited at West's house in 1806. In the advertisement for his exhibition Blake had indeed described his pictures as 'grand Apotheoses of NELSON and PITT'.

195 *When the Morning Stars Sang Together*, illustration to The Book of Job, no.14, *c*.1805–6 (entry on p.100)

214 *The Virgin and Child in Egypt,* 1810 (entry on p.111)

This picture is much damaged, only about a half of Blake's original paint remaining. There is a preliminary drawing in the British Museum.

206 *The Spiritual Form of Pitt Guiding Behemoth* 1805 (?)

Tempera heightened with gold on canvas, $29\frac{1}{8} \times 24\frac{3}{4}$ (74 × 62.7). Signed 'WBlake 1805 [? –the last digit is obscure]'.

Tate Gallery, London

The second work in Blake's exhibition, and companion to No.205. Blake's title continues, 'he is that Angel who, pleased to perform the Almighty's orders, rides on the whirlwind, directing the storms of war: He is ordering the Reaper to reap the Vine of the Earth, and the Plowman to plow up the Cities and Towers'. The imagery parallels that in the Book of Revelation and other biblical and apocryphal texts: the reaper and plowman are the angels who prepare 'the great winepress of the wrath of God' or, as Blake put it in his own poem *Milton, c.*1804–10, the 'Wine-press of Los . . . call'd War on Earth'. In Blake's *Jerusalem, c.*1804–20, the two biblical monsters Leviathan and Behemoth appear as 'the War by Sea enormous & the War by Land astounding'. The two 'Spiritual Forms' are, therefore, allegories of apocalyptic war, brought up-to-date with contemporary protagonists (William Pitt died a year after Nelson, in 1806); such wars preceded the Last Judgment, the subject of several works by Blake during these years (see p.104 and Nos.211 and 213).

In his catalogue Blake goes on to explain that these two pictures 'are compositions of a mythological cast, similar to those Apotheoses of Persian, Hindoo, and Egyptian Antiquity, which are still preserved on rude monuments, being copies from some stupendous originals now lost or perhaps buried till some happier age. The Artist having been taken in vision into the ancient republics, monarchies, and patriarchates of Asia, has seen those wonderful originals called in the Sacred Scriptures the Cherubim, which were sculptured and painted on walls of Temples, Towers, Cities, Palaces . . . being originals from which the Greeks and Hetrurians copied Hercules Farnese, Venus of Medicis, Apollo Belvidere, and all the grand works of ancient art. They were executed in a very superior style to those justly admired copies . . .'. Blake sees the art of Antiquity as a mere secular reflection of the lost religious art of the Old Testament; similarly with 'Homer's Mythology, or Ovid's': 'The Greek Muses are daughters of Mnemosyne, or Memory, and not of Inspiration or Imagination'.

Blake claimed that the originals seen in his visions were 'some of them one hundred feet in height'. He wished that 'it was now the fashion to make such monuments, and then he should not doubt of having a national commission to execute these two Pictures on a scale that is suitable to the grandeur of the nation, who is the parent of his heroes, in high finished fresco . . .'.

He concludes with an attack on oil as a medium, for turning 'every permanent white to a yellow and brown putty . . .'; moreover 'real gold and silver cannot be used with oil, as they are in all the old pictures and in Mr. B.'s frescos', such as the 'Spiritual Forms' and 'The Bard' (No.207). 'All the genuine old little pictures, called Cabinet Pictures, are in fresco and not in oil' – how unlike his letter to Trusler in 1799, quoted under No.141.

This picture belonged to Samuel Palmer, for whom it was restored by George Richmond. It has been cleaned again for this exhibition, but much had irretrievably darkened. It seems that Palmer also owned a 'Spiritual Form of Napoleon', whether from this period or later is not known; this alas is now lost and is known only from a description made in 1876.

207 *The Bard, from Gray* 1809(?)

Tempera heightened with gold on canvas, $23\frac{5}{8} \times 17\frac{3}{8}$ (60 × 44.1). Signed 'WBlake' with traces of date.

Tate Gallery, London

The fourth work in Blake's exhibition. It illustrates Gray's poem 'The Bard', to which Blake had already devoted fourteen watercolours in his illustrations to Gray's *Poems* for the Flaxmans of *c*.1797–8. 'The Bard' recounts how Edward I, invading Wales, had condemned all the Welsh bards to death, only to be confronted by a lone survivor who prophesied the doom of the king and all his successors from a high rock above the river Conway, accompanied by the ghosts of the other bards. The confrontation of poetic inspiration and secular oppression was one that would have had a special appeal for Blake.

In his catalogue Blake quotes two lines of Gray's poem,

> *Weave the warp, and weave the woof*
> *The winding sheet of Edward's race,*

as typical of poetry's power of expression 'by means of sounds of spiritual music and its accompanying expressions of articulate speech.' By contrast, should 'Painting be confined to the sordid drudgery of fac-simile representations of merely mortal and perishing substances . . . ? No, it shall not be so! Painting, as well as poetry and music, exists and exults in immortal thoughts.'

Blake goes on to defend his 'mode of representing spirits [the dead bards] with real bodies', a criticism that had been made of his illustrations to *The Grave*, by citing the admired Greek statues of the gods as 'all of them representations of spiritual existences . . . to the mortal perishing organ of sight. . . . The Prophets describe what they saw in Vision as real and existing men, whom they saw with their imaginative and immortal organs; the Apostles the same; the clearer the organ the more distinct the object. A Spirit and a Vision are not, as the modern philosophy supposes, a cloudy vapour, or a nothing: they are organized and minutely articulated beyond all that the mortal and perishing nature can produce. He who does not imagine in stronger and better lineaments, and in stronger and better light than his perishing and mortal eye can see, does not imagine at all.'

Blake's note ends, rather confusingly, 'The execution of this picture is also in Water Colours, or Fresco'. It has recently been cleaned but, like so many of Blake's earlier temperas, is much darkened. The picture belonged to Samuel Palmer who wrote on a label on the back that it was 'Signed "W.Blake 1809"'; only the signature remains. He subsequently gave it to George Richmond, who gave it to his son William Blake Richmond. There are two sketches in the Philadelphia Museum.

208 *Satan Calling up his Legions* c.1800–09

Tempera on canvas, approx. $21\frac{1}{2} \times 16\frac{1}{2}$ (54.5 × 42).
Victoria and Albert Museum, London

208

An illustration to Milton's *Paradise Lost* 1, 300–34; the ninth of Blake's exhibits. In his Catalogue Blake described this as 'a composition for a more perfect Picture, afterwards executed for a Lady of high rank [No.209]. An experiment Picture'. By this last he meant an experiment in technique, and he describes how it was 'painted at intervals, for experiment on colours without any oily vehicle. . . . The great labour which has been bestowed on it, that is, three or four times as much as would have finished a more perfect Picture . . . has destroyed the lineaments; it was with difficulty brought back again to a certain effect, which it had at first, when all the lineaments were perfect'. His difficulties were the result of the 'temptations and perturbations . . . of that infernal machine called Chiaro Oscuro, in the hands of Venetian and Flemish Demons . . .'. He continued by attacking Titian, Rubens ('a most outrageous demon') and Correggio ('a soft and effeminate, and consequently a most cruel demon').

His concluding words, that 'These experiment Pictures have been bruised and knocked about without mercy, to try all experiments', seem, alas, only too true. The two other 'experiment pictures' in his exhibition, 'The Goats' (a subject 'taken from the Missionary Voyage', in which the missionaries' goats had stripped off the vine leaves that clothed the savage girls) and 'The Spiritual Preceptor' (a subject 'taken from the Visions of Emanuel Swedenborg'), have disappeared, as have two further temperas in Blake's exhibition, 'The Ancient Britons' and 'A Spirit vaulting from a Cloud . . .' (see No.254). This picture, like Nos.206–7, belonged to Samuel Palmer.

209 *Satan Calling up his Legions* c.1805

Tempera on canvas, approx. 21 × 16 (53.5 × 40.5).
Signed '. . . Blake . . .' with illegible letters or figures (?) before and after.

H. M. Treasury and the National Trust, Petworth House, Sussex

This picture, which was not in Blake's exhibition, is that referred to by Blake in his catalogue entry on No.208 as the 'more perfect Picture, afterwards executed for a Lady of high rank', presumably the Countess of Egremont, the wife of Turner's great patron the third Earl of Egremont. The composition follows that of the other work with minor changes, but the forms, even allowing for the better state of preservation, are more clearly outlined. The Egremonts seem to have got to know Blake during his stay at Felpham, 1800–03, and the picture seems to be earlier than the 'Vision of the Last Judgment' he painted for Lady Egremont in 1808, No.211. In addition, the composition of the two tempera paintings of this subject are looser and less disciplined than those of the two watercolour versions of 1807 and 1808 (see No.216).

210 *Chaucer's Canterbury Pilgrims* 1810

Line engraving coloured with watercolour, 11¾ × 36½
(29.9 × 92.7); platemark 13¾ × 37½ (35 × 95.2).
Inscr. 'CHAUCERS CANTERBURY PILGRIMS', 'Painted in Fresco by William Blake & by him Engraved & Published October 8 . 1810, at Nº 28. Corner of Broad Street Golden Square', and with the names of the characters.

Private collection, England

This is a unique hand-coloured example of the first state of Blake's own engraving after the tempera painting, signed and apparently dated 1808, that he included as the third work in his exhibition with the title 'Sir Jeffery Chaucer and the Nine and Twenty Pilgrims on their Journey to Canterbury'. The painting was the occasion of Blake's second quarrel with Robert Cromek and also of his falling out with his old friend Thomas Stothard. Blake's version of the incident, as told by John Linnell, was that Cromek commissioned the painting for twenty guineas, the price to be supplemented when Blake engraved it, but that Cromek secretly planned to have it engraved by William Bromley. Blake, suspecting this, refused to let him have the painting, whereupon Cromek got Stothard to do a painting of the subject exactly the same size (this is now in the Tate Gallery; the engraving, by Schiavonetti in the end, not Bromley, was apparently ready by November 1809). Stothard's story, according to J. T. Smith, was that he had acted in completely good faith, knowing nothing of Blake's interest in

the matter when Cromek approached him (and, incidentally, offered him sixty guineas, later raised to a hundred).

The story, in whichever version, suggests that Blake may have begun work on his picture as early as 1805 or '06, before he finally became disillusioned with Cromek over *The Grave* (see p.79). At all events the date on the painting, now damaged, was formerly read as '1808', and Blake's engraving was announced in May 1809 and published on 8 October 1810.

Blake devoted no fewer than thirty-six pages in his *Descriptive Catalogue* to this picture, largely analysing Chaucer's characters, which he regarded as 'the physiognomies or lineaments of universal life'. Charles Lamb, who, according to Henry Crabb Robinson, preferred Blake's picture greatly to Stothard's, 'declared that Blake's description was the finest criticism he had ever read of Chaucer's poem'.

The figures, which are identified by Blake on the engraving, are led by the Knight with his son as Squire; in the centre is the Host and Chaucer himself can be seen on the left. Perhaps surprisingly, Blake describes the Knight, who 'has ever been a conqueror', as 'a true Hero, a good, great, and wise man', perhaps because he 'is that species of character which in every age stands as the guardian of man against the oppressor'. On the whole, indeed, Blake's appreciation of Chaucer's characters is remarkably tolerant. Even the Pardoner, 'the Age's Knave', is justified as a man 'sent in every age for a rod and scourge, and for a blight, for a trial of men . . . , and he is suffered by Providence for wise ends'.

Blake identified most with the Good Parson, 'a real Messenger of Heaven', and with the Plowman. Grecian Gods, being 'the ancient Cherubim of Phœnicia' and 'visions of the eternal attributes', can 'when erected into gods, become destructive to humanity'. Thus the Plowman 'is Hercules in his supreme eternal state, divested of his spectrous shadow; which is the Miller, a terrible fellow, such as exists . . . for the trial of men . . . to curb the pride of Man'.

As for the Women, these 'Chaucer has divided into two classes, the Lady Prioress and the Wife of Bath'. The latter is shown as the Whore of Babylon, much as in Blake's contemporary watercolour, No.190.

Blake concludes his survey of Chaucer's characters with the Clerk of Oxenford, 'the contemplative philosopher', as opposed to Chaucer himself, 'the poetical genius'. 'The painter has put them side by side, as if the youthful clerk had put himself under the tuition of the mature poet. Let the Philosopher always be the servant and scholar of inspiration and all will be happy.'

He goes on to contrast his own 'unbroken lines, unbroken masses, and unbroken colours' with the 'broken' equivalent of Rubens, Rembrandt and the 'Venetian and Flemish practice'. This leads to an attack on Stothard's version: 'All is misconceived, and its mis-execution is equal to its misconception'.

Years later, in a conversation with Crabb Robinson, Blake defended himself from the charge of having stolen one of his figures from a picture in the collection of Charles Aders, which consisted largely of Flemish and German Primitives: 'I did it 20 years before I knew of the picture'. However, 'in my youth I was always studying this kind of painting. No wonder there is a resemblance'. More remarkable is the influence of the Parthenon frieze, particularly as the Elgin marbles had only been unpacked in 1807. Blake shared this early enthusiasm with Flaxman, Fuseli, Stothard and the young Benjamin Robert Haydon.

The painting was sold, like so many others, to Thomas Butts, was later in the Stirling Maxwell collection, and passed with other works at Pollok House to the Corporation of Glasgow.

Blake announced the engraving after his picture in a prospectus of 15 May 1809. The price was given as four guineas, but this was reduced to three guineas before the engraving was actually published. An advertisement illustrated by an engraving of a detail from the left of the composition was published on 26 December 1811. Blake also planned, but never published, a long 'Public Address' arising out of the publication of the engraving, attacking the English for condemning drawing while concentrating on engraving technique with 'absurd Nonsense about dots & Lozenges & Clean Strokes . . . . I defy any Man to Cut Cleaner Strokes than I do, or rougher where I please. . . . Painting is drawing on Canvas, & Engraving is drawing on Copper, & nothing Else, & he who draws best must be the best Artist . . .'.

There are a number of coloured copies of Blake engravings with a good claim to have been coloured by Blake himself, including the illustrations to Young's *Night Thoughts* and Hayley's *Ballads*, the prints of The Book of Job, and Blake's engravings after Maria Flaxman's illustrations to Hayley's *Triumphs of Temper*, 1807. Two coloured copies of the 'Canterbury Pilgrims' are known: this example, which, by comparison with the best examples of other of Blake's coloured engravings, seems certainly to have been done by him, and a copy of the second state (or perhaps of an otherwise unknown transitional state between the second and the third) in the United States. There is a drawing for the engraving, reduced in scale from the painting, on loan to the National Gallery of Victoria.

211 *A Vision of the Last Judgment* 1806

Pen and watercolour over pencil, $19\frac{1}{2} \times 15\frac{5}{16}$ (49.5 × 39) on paper $22\frac{3}{8} \times 17\frac{7}{8}$ (56.8 × 45.5).
Signed 'WBlake inv. 1806'.
Glasgow Museums and Art Galleries, Pollok House, Stirling Maxwell Collection

Blake had probably first treated this subject in 1805 as one of his illustrations to *The Grave*, engraved three years later by Schiavonetti. This watercolour, painted for Thomas Butts, is an enlarged and elaborated version of that design. It was itself developed in a watercolour painted two years later which was accompanied by a long letter explaining the subject; see No.213. Most of the details described by Blake are the same as in this version though he changed the position of certain figures: for instance here, at the bottom of the design, the Apocalyptic Dragon with seven heads appears above the Harlot rather than the other way round. The general composition and many of the actual figures are derived from Michelangelo's 'Last Judgment' on the altar wall of the Sistine Chapel.

For the companion 'Fall of Man', painted the following year, see No.212. Both works passed from the Butts Collection to Sir William Stirling Maxwell.

212 *The Fall of Man* 1807

Pen and watercolour, $19 \times 15\frac{1}{4}$ (48.3 × 38.7) with $\frac{5}{16}$ (0.7) added at the bottom.
Signed '1807 WBlake inv' and inscr. on the back with a description of the subject; see below.
Victoria and Albert Museum, London

The description on the back, if not actually written by Blake himself as seems most likely, must reflect his account: 'The Father indignant at the Fall – the Saviour, while the Evil Angels are driven, gently conducts our first parents out of Eden through a Guard of weeping Angels – Satan now awakes Sin, Death & Hell, to celebrate with him the birth of War & Misery: while the Lion seizes the Bull, the Tiger the Horse, the Vulture and the Eagle contend for the Lamb'. Unlike Milton's account of the Expulsion in *Paradise Lost* and Blake's illustrations of it in 1807 and 1808 (see No.227), Blake here shows Christ, the Saviour, leading Adam and Eve out of the Garden of Eden rather than the Archangel Gabriel. His action is contrasted with the fury of God the Father above, surrounded by avenging angels. Below are the various horrors resulting from the Fall, which necessitate the 'Last Judgment' as depicted in the companion watercolour of 1806, No.211.

214

Fig. 16 William Blake, *Adam naming the Beasts*, 1810 (Pollok House, Glasgow)

213 *The Last Judgment* 1808

Pen and watercolour over pencil, approx. 20 × 15½ (51 × 39.5). Signed 'WBlake inv and del: 1808'.

H.M. Treasury and the National Trust, Petworth House, Sussex

This version of the subject was commissioned in 1807 by the Countess of Egremont on the recommendation of Ozias Humphry. Blake described his composition in a lost letter to Humphry, of which however three drafts, made in January and February 1808, survive:

> Christ seated on the Throne of Judgment; before his feet & around him the heavens in clouds are rolling like a scroll ready to be consumed in the fires of the Angels who descend with the[ir] Four Trumpets sounding to the Four Winds.
>
> Beneath, the Earth is convulsed with the labours of the Resurrection – in the Caverns of the Earth is the Dragon with Seven heads & ten Horns chained by two Angels, & above his Cavern on the Earth's Surface is the Harlot siezed [*sic*] & bound by two Angels with chains . . .
>
> The right hand of the Design [as seen from the point of view of those within the picture] is appropriated to the Resurrection of the Just; the left hand of the Design is appropriated to the Resurrection & Fall of the Wicked.
>
> Immediately before the Throne of Christ is Adam & Eve kneeling in humiliation as representatives of the whole Human Race. Abraham & Moses kneel on each side beneath them . . .; beneath Moses . . . is seen Satan wound round by the Serpent & falling headlong.

The Pharisees 'pleading their own righteousness' are among those about to fall into the 'Abyss of Hell' to the right of 'the Harlot's Seat'.

> Before the Throne of Christ on the Right [left] hand, the Just in humiliation & in exultation rise thro the Air with their Children & Families . . .; among them is a Figure crownd with Stars & the Moon beneath her feet with six infants around her. She represents the Christian Church. . . . Parents & Children, Wives & Husbands embrace & arise together & in exulting attitudes of great joy tell each other that the New Jerusalem is ready to descend upon Earth. . . .
>
> The Whole upper part of the Design is a View of Heaven opened around the Throne of Christ; in the Cloud which rolls away are the Four Living Creatures filled with Eyes attended by the Seven Angels with the Seven Vials of the Wrath of God & above these there are

Fig. 17 William Blake, *Eve naming the Birds*, c. 1810 (Pollok House, Glasgow)

Fig. 18 William Blake, *Christ Blessing*, c. 1810 (Fogg Art Museum, Cambridge, Mass.)

Seven Angels with Seven Trumpets . . .; the Four & Twenty Elders [are] seatèd on Thrones to Judge the Dead.

Behind the Seat & Throne of Christ appears the Tabernacle with its veil opened, the Candlestick on the right [left], the Table with the Shew bread on the left; in the midst is the Cross in place of the Ark with the two Cherubim bowing over it.

On the Right [left] hand of the Throne of Christ is Baptism, On the left is the Lord's Supper . . .; many Infants appear in the Glory representing the Eternal Creation flowing from the Divine Humanity in Jesus who opens the Scroll of Judgment upon his knees before the Living & the Dead.

The composition is closely based on that of two years earlier (No.211).

214 *The Virgin and Child in Egypt* 1810

Tempera on canvas, 30 × 25 (76.2 × 63.5).
Signed 'Fresco by Willm Blake 1810'.
Victoria and Albert Museum, London

Matthew 2:14–15. In the background are the pyramids of Egypt, symbols of the materialism and repressive religion that Christ's birth was to overthrow.

This painting seems to form part of a set of four together with 'Adam naming the Beasts', which is signed and dated 1810 in the same form, its companion 'Eve naming the Birds' (both at Pollok House, Glasgow), and 'Christ Blessing' (Fogg Museum). All share the same size and general format with a half-length figure, and all belonged to Thomas Butts and were later, except for 'Christ Blessing', in the Stirling Maxwell collection. In each pair of pictures, 'Adam' and 'Eve', 'The Virgin and Child' and 'Christ Blessing', the same placing of the hands, subtly varied, is contrasted as between male and female (see figs.16–18). The two pairs represent the male and female protagonists of the Creation and Fall on the one hand, and of Man's Salvation on the other.

215 *The Judgment of Paris* 1811(?)

Pen and watercolour over pencil, $15\frac{3}{16} \times 18\frac{1}{8}$ (38.5 × 46).
Signed 'WB inv [as monogram] 1811 [?]' and inscr. 'ΠΑΡΙΣ ['Paris']' on the collar of Paris's dog.
Trustees of the British Museum, London

One of Blake's rare illustrations of a Classical subject. 'Philoctetes and Neoptolemus on the Island of Lemnos' of 1812, though slightly different in size, was probably painted as a companion: 'The Judgment of Paris' shows the origins of the Trojan War, while Philoctetes' arrival at Troy at the instigation of Neoptolemus led to the death of Paris and the victory of the Greeks.

The subject would have appealed to Blake as an example of the fatal effect of the division of the female principle, itself a dividing off from the united Man (see No.80). Paris's gift of the apple to Aphrodite, personification of sensuous pleasure, enrages Athena (on the right), the goddess of wisdom and arts but here debased in the service of war, and Hera, who calls for war to avenge Paris's insult to herself and to the institution of marriage. Hermes, messenger of the gods, and Discord are seen above, while Eros, who has inspired Paris's choice, starts away on the left.

The form of signature, 'WB inv' as a monogram, is an exception to what seems to be the general rule that Blake abandoned this form after 1805 in favour of a written out 'WBlake' or 'WB inv' all on one line. The last digit of the date differs from the figure one before it and could possibly be a seven, but this seems unlikely in view of the style of the watercolour, still close to works of 1805–10, and the date of the 'Philoctetes', 1812. The watercolour was in the Butts and W. Graham Robertson collections.

Illustrations to Milton and other writers, c.1807–20

In 1801, while Blake was painting his illustrations to the Bible for Thomas Butts, he received his first commission for a series of illustrations to Milton. Further series continued to occupy him over the next fifteen years. Though some of these were painted for Butts, to begin with they were the result of the initiative of another patron, the Rev. Joseph Thomas of Epsom, to whom Blake had been introduced once again by his friend John Flaxman, who wrote to him on the 31 July 1801 to say that 'the Revᵈ Joseph Thomas of Epsom desires you will at your leisure, make a few sketches of the same size, which may be any size you please from Milton's Comus for Five Guineas' (these are now in the Huntington Library, San Marino). Flaxman went on to inform Blake that Thomas also desired him to paint some illustrations to be inserted in a folio edition of Shakespeare (see No.254). Two further series of illustrations to Milton were painted for Thomas, of subjects from *Paradise Lost* in 1807 (Huntington Library) and from *The Ode on the Morning of Christ's Nativity* in 1809 (Whitworth Institute, Manchester). Already, in 1808, Blake had done a second series of *Paradise Lost* illustrations (Nos.216–27), larger and with one of the subjects altered, for Thomas Butts, for whom he later did a second series of illustrations to *Comus* (Nos.231–8) and to *The Ode on the Morning of Christ's Nativity* (Huntington Library), both of c.1815. For Butts he also did a new series illustrating *L'Allegro* and *Il Penseroso* on paper watermarked 1816. Also on paper watermarked 1816 are the illustrations to *Paradise Regained*; these may also have been intended for Butts but were bought in 1825 by John Linnell, the great patron of Blake's last years. Linnell also seems to have commissioned a third set of illustrations to *Paradise Lost* but only three designs were completed, in 1822 (Nos.228–30).

The illustrations to Milton thus provide a good survey of Blake's later development, spanning the years 1801–22. The linear, flatly-coloured style of the early years of the century gave way to a more highly worked, often jewel-like finish in richer colours applied with a broken technique rather than in flat washes; the figures are more firmly but at the same time more impressionistically modelled.

216

Illustrations to John Milton's 'Paradise Lost' 1808

216 Satan Arousing the Rebel Angels
Pen and watercolour, irregular, 20⅜ × 15½ (51.8 × 39.3).
Signed 'WBlake 1808'.
Victoria and Albert Museum, London

Paradise Lost 1: 300–34: 'Awake! arise, or be for ever fallen'. The fallen Satan summons the rebel angels to conference.

The composition is more symmetrical and condensed, with fewer figures, than in the two tempera paintings, Nos.208 and 209; the corresponding watercolour in the smaller series of *Paradise Lost* watercolours painted for the Rev. Joseph Thomas in 1807 marks an intermediate stage. The development is typical of Blake's final abandonment of the pictorial tradition in favour of a two-dimensional display of emblematic figures. Blake also plays down the drama of the situation, in keeping with his interest in the theological aspects of Milton's poem; this led him to include such unusual subjects as 'Christ Offers to Redeem Man', No.218.

The composition, particularly in this final, refined form, has been seen as a restatement in negative terms of the traditional way of representing the Resurrection. The figures are once again typical of Blake's repertoire of expressive poses stemming by way of Michelangelo from the Antique.

This watercolour, like Nos.217 and 225, belonged to Thomas Butts but was separated in the middle of the nineteenth century from the main body of the series, the nine watercolours now at Boston (Nos.218–24, 226–7). Whereas the Boston watercolours were sold at Foster's on 29 June 1853 and were bought by J. C. Strange, the other three were in another sale, referred to by William Rossetti but now untraced; by 1863 they belonged to the dealer Fuller from whom they passed to Turner's great patron H. A. J. Munro of Novar, only to be dispersed after the sale of his collection in 1868.

217 **Photograph of 'Satan, Sin and Death, Satan Comes to the Gates of Hell'**

Pen, gold and watercolour, $19\frac{1}{2} \times 15\frac{7}{8}$ (49.5 × 40.3).
Signed 'WB inv' as monogram.
Henry E. Huntington Library, San Marino

Paradise Lost 2:645–734: '''O father, what intends thy hand . . . Against thy only son?'' Satan, in search of the rumoured newly created Earth, comes to the Gates of Hell which he finds guarded by Sin, a woman down to the waist but serpent-like below and girt around with hell-hounds, and by Death. Satan and Death are about to fight when Sin tells them that Death is her son by Satan.

This was a common subject in the late eighteenth and early nineteenth centuries. Burke had singled it out as an example of the Sublime and engravings had spread the fame of Hogarth's painting, now in the Tate Gallery. Blake himself had already treated the subject in one of his pen and wash drawings of *c*.1780, as well as in the Thomas series of *Paradise Lost* watercolours of 1807. Blake manages to convey Death's lack of substance while retaining his usual clarity of form by showing the figure as transparent but fully formed with a clear outline.

The form of signature, 'WB inv' as a monogram, is that which Blake seems on the whole to have abandoned after 1805 (but see No.215). It is just possible that this watercolour, treating such a common subject, was done on its own before the main series, most of which bear Blake's typical post-1805 written-out signature. However, the composition seems to represent an advance on that in the Thomas series of *Paradise Lost* watercolours of 1807. There is a preparatory sketch, the same size as the Thomas version but sharing features with this larger watercolour and therefore presumably drawn sometime between the two, at Johns Hopkins University, Baltimore.

218 **Christ Offers to Redeem Man**

Pen and watercolour, $19\frac{1}{2} \times 15\frac{1}{2}$ (49.6 × 39.3).
Signed 'WBlake 1808'.
Museum of Fine Arts, Boston: Gift by subscription, 1890

Paradise Lost 3:222–352. Christ offers to die for Man that he may live, while the multitude of angels cast down their crowns. Blake wrote his own version of the scene on plate 96 of *Jerusalem*, at much the same time as the *Paradise Lost* illustrations: Jesus says to Albion,

> . . . unless I die thou canst not live;
> But if I die I shall arise again & thou with me.
> This is Friendship & Brotherhood: without it Man is not.

In choosing this unusual subject Blake not only showed his particular interest in the theological aspects of Milton's poem but also used it to demonstrate his criticism of Jehovah as the Creator and cause of sin. He contrasted the ecstatic, open-gestured figure of Christ with the closed, slumped form of God the Father; Satan, as yet unaware, floats below.

219 **Satan Watching the Endearments of Adam and Eve**

Pen and watercolour, $20 \times 15\frac{1}{16}$ (50.7 × 38.2).
Signed 'WBlake 1808' (twice).
Museum of Fine Arts, Boston: Gift by subscription, 1890

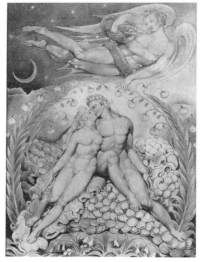

Paradise Lost 4:325–535. Adam and Eve embrace in innocent nakedness while the envious Satan, entwined by the Serpent, eyes them with 'jealous leer malign'. In the first set of *Paradise Lost* watercolours this subject followed a watercolour of 'Satan spying on Adam and Eve, and Raphael's Descent into Paradise' (*Paradise Lost* 4:288–324, and 5:276–85). In the second series Blake tightened up his scheme, devoting three watercolours to the preliminaries (Satan's rebellion and Christ's offer of redemption), three to Adam and Eve before the Fall, three to the ultimate causes of the

220

221

222

Fall and the Fall itself, and three to the consequences of the Fall.

As well as the Thomas version, Blake had already treated this subject in a finished watercolour of 1806 (Fogg Art Museum). There is a preliminary drawing for this in a private English collection and another sketch, apparently done between the Thomas and Butts versions, in the British Museum.

220 · Adam and Eve Asleep
Pen and watercolour, $19\frac{3}{8} \times 15\frac{5}{16}$ (49.2 × 38.8).
Signed 'WBlake 1808'.
Museum of Fine Arts, Boston: Gift by subscription, 1890
Paradise Lost 4:771–809. Satan, in the shape of a toad, seduces Eve's mind in her sleep while the angels Ithuriel and Zephon hover over the sleeping couple. This subject was added by Blake in the Butts series to replace 'Raphael's Descent into Paradise', partly to reinforce Satan's part in the Fall. In Blake's own terms the soft delights of Paradise before the Fall would have represented the world of Beulah, a stage lower than the true Eden, during which the innocent mind was not only open to temptation but needed experience to achieve complete fulfilment. This he had already shown as early as *Tiriel*, in the negative innocence of Har and Heva; see No.41.

221 Raphael Warns Adam and Eve
Pen and watercolour, $19\frac{9}{16} \times 15\frac{5}{8}$ (49.7 × 39.7).
Signed 'WBlake 1808'.
Museum of Fine Arts, Boston: Gift by subscription, 1890
Paradise Lost 5:377–85,443–50,512–28. The Archangel Raphael warns Adam, who has been told not to eat of the Tree of the Knowledge of Good and Evil, of the sin of disobedience; meanwhile Eve ministers to them. This is a slightly earlier moment than that shown in the corresponding watercolour from the Thomas set, in which Adam and Eve sit side by side being admonished by Raphael. The change not only gives Eve a distinct role but also increases the hierarchical symmetry and monumentality of the composition, which is also notable for Blake's exquisite creation of Gothic arches and tracery from natural forms.

There is a sketch for the earlier, Thomas version in the British Museum.

222 The Rout of the Rebel Angels
Pen and watercolour, $19\frac{5}{16} \times 15\frac{1}{16}$ (49.1 × 38.2).
Signed 'WBlake 1808'.
Museum of Fine Arts, Boston: Gift by subscription, 1890
Paradise Lost 6:835–66. Blake, following the order of Milton's poem, now reaches the prime cause of the Fall, the rebellion and the rout by the Messiah of the rebel angels, which is described by Raphael in his discourse to Adam and Eve. Blake turns the scene into a completely hierarchic composition, emblematic rather than dramatic, though the actual contrast in forms as between the upper and lower halves of the design has considerable expressive effect. Cf. the early drawing, No.12, and No.121.

223 The Creation of Eve
Pen and watercolour, $19\frac{11}{16} \times 15\frac{3}{4}$ (49.9 × 40).
Signed 'WBlake 1808'.
Museum of Fine Arts, Boston: Gift by subscription, 1890
Paradise Lost 8:452–77. Adam tells Raphael of the creation of Eve. Blake, unlike his depiction of the subject in the series of Biblical watercolours for Thomas Butts, 'The Angel of the Divine Presence bringing Eve to Adam' (No.159), here shows Christ, not Jehovah, as the creator. Fuseli, in his Milton Gallery, had left the figure vague, though he wrote in a letter to William Roscoe of 14 August 1795, 'for believers, let it be the Son, the

223

Visible Agent of his father; for others it is merely a superior Being entrusted with creation'. For Blake the creation of Eve was all part of Christ's redemption of Man, causing His descent to Earth and, paralleling the creation of Enitharmon in Blake's own mythology, giving concrete form to yet another stage of Man's fall into error. The passivity of Adam's sleeping body, on a great leaf, expresses Blake's condemnation of Adam's vegetative, unimaginative role in the act.

224   The Temptation and Fall of Eve

Pen and watercolour, $19\frac{5}{8} \times 15\frac{1}{4}$ (49.7 × 38.7).
Signed 'WBlake 1808'.
Museum of Fine Arts, Boston: Gift by subscription, 1890

Paradise Lost 9:780–4. Blake shows Adam amazed at the storm that in the text only occurs at the very end of the book. In this version, though not in the earlier watercolour of 1807 done for Thomas, the flashes of lightning appear to touch Adam's hands and one of his feet, an allusion to the Stigmata and to Man's eventual salvation through the Crucifixion. Blake also departs from the text in that, rather than showing Eve plucking the fruit, he shows her being fed it mouth to mouth by the Serpent, thus stressing the sexual implications of the Fall.

225   The Judgment of Adam and Eve

Pen and watercolour over pencil, sight $19\frac{9}{16} \times 15\frac{3}{8}$ (49.6 × 39).
Signed 'WBlake 1808'.
Houghton Library, Harvard University, Cambridge, Massachusetts

Paradise Lost 10:163–210. 'So judged he man, both Judge and Saviour sent.' Blake's design expresses the dual role of Christ, sent by the Father to judge Adam and Eve but also determined to temper justice with mercy: as He judges so also does He deflect the full wrath of the Father above.

Like Nos.216 and 217, this watercolour became separated from the rest of the series and belonged to Munro of Novar; it was later in the collections of Marsden J. Perry and W. A. White.

224

226   The Archangel Michael Foretelling the Crucifixion

Pen and watercolour, $19\frac{3}{4} \times 15$ (50.1 × 38.1).
Museum of Fine Arts, Boston: Gift by subscription, 1890

Paradise Lost 12:411–19, 427–31. The Archangel Michael reveals how Sin and Death, turned loose on Mankind at the Fall, will be overcome by Christ's sacrifice on the Cross. Blake adapts the legend that the Cross was planted on the grave of Adam and Eve by showing it rising from the bodies of Sin and Death, who lie inert with the bodies of the 'dogs of war'. Blake follows early Christian symbolism in showing the Serpent's head pinned with the nail that pierces Christ's feet. Eve lies asleep, at one with the material earth that will be left behind when Man, reunited as a single being, shall be redeemed.

227   The Expulsion of Adam and Eve from the Garden of Eden

Pen and watercolour, $19\frac{11}{16} \times 15\frac{1}{4}$ (50 × 38.8).
Signed 'WBlake 1808'.
Museum of Fine Arts, Boston: Gift by subscription, 1890

Paradise Lost 12:637–44. The Archangel Michael leads Adam and Eve out of the eastern gate of Paradise. Blake shows the 'dreadful faces' above the gate as four horsemen, presumably an allusion to the four horsemen of the Book of Revelation and Man's final Judgment; in the Thomas version of 1807 Adam and Eve look up towards them with expressions of wonder and joy, but here they look down at the serpent, thorns and thistles that represent the world they are about to enter.

225

226

227

228

Three Illustrations to John Milton's 'Paradise Lost': The Unfinished Linnell Set 1822

These three reworkings of compositions from the 1808 Butts set of illustrations to *Paradise Lost* were presumably commissioned by John Linnell as the beginning of a complete set. Linnell noted in his journal under 9 May 1822, 'Mr Blake – began copies from his Drawings from Miltons P. L.'. The dating is supported by William Rossetti who was in touch with Linnell while he and his brother Dante Gabriel Rossetti were seeing Alexander Gilchrist's *Life of William Blake* through the press; he lists the three watercolours under the year 1822.

Though closely based on the compositions of the Butts set, these watercolours are typical of Blake's late style in their freer, more broken treatment and richer colouring.

228 Satan Watching the Endearments of Adam and Eve
Pen and watercolour, 20$\frac{7}{16}$ × 15$\frac{5}{8}$ (51.9 × 39.7).
Signed 'WBlake inv'.
National Gallery of Victoria, Melbourne
A reworking of No.219.

229 The Creation of Eve
Pen and watercolour over pencil, 19$\frac{7}{8}$ × 16 (50.5 × 40.7).
National Gallery of Victoria, Melbourne
A reworking of No.223.

230 The Archangel Michael Foretelling the Crucifixion
Pen and watercolour over pencil, 19$\frac{3}{4}$ × 15$\frac{1}{8}$ (50.2 × 38.5).
Syndics of the Fitzwilliam Museum, Cambridge
A reworking of No.226. Blake has added the rays emanating from the Crucified Christ.

Illustrations to John Milton's 'Comus' c.1815

Instead of Milton's straightforward account of the Lady's rescue from the importunities of Comus by her Brothers aided by the Attendant Spirit, it has been suggested that Blake portrays the spiritual journey of the Lady in a way that parallels that of the protagonist in Blake's own *Book of Thel*, 1789 (see Nos.47–8). The Attendant Spirit would stand for the poet, seeking to enlighten both the Lady and her Brothers, but his final flight reveals his failure (see No.238).

Compared with the two series of *Paradise Lost* watercolours of 1807 and 1808 there is a much greater development in style between the first set of illustrations to *Comus*, painted for the Rev. Joseph Thomas c.1801, and that done for Thomas Butts, sold in 1853 to J. C. Strange and now in the Boston Museum. The date of the Butts set is not documented, but comparison with the illustrations to *L'Allegro* and *Il Penseroso* (Nos.239–50) and *Paradise Regained* (Fitzwilliam Museum, Cambridge), both of which are on paper watermarked 1816, suggests a date of about 1815.

231 Comus with his Revellers
Pen and watercolour, 6$\frac{1}{16}$ × 4$\frac{3}{4}$ (15.4 × 12).
Museum of Fine Arts, Boston: Gift of Mrs John L. Gardner and George N. Black
Comus, 64–82, 170–81, and stage directions: Comus, son of Circe by Bacchus, and his crew of followers translated into brutish form by his magic drink. The Lady enters hearing their noise, having become separated from her brothers in the wood.

232 Comus, Disguised as a Rustic, Addresses the Lady in the Wood
  Pen and watercolour, $6\frac{1}{16} \times 4\frac{3}{4}$ (15.4 × 12).
  Signed 'WBlake'.
  Museum of Fine Arts, Boston: Gift of Mrs John L. Gardner and
  George N. Black
Comus, 83–5, 145–67, 244–70. Comus addresses the Lady, 'that she shall
be my queen'; the Attendant Spirit hovers and observes the scene.

233 The Brothers Observed by Comus Plucking Grapes
  Pen and watercolour, $6\frac{1}{16} \times 4\frac{3}{4}$ (15.4 × 12).
  Signed 'WBlake'.
  Museum of Fine Arts, Boston: Gift of Mrs John L. Gardner and
  George N. Black
Comus, 290–303. Comus tells the Lady that he has seen her brothers
picking grapes at the time the 'laboured ox' goes home from ploughing. The
Lady is seen sitting at the edge of the wood in the distance with the
Attendant Spirit hovering overhead.

234 The Brothers Meet the Attendant Spirit in the Wood
  Pen and watercolour, $6\frac{1}{16} \times 4\frac{11}{16}$ (15.3 × 12).
  Signed 'WBlake'.
  Museum of Fine Arts, Boston: Gift of Mrs John L. Gardner and
  George N. Black
Comus, 489–658. The Spirit, now disguised as a shepherd, tells the
brothers of the danger to the Lady's chastity and gives them a magic root.
However, in Blake's designs the Spirit holds not a root but a flower. This is
one of the deviations from Milton's text that suggests that Blake was adding
his own gloss: the flower probably represents sexual delight (like the 'flower
as May never bore' in 'My Pretty Rose Tree' from *Songs of Experience*),
introduced to suggest that the insistence on virginity is mistaken. Above,
Blake shows a Diana-like figure drawn by dragons. Scaly dragons are in
fact mentioned in some lines from the poem usually omitted but printed in
H. J. Todd's editions of 1798, 1801 and 1809, but the figure is Blake's; if
she is Diana this would be an allusion to her chastity.

234

235

235 The Magic Banquet with the Lady Spell-Bound
Pen and watercolour, $6\frac{1}{16} \times 4\frac{11}{16}$ (15.3 × 12).
Signed 'WBlake'.
Museum of Fine Arts, Boston: Gift of Mrs John L. Gardner and George N. Black

Comus, 659–65, 811–13, and stage directions. The Lady sits in an enchanted chair, fixed to the spot by Comus's wand while he tries to persuade her to drink from his magic glass. Unlike the earlier watercolour painted for Thomas, in which Comus's companions all have bird-like heads, here they include a near-human, various animals and a long-beaked bird with, it must be admitted, somewhat comical effect.

236 The Brothers Driving out Comus
Pen and watercolour, $6\frac{1}{16} \times 4\frac{3}{4}$ (15.4 × 12.1).
Signed 'WBlake'.
Museum of Fine Arts, Boston: Gift of Mrs John L. Gardner and George N. Black

Comus, 814, and stage directions. The Brothers break Comus's spell by smashing his lamp, whereupon Comus's palace vanishes without trace. Comus starts away in alarm while his companions disappear, transformed into horrid, partly bat-winged near-human heads. The Lady sits as she did in the previous scene, still spell-bound.

237 Sabrina Disenchanting the Lady
Pen and watercolour, $6 \times 4\frac{11}{16}$ (15.3 × 11.9).
Signed 'WBlake'.
Museum of Fine Arts, Boston: Gift of Mrs John L. Gardner and George N. Black

Comus, 908–21. Sabrina, naiad of the River Severn, sprinkles water from her river on the Lady, whereupon she awakes from Comus's spell.

238 The Lady Restored to her Parents
Pen and watercolour, $6\frac{1}{16} \times 4\frac{3}{4}$ (15.4 × 12.1).
Signed 'W.Blake'.
Museum of Fine Arts, Boston: Gift of Mrs John L. Gardner and George N. Black

Comus, 946–7, and stage directions. As the sun rises the Attendant Spirit, now back in his true guise, takes his leave. The scene however is not such a positive scene of rejoicing as one would expect, neither in the rather stiff

236

237

238

poses of the mortal figures, nor in their expressions and that of the Spirit (the overall gloom is even stronger in the earlier Thomas watercolour). Blake's conclusion is therefore a negative one: the Lady and her Brothers return to the unenlightened moral code of their aged parents.

Illustrations to John Milton's 'L'Allegro' and 'Il Penseroso' c.1816–20

Although previous illustrations to these poems had sometimes introduced the poet himself, Blake seems to have gone further, using the series to illustrate the whole development of Milton's poetic life from an early state of Innocence, inspired by Mirth, through the Experience of Melancholy to the final maturity that produced *Paradise Lost*.

239

239 Mirth
Pen and watercolour, $6\frac{3}{8} \times 4\frac{13}{16}$ (16.1 × 12.2).
Signed 'Inv WBlake'.
Watermarked 'M & J LAY 1816'.
Pierpont Morgan Library, New York: Gift of the Fellows, purchased
with the special assistance of Mr Paul Mellon and Mrs L. K. Thorne
L'Allegro, 13, 25–8, 31–6. Mirth, 'Mountain Nymph' of 'Sweet Liberty', is summoned with her attendants,

> Jest & youthful jollity
> Quips & Cranks & Wanton Wiles
> Nods & Becks & wreathed smiles
> Sport that wrinkled Care derides
> And Laughter holding both his Sides.

Blake accompanied each watercolour in this series with a separate sheet of paper bearing his title, his transcript of the appropriate verses, and a description of his illustration. In this design, as he states, 'These Personifications are all brought together . . . Surrounding the Principal Figure which is Mirth herself'.

For the engravings after this design see Nos.251 and 252. They are the same size and it is just possible that Blake intended to engrave the whole series as he did later in the case of the 'Job' and 'Dante' series commissioned by John Linnell.

240

240 Night Startled by the Lark
Pen and watercolour, $6\frac{3}{8} \times 4\frac{13}{16}$ (16.1 × 12.3).
Signed 'WBlake inv:'.
Watermarked 'M & J LAY 1816'.
Pierpont Morgan Library, New York: Gift of the Fellows, purchased
with the special assistance of Mr Paul Mellon and Mrs L. K. Thorne
L'Allegro, 41–4. In his accompanying text Blake describes the watercolour as follows: 'The lark is an Angel on the Wing; dull Night starts from his Watch Tower on a Cloud. The Dawn with her dappled Horses arises above the Earth; the Earth beneath awakes at the Lark's voice.' This follows Milton except for the personification of the Earth, which is Blake's own contribution.

In Blake's own poem *Milton*, c.1804–10, 'the Lark is Los's Messenger', so Blake probably saw this illustration in more general terms as showing how the artistic imagination drives away darkness and awakens man from his material life.

241

241 The Sun at his Eastern Gate
Pen and watercolour, $6\frac{5}{16} \times 4\frac{13}{16}$ (16 × 12.2).
Signed 'WBlake inv'.
Pierpont Morgan Library, New York: Gift of the Fellows, purchased
with the special assistance of Mr Paul Mellon and Mrs L. K. Thorne

L'Allegro, 57–68. Blake describes the illustration in his accompanying notes, again largely following Milton's text: 'The Great Sun is represented clothed in Flames Surrounded by the Clouds in their Liveries in their various Offices at the Eastern Gate. Beneath in Small Figures Milton walking by Elms on Hillocks green, The Plowman, The Milkmaid, the Mower whetting his scythe & the Shepherd & his Lass under a Hawthorne in the dale'. Blake adds the angel trumpeters and the little flying spirits in the trees.

This magnificent picture of the Great Sun as Apollo probably also meant for Blake the appearance of Los, the Poetic Genius, heralded by the Lark in the previous illustration, No.240. It is significant that the figure of the Great Sun is close to Flaxman's 'Triumph of Christ', an illustration to Dante's *Paradiso*: thus Milton is shown receiving the first full impact of heavenly inspiration.

242 A Sunshine Holiday

Pen and watercolour, $6\frac{3}{8} \times 4\frac{3}{4}$ (16.2 × 12.1).
Signed 'WBlake inv'.
Pierpont Morgan Library, New York: Gift of the Fellows, purchased with the special assistance of Mr Paul Mellon and Mrs L. K. Thorne

L'Allegro, 73–4, 91–8. As Blake points out in his accompanying description, he introduces from an earlier part of the poem a personified treatment of the Mountains and Clouds to form a background to Milton's straightforward account of peasant merrymaking. Blake's text, partly quoting from Milton, reads, 'In this design is Introduced

Mountains on whose barren breast
The labring Clouds do often rest

Mountains, Clouds, Rivers, Trees appear Humanized on the Sunshine Holiday. The Church Steeple with its merry bells. The Clouds arise from the bosoms of Mountains While Two Angels sound their Trumpets in the Heavens to announce the Sunshine Holiday'. Blake in fact sets the scene of merrymaking in a rich allegory of nature which forms an oppressive accompaniment, perhaps signifying the negative materialism of this state of Innocence.

243 The Goblin

Pen and watercolour, $6\frac{7}{16} \times 4\frac{13}{16}$ (16.4 × 12.2).
Signed 'WBlake inv'.
Pierpont Morgan Library, New York: Gift of the Fellows, purchased with the special assistance of Mr Paul Mellon and Mrs L. K. Thorne

L'Allegro, 100–9, 113–14. Blake's accompanying description follows Milton's account of a number of stories told to accompany 'the Spicy Nut brown Ale': 'The Goblin crop full flings out of doors from his Laborious task dropping his Flail & Cream bowl, yawning and stretching vanishes into the Sky, in which is seen Queen Mab Eating the Junkets. The Sports of the Fairies are seen thro the Cottage where "She" lays in Bed "pinchd & pulld" by Fairies as they dance on the Bed, the Cieling & the Floor, & a Ghost pulls the Bed Clothes at her Feet. "He" is seen following the Friar's Lantern towards the Convent'.

However, Blake transforms Milton's cosy evening story-telling into an image of horror, with the giant spirit-figure of the Goblin dominating the whole scene. Something seems to have gone very wrong with mirthful Innocence. Milton does not in fact mention a convent, and it may be that Blake is here showing Milton submitting to the constraints of institutionalised religion and the consequent superstitious images of horror.

221 *Raphael Warns Adam and Eve*, illustration to *Paradise Lost*, 1808 (entry on p.114)

241 *The Sun at his Eastern Gate*, illustration to *L'Allegro, c.*1816–20 (entry on p.119)

244 The Youthful Poet's Dream
Pen and watercolour, $6\frac{5}{16} \times 4\frac{3}{4}$ (16.1 × 12).
Signed 'WBlake inv'.
Watermarked 'M & J LAY 1816'.
Pierpont Morgan Library, New York: Gift of the Fellows, purchased
with the special assistance of Mr Paul Mellon and Mrs L. K. Thorne
L'Allegro, 125–6, 128–34. Blake's description adds to Milton's more
simple vision of Hymen and his references to Ben Jonson and Shakespeare
by setting the vision in the 'Sun of Imagination'. 'The youthful Poet
sleeping on a bank by the Haunted Stream by Sun Set sees in his dream the
more bright Sun of Imagination. under the auspices of Shakespeare &
Johnson [sic] in which is Hymen at a Marriage & the Antique Pageantry
attending it'. The 'learned' Jonson with his book and Shakespeare with his
papers, warbling 'his native woodnotes wild', support the visionary sun in
which a classical scene of Antique pageantry appears; Blake thus shows
the three main sources of Milton's early inspiration. Three figures, floating
above the water, express alarm, presumably at the youthful poet's
misguidedness, and trees overshadow the visionary sun, representing the
opacity of his vision.

245

245 Melancholy
Pen and watercolour, $6\frac{3}{8} \times 4\frac{13}{16}$ (16.2 × 12.2).
Signed 'WBlake inv'.
Pierpont Morgan Library, New York: Gift of the Fellows, purchased
with the special assistance of Mr Paul Mellon and Mrs L. K. Thorne
Il Penseroso, 31–4, 37–9, 45–54, 56–60: Melancholy, a 'pensive Nun
devout & pure', with Peace, Quiet, Spare Fast, and Leisure, hears the Muses
in a ring round Jove's altar (seen above Spare Fast on the right). Milton also
mentions the cherub Contemplation, who guards the Fiery-wheeled
Throne above, Philomel 'smoothing the rugged Brow of Night' on the left,
and Cynthia checking the dragon yoke on the right. Blake, as he says in his
accompanying note, brings all these personifications together 'surrounding the Principal Figure who is Melancholy herself'.

This illustration is the counterpart of the first in the series, 'Mirth',
No.239.

246

246 The Wandering Moon
Pen and watercolour, $6\frac{5}{16} \times 4\frac{13}{16}$ (16.1 × 12.3).
Signed 'WBlake inv'.
Pierpont Morgan Library, New York: Gift of the Fellows, purchased
with the special assistance of Mr Paul Mellon and Mrs L. K. Thorne
Il Penseroso, 67–76. Described by Blake as follows: 'Milton in his Character
of a Student at Cambridge, Sees the Moon terrified as one led astray in the
midst of her path thro heaven. The distant Steeple seen across a wide water
indicates the sound of the Curfew Bell.' It is Blake who links Milton's
reference to the moon 'Like one that has been led astray' to Milton's own
studies at Cambridge. Blake associated the moon with Beulah, a state in
which the lulled senses may easily be led astray.

247 The Spirit of Plato
Pen and watercolour, $6\frac{3}{8} \times 4\frac{13}{16}$ (16.3 × 12.2).
Signed 'WBlake inv'.
Watermarked 'M & J LAY 1816'.
Pierpont Morgan Library, New York: Gift of the Fellows, purchased
with the special assistance of Mr Paul Mellon and Mrs L. K. Thorne
Il Penseroso, 87–94. Blake's description reads, 'The Spirit of Plato unfolds
his Worlds to Milton in Contemplation. The Three destinies sit on the
Circles of Plato's Heavens weaving the Thread of Mortal Life; these Heavens
are Venus, Jupiter & Mars. Hermes flies before as attending on the Heaven

247

248

of Jupiter, the Great Bear is seen in the Sky beneath Hermes & The Spirits of Fire, Air, Water & Earth Surround Milton's Chair'. Blake took the general idea and the images of Hermes (upper right), the Great Bear, the Spirit of Plato (standing) and the Spirits of Fire, Air, Water and Earth from Milton's text but the rest is his own, in particular the three destinies and the division of Plato's Heavens between Venus, Jupiter and Mars, corresponding to Plato's division of the soul into the senses, reason and energy. In Venus's Heaven (directly behind Plato on the left) one couple is bound back to back by serpents while another is separating in despair. Mars, in the centre, sits enthroned and tyrannical. Jupiter, on the right, plays with the compasses of unenlightened reason. The design is therefore an attack on the Platonic system and hence on Milton at this stage in his development; the static composition, based on rectangular forms, reinforces the mood.

249

248 The Sun in his Wrath

Pen and watercolour, $6\frac{3}{8} \times 4\frac{7}{8}$ (16.2 × 12.3).
Signed 'W Blake inv'.
Watermarked 'M & J LAY 1816'.
Pierpont Morgan Library, New York: Gift of the Fellows, purchased
with the special assistance of Mr Paul Mellon and Mrs L. K. Thorne
Il Penseroso, 131–4. Blake's description adds even more than in previous cases to Milton's simple description of how,

> . . . when the Sun begins to fling
> His flaring Beams, me, Goddess bring
> To arched walks of twilight Groves
> And shadows brown that Sylvan loves
> Of pine or monumental oak;

'Milton led by Melancholy into the Groves away from the Sun's flaring Beams, who is seen in the Heavens throwing his darts & flames of fire. The Spirits of the Trees on each side are seen under the domination of Insects raised by the Sun's heat'. For Blake, the poet has been led away from the Sun of Inspiration into a monster-infested wood. Milton still clutches the book that had so misled him in the previous design, No.247.

249 Milton's Mysterious Dream

Pen and watercolour, $6\frac{3}{8} \times 4\frac{7}{8}$ (16.3 × 12.4).
Signed 'W Blake inv'.
Pierpont Morgan Library, New York: Gift of the Fellows, purchased
with the special assistance of Mr Paul Mellon and Mrs L. K. Thorne
Il Penseroso, 139–40, 145–54. Milton sets the scene by 'some Brook' with, 'as I wake', sweet music,

> Above, about, or underneath
> Sent by some Spirit to mortals good
> Or th'unseen Genius of the wood,

250

and describes the dream as mysterious, the product of 'dewy-feathered Sleep'. Blake's description qualifies it further: 'Milton sleeping on a Bank. Sleep descending, with a Strange Mysterious dream upon his Wings of Scrolls & Nets & Webs unfolded by Spirits in the Air, & in the Brook around Milton are Six Spirits or Fairies hovering on the air with Instruments of Music'. For Blake scrolls and nets and webs are usually the outward signs of restricted vision (see No.57) but here they seem to be loosening; perhaps the dream, by giving form to Milton's restricted vision, is enabling him to go beyond it, inspired by the spirit musicians. Above the poet is a tight group of figures emerging from one of the scrolls, either bearded like Urizen or clasping themselves to keep out enlightenment; these too seem to be being driven away.

250 Milton in his Old Age
Pen and watercolour, $6\frac{1}{4} \times 4\frac{7}{8}$ (15.9 × 12.5).
Signed 'WBlake inv'.
Watermarked 'M & J LAY 1816'.
Pierpont Morgan Library, New York: Gift of the Fellows, purchased
with the special assistance of Mr Paul Mellon and Mrs L. K. Thorne
Il Penseroso, 167–74. Blake's description largely follows Milton's text but
expresses the last lines quoted,

Till old Experience do attain
To somewhat like Prophetic Strain,

in a much more positive way: 'Milton in his Old Age sitting in his Mossy Cell
Contemplating the Constellations, Surrounded by the Spirits of Herbs &
Flowers, bursts forth into a rapturous Prophetic Strain'. The aged, blind
Milton is shown endowed with visionary sight, the source rather than the
recipient of inspiration as from the Great Sun in No.241. The 'Spirits of
Herbs & Flowers' join in his spiritual life, while the stars above are
expressed as living zodiacal figures.

Mirth
Line and stipple engraving, $6\frac{3}{8} \times 4\frac{13}{16}$ (16.1 × 12.2); platemark
$6\frac{7}{8} \times 5\frac{7}{16}$ (17.5 × 13.8).

251 First State c.1816–20
Trustees of the British Museum, London

252 Second State c.1820–25
Inscr. 'Solomon says Vanity of Vanities all is Vanity & what can be
Foolisher than this' below, and 'SPORT', 'that wrinkled CARE
derides', and 'LAUGHTER holding both his sides' by the appropriate
characters.
Private collection, England

Whereas the first state of the engraving is a conventional translation of the
original watercolour, No.239, into the new medium (and was once even
doubted as the work of Blake himself), the second is a fascinating example
of the transformation possible on the metal plate itself. Only the ground and
distant trees remain of the original state; everything else has been
reworked in a way that exaggerates the features of Blake's late style to give
an impression of gay movement appropriate to the subject, though the
inscription added by Blake suggests that he did not altogether approve of
the frivolous vanities he so convincingly expressed. An example of Blake's
sleight-of-hand is the way he has moved Mirth's raised hand without
disturbing the position of the tiny figures round it. The tilt of her head has
also been slightly altered. Otherwise the drastically altered appearance of
the print has been entirely achieved by opening up the textures of the
original state.

Neither state exists in more than the one copy exhibited here, and the
second state may in fact be unfinished. The British Museum print comes
from the Linnell Collection. The early history of the other is not known.

253 *The Vision of Queen Katherine* 1807
Pen and watercolour over pencil, $15\frac{3}{4} \times 12\frac{5}{16}$ (40.1 × 31.3).
Signed 'WB. inv 1807'.
Syndics of the Fitzwilliam Museum, Cambridge

An illustration of the stage direction in Act IV, Scene 2 of Shakespeare's
King Henry VIII, in which six personages dance and, two by two, hold
garlands over Queen Katherine's head. At the end – 'as it were by
inspiration – she makes in her sleep signs of rejoicing, and holdeth up her
hands to heaven.' Her attendants Griffith and Patience sit at her side,
unaware of the vision. In Blake the six personages become airborne,
echoing Katherine's exclamation on awakening, 'Spirits of peace, where
are ye? are ye all gone?'; Blake also increases their number.

251

252

253

Blake had already illustrated this subject in a smaller watercolour, probably of the early 1790s, also in the Fitzwilliam Museum, but there the composition is much stiffer and the attendants are not present. In 1809 he treated the subject again for the Rev. Joseph Thomas's extra-illustrated Shakespeare folio (see No.254); rather surprisingly that version too is stiffer than this one. Late in his life Blake did a new version for Sir Thomas Lawrence (Rosenwald Collection); this closely follows the 1807 composition, save for the more relaxed handling typical of his late style.

Blake's composition is considerably indebted to two of Fuseli's treatments of the subject, that engraved by Bartolozzi in 1788 and that engraved by Blake himself in 1804 for Chalmers' edition of Shakespeare. The circular movement of the spirits reflects such works as Fuseli's 'Shepherd's Dream', painted for his Milton Gallery in 1793 and now in the Tate Gallery.

254

254 *As if an Angel Dropped Down from the Clouds* 1809
Pen and watercolour, irregular, $9\frac{1}{8} \times 6\frac{13}{16}$ (23.1 × 17.3) on paper $12\frac{1}{16} \times 7\frac{1}{2}$ (30.8 × 19.1).
Signed 'WBlake 1809'.
Trustees of the British Museum, London

An illustration to Act IV, Scene 1 of *Henry IV, Part I*, one of six watercolours done by Blake for the Rev. Joseph Thomas to be inserted into a 1632 second folio Shakespeare. Blake seems to have been put in touch with Thomas by John Flaxman, and the commission is first mentioned in the postscript to Flaxman's letter of 31 July 1801 to Hayley that also mentioned the first series of illustrations to Milton's *Comus* (see p.112). However, Blake must have delayed, as all but one of his watercolours are dated 1806 or 1809. Thomas's second folio also contained thirty further watercolours by other artists, including Flaxman, William Hamilton, Robert Ker Porter and Mulready, as well as a view of Stratford by John Varley; they include works dated 1801, 1803, 1808 and 1809. To begin with Thomas asked for the illustrations to be in bistre or Indian ink, and this was followed by many of the artists; Blake however, introduced colour into his illustrations, particularly those of 1809.

Blake illustrated Shakespeare's simile with the inspired literalness of his 'Pity', No.95. Richard Vernon is describing how he saw Prince Henry, in full armour,

> *Rise from the ground like feather'd Mercury,*
> *And vaulted with such ease into his seat,*
> *As if an angel dropp'd down from the clouds,*
> *To turn and wind a fiery Pegasus,*
> *And witch the world with noble horsemanship.*

However, Blake added the nude girl with a book, presumably the imagined reader, reclining on a cloud above Shakespeare's angel and fiery Pegasus.

Another version of this subject, in tempera, was included in Blake's exhibition, 1809–10. Blake's title gives a clue to his typically personal symbolism: 'A Spirit vaulting from a cloud to turn and wind a fiery Pegasus – Shakespeare. The Horse of Intellect is leaping from the cliffs of Memory and Reasoning; it is a barren Rock: it is also called the Barren Waste of Locke and Newton.'

255

255 *Unidentified Book Illustration* c.1820
Pen and sepia wash, $6\frac{3}{8} \times 4\frac{9}{16}$ (16.3 × 11.6).
Bateson Collection

A late drawing in the style of the illustrations to *L'Allegro* and *Il Penseroso*, c.1816 or later (Nos.239–50). The subject is uncertain, though it has been thought to be an illustration to Oliver Goldsmith's *Vicar of Wakefield*. The costumes are contemporary and the drawing appears to show a lover returning just too late to find his beloved married to another; his figure symbolically blocks out the setting sun.

256 *The Fall of Fair Rosamund* c.1815

Pencil, sight $12\frac{1}{16} \times 17\frac{1}{16}$ (30.2 × 43.3).
Private collection, England

Although formerly known as 'The Wise and Foolish Virgins' (see Nos.172–3) this drawing has been identified by George Goyder as an illustration to the story of Fair Rosamund. Blake had engraved the subject, from Thomas Hull's verse play *Henry the Second, or the Fall of Rosamund*, 1773, after a design by Thomas Stothard in 1783, though this drawing is completely different in composition and must date from many years later.

Fair Rosamund (died 1176?), the daughter of Walter de Clifford, was the mistress of Henry II. Legend has it that she was concealed from the jealousy of Queen Eleanor at Woodstock in a secret chamber approached through an intricate maze. The Queen finally tracked her down by following an unravelled thread and forced her to take poison. In the drawing she stands over the kneeling Rosamund, threatening her with a dagger. Rosamund holds a goblet and the fatal thread joins the two characters. The choice of subject, like those of Jane Shore and Queen Emma earlier in Blake's career (see Nos.16, 17 and 19), is typical of his defence of women against the rigours of conventional morality.

On the back is the top half of a large drawing of a nude demon. The other half is on the back of a sketch, untraced since 1956, for the watercolour of 'Non Angli sed Angeli', a subject from English History of *c.*1793 or earlier in the Victoria and Albert Museum; Blake's economical use of paper often resulted in single sheets bearing drawings widely differing in date.

256

'Jerusalem', c.1804–20

Work on *Jerusalem* seems to have occupied Blake during much of the relatively unknown period of his career, between the failure of his exhibition and his meeting with John Linnell in 1818. In fact, these years were not quite as devoid of work as has often been supposed. Besides a number of miscellaneous works, he continued with his illustrations to Milton. His illuminated book of that name, dated like *Jerusalem* 1804 on the title page, had occupied him up to about 1810, with further additions until about 1815. He continued to colour books first printed earlier in his life up to his death.

Jerusalem, the last of his major illuminated books, took considerably longer than the earlier examples. Begun, presumably, in 1804, sixty of the 100 plates were reported by George Cumberland to have been engraved by 1807. The poet Robert Southey was shown some pages by Blake in July 1811 but later wrote, in a letter of 8 May 1830 following a reference to *The Grave*, that Blake's 'still stranger designs for his own compositions in verse were not ready for sale when I saw him'. However, 'Detached specimens of an original illuminated Poem, entitled *Jerusalem* . . .' were exhibited in 1812 with the Associated Painters in Water Colour (typically a break-away body from the Society of Painters in Oil and Water Colours). Some passages in the text refer to events of 1808–9, others to 1811–15, and every complete copy of the book contains pages watermarked 1820. Some of the proof pages were probably coloured earlier, and Linnell bought chapter 2 in 1818, though the rest of his copy could not have been finished until 1820.

In many ways, despite its length, *Jerusalem* (like *Milton*) is less ambitious than the books of the mid-1790s. There are proportionally fewer full-page and half-page illustrations, and many pages of text alone, though all of these are enlivened by small decorative figures and motifs in the margins and between the lines of the text. The colouring of the one known completely coloured copy (Nos.265–74), like that of the coloured copy of chapter 1 (Nos.258–64), is however much richer than that of the books coloured in earlier years, despite Blake having reverted to watercolour instead of the colour printing of the 1790s. The whole page is coloured, not just the designs, and this colouring echoes that of Blake's contemporary watercolours, being much subtler and richer; on some pages, gold is used. The same richer colouring is found in copies of the earlier books that were coloured at this time, the bright, glowing tones being in strong contrast not only to the pale delicacy of about 1790, but even more to the sombre heaviness of the mid-1790s. The engraving of the plates is also more elaborate than in the earlier books; both relief etching and white-line engraving are used (see p.25 and below, pp.127–8) and the combined grace and richness of the figures and other forms are typical of Blake's later style.

257

257 *'Jerusalem': plate 1, frontispiece* c.1804–7/c.1815–20
Line engraving, printed in relief, $8\frac{3}{4} \times 6\frac{3}{8}$ (22.3 × 16.2) on paper $10\frac{1}{4} \times 7\frac{11}{16}$ (26 × 19.5).
Inscr. as below.
Private collection, England

This is a unique proof of the frontispiece taken before Blake deleted the inscriptions.

Above the archway Blake sets the scene for the whole book with one of his paradoxical statements about the nature of the material world, beginning,

> *There is a Void, outside of Existence, which if entered into*
> *Englobes itself & becomes a Womb; such was Albion's Couch*
> *A pleasant Shadow of Repose calld Albion's lovely Land.*

On the right are lines identifying Los with the Traveller, shown pushing through the doorway into the Void:

> *Half Friendship is the bitterest Enmity said Los*
> *As he enterd the Door of Death for Albion's sake Inspired.*
> *The long sufferings of God are not for ever: there is a Judgment.*

On the left, in reversed writing, is,

> *Every Thing has its Vermin, O Spectre of the Sleeping Dead!*

The colouristic effect obtained by printing the plate in two shades of ink is remarkable. Like a number of other proofs from *Jerusalem*, this is on the back of a proof of the title-page from *Europe*. Like Nos.69–71 it was probably printed c.1815–20. This proof comes from the collection of William Bell Scott.

258

Jerusalem c.1804–15/c.1818–20

258 **Frontispiece**

259 **Title-Page**
Inscr. '1804 Printed by W. Blake Sth Molton St.'

260 **Plate 7**

261 **Plate 11**

262 **Plate 20**

263 **Plate 23**

264 **Plate 25**
Relief etchings save for the designs on Nos.258–9 and 261 which
are line engravings printed in relief, all finished in watercolour,
approx $8\frac{5}{8} \times 6\frac{1}{4}$ (22 × 16) on paper $14\frac{3}{4} \times 10\frac{1}{2}$ (37.5 × 26.5).
Private collection, England

From Copy B, which consists of the first chapter only. Some pages are
watermarked 1818 and this copy could have been printed and coloured as
early as this. It was probably bought by P. A. Hanrott by c.1821 and was
acquired by Henry Cunliffe in the mid-nineteenth century. The date '1804'
on the title-page is presumably the date at which Blake started writing the
text; he lived at 17 South Molton Street from 1803 to 1821.

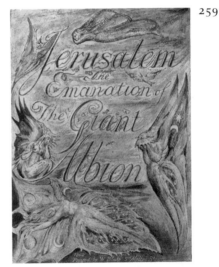

259

The colouring of this copy is elaborate, both designs and text having
been coloured in thin but subtle watercolour washes, but it is relatively
light in tone as compared with the unique complete coloured copy,
Nos.265–74.

Jerusalem is the last of Blake's great prophetic books. As the subtitle 'The
Emanation of the Giant Albion' suggests, the protagonists are Albion or
Mankind and his female emanation Jerusalem, with whom he is reunited
as part of Man's Redemption through Christ. In her fallen state she
becomes Vala, or Nature, and Albion's struggle with her is paralleled by the
struggle of Los, the poetic principle, with his emanation Enitharmon as he
tries to give form to the actual poem *Jerusalem*. The theme is established by
the opening lines,

> *Of the Sleep of Ulro! and of the passage through*
> *Eternal Death! and of the awakening to Eternal Life.*

Ulro is Blake's term for the lowest state of being, total despair, and
throughout the poem there is a strange combination of his own imaginary
mythological world and specific references to English place-names. These
puzzled the poet Robert Southey who told Crabb Robinson on 24 July 1811
that Blake had shown him 'a perfectly mad poem called Jerusalem – Oxford
Street is in Jerusalem'. Blake defended his identification of Jerusalem with
Albion in his address 'To the Jews' on plate 27, where he answers the
question 'Was Britain the Primitive Seat of the Patriarchal Religion?' with
'It is True and cannot be controverted. Ye are united, O ye Inhabitants of
Earth, in One Religion, The Religion of Jesus . . . "All things Begin & End in
Albion's Ancient Druid Rocky Shore".' This identification of the Druids
with the Patriarchs was a common one among the eighteenth-century
British mythologists such as John Toland, William Stukeley and Edward
Davies (see also the note on plate 70 of *Jerusalem*, No.271).

260

The frontispiece shows Blake's Traveller, looking for enlightenment as
he pushes through a Gothic door with his lamp. An early proof of the plate
(No.257) has a long inscription, later removed, identifying the Traveller
with Los. For an earlier example of Blake's recurrent image of the entry into
the grave as a step towards redemption see No.152.

Many of Blake's designs illustrate the poem obliquely, through an
imagery of fairy-like creatures, beginning with the title-page in which bird-
like and insect-like figures enact the lamentation of the daughters of Albion
over Jerusalem. Similar figures are found on plate 11, which like the title-
page is printed as a white-line engraving, a technique reserved on the
whole, though not exclusively, for such designs; the plates were etched like
ordinary line engravings but printed from the remaining surface of the

261

262

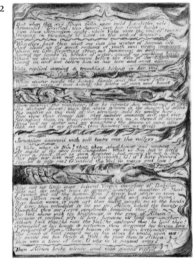

263

264

plate, not from the incised depressions. The significance of the swan-like and fish-like creatures on plate 11 is not clear, but they may be Sabrina (the naiad of the River Severn) and Ignoge, two of the daughters of Albion.

Plate 25 concludes the first chapter with a striking image of horror in which Albion is disembowelled by his three daughters. The accompanying text is an attack on the vengeance of institutionalised religion, and the figure of Albion, though not the actual form of torture, repeats that of the man being stoned in 'The Blasphemer', one of the watercolours of biblical subjects painted for Butts c.1800–05 (No.164), which is an attack on the Mosaic law of an eye for an eye and a tooth for a tooth. The figure appears again in two drawings of sacrificial scenes known as 'The Death Chamber' (No.276 and Fogg Art Museum).

The other three plates are examples of the small-scale designs that decorate many of the pages of *Jerusalem*. On plate 7 the Apollo-like figure in the margin seems to represent Los standing firm despite his spectre's tale of woe, reflecting their two contrasted speeches on this page. On plate 20 the interlinear designs seem to show slaves labouring with fiery harrows and plough, supplementing rather than directly illustrating Vala's description of winter misery; soaring female figures on the right of each design add a positive element to this fiery harvest. On plate 23 Jerusalem is shown caught up in the 'Veil of Vala' bemoaned in the text by the lamenting Albion. Below, workers labour in the 'caverns of Derbyshire & Wales', victims of God's 'Moral Justice' as exemplified by the Veil:

Lo, here is Vala's Veil whole, for a Law, a Terror & a Curse.

The interaction of text and design is in fact much more subtle than can be indicated here; only thorough reading of the verses in conjunction with the designs can give anything like the full meaning.

'Jerusalem' c.1804–15/c.1820–25

265 **Title-Page**
 Inscr. '1804 Printed by W. Blake Sth Molton S^t'.
266 **Plate 28**
267 **Plate 35** (31)
268 **Plate 37** (33)
269 **Plate 46** (41)
270 **Plate 53**
271 **Plate 70**
272 **Plate 76**
 Inscr. 'Albion' and 'Jesus'.
273 **Plate 84**
274 **Plate 99**
 Relief etchings save for the designs on Nos.265–70 and 272 which are line engravings printed in relief, all finished in watercolour and gold, approx. $8\frac{5}{8} \times 6\frac{1}{4}$ (22 × 16) on paper $13\frac{1}{2} \times 10\frac{5}{8}$ (34.5 × 27).
 Mr and Mrs Paul Mellon

From Copy E, the only complete coloured copy of the book. Unlike Copy B (see Nos.258–64) each chapter includes pages watermarked 1820. On 12 April 1827 Blake wrote to Allan Cunningham saying that he had one 'Finished', presumably coloured, copy, 'but it is not likely that I shall get a Customer for it'. According to Cunningham Blake 'wrought incessantly upon what he counted his masterpiece, the "Jerusalem", tinting and adorning it, with the hope that his favourite would find a purchaser. No one, however, was found ready to lay out twenty-five guineas on a work which no one could have any hope of comprehending, and this disappointment sank to the old man's heart'. It passed to Frederick Tatham, whose manuscript life of Blake was formerly bound with it, and was later in the George Blamire and Stirling collections. Blake altered the order of certain of the plates in chapter 2, hence the alternative numbers given in brackets above.

The title-page from this copy is included for a direct comparison between the colouring of Copies E and B. Copy E is richer, more elaborate and often more sombre; gold is used to increase the effect.

Plate 28, the headpiece to chapter 2, is another 'fairy' design printed in relief like the title-page and plate 11. In an early state of the plate in the Pierpont Morgan Library the embrace is more overtly erotic, and it probably alludes to the past joys of the Garden of Eden, 'every labour of love', having now become a Crime, with 'Albion the punisher & judge'. The couple appear again in a detail of one of Blake's illustrations to Dante, No.321.

Plate 35, at first sight a scene paralleling the creation of Eve, seems rather to show Christ, with the stigmata, soaring above Albion, within whose bosom 'the Divine hand found the Two Limits, Satan and Adam', one aware of His presence, the other not. As in some of the *Night Thoughts* and Gray illustrations (see Nos.104–31), the design is conceived as continuing behind the text. This plate too is in white-line engraving, breaking the general rule that Blake reserved this technique for his 'fairy subjects'.

Plate 37, also in white-line engraving, combines both human figures and strange bat-winged ones. The latter represent the prophecy of Los ('One' who 'stood forth from the Divine family') of Albion's burial in the 'Sepulcher . . . and a Death of Eight thousand years', should Albion persist in forbidding with Laws

 Our Emanations, and to attack our secret supreme delights.
Above, Los leans back supported by Christ, presumably as a result of seeing 'blue death in Albion's feet'.

The monster-drawn chariot on plate 46, again in white-line engraving, was perhaps suggested by 'the scythed chariots of Britain' mentioned on

268

269

270

the facing page, but fits in the wider context of the parallels to the Book of Revelation of the whole book. Visually the design recalls both the Whore of Babylon and the various dragons of the Apocalypse (see Nos. 115, 186–90, and the later vision of the Whore of Babylon in the Dante illustrations, No. 335) and the colour print of 'God judging Adam' (No. 87); indeed, the Great Red Dragon reappears on plate 50 as the tailpiece to this chapter. More surprisingly, the human-faced bulls seem to derive from engravings after similar beasts at Persepolis. The nearest parallel in the text, though by no means an exact one, is probably 'the Plow of Jehovah and the Harrow of Shaddai' that will pass 'over the Dead to awake the Dead to Judgment'.

The headpiece to chapter 3, plate 53, is another 'fairy' design in white-line engraving. It shows Vala in her fallen state as Rahab (referred to as 'eternal state' at the head of the interpolated address 'To the Deists' on the previous plate), in other words the Whore of Babylon, the Church at its most oppressive, as is shown by the Papal tiara she wears (for a parallel in Blake's interpretation of Dante's attitude to the Church see Nos. 334–5 and 339). Again there seems to be an eastern prototype, an engraving of a goddess seated on a sunflower from E. Moor's *Hindu Pantheon*.

The giant trilithon on Plate 70, dwarfing the tiny human figures, echoes that on Plate 6 of *Milton* where it represents 'stony Druid Temples'. Here the imagery is more complex in that it seems to represent a stage in the transformation of the twelve sons of Albion, first into the triple-headed Hand, then back to twelve, whence the 'Giant-brood',

> . . . combine into Three Forms named Bacon & Newton & Locke
> In the Oak Groves of Albion which overspread all the Earth,

the Oak Groves being traditionally associated with the Druids. As in *Europe* and *The Song of Los* (see also 'Newton', No. 92) the very narrowness of vision of these rationalistic thinkers contributes, by defining and giving form to error, to Man's ultimate salvation, but Blake's lumping together of the Age of Reason and Druidic oppression is startling, to say the least. Blake more usually followed the eighteenth-century British mythologists in associating the Druids with patriarchs of the Old Testament. As he wrote in his address 'To the Jews' on plate 27 of *Jerusalem*, 'Your Ancestors derived their origin from Abraham, Heber, Shem, and Noah, who were Druids: as the Druid Temples (which are the Patriarchal Pillars & Oak Groves) over the whole Earth witness to this day'.

The design on plate 84 is a revival, in reverse, of one of the illustrations to *Songs of Experience*, the headpiece to 'London'. Here it illustrates the lines,

> I see London blind & age-bent begging thro' the Streets
> Of Babylon, led by a child; his tears run down his beard.

The child leads him towards the Gothic church, the Cross on the top of which is silhouetted against a bright rift in the clouds while, in this copy of the book, the sun rises on the left.

The specifically Christian promise of plate 84 is typical of the conclusion of *Jerusalem* as a whole. Chapter 4 is preceded and concluded by two ecstatic Christian images, plates 76 and 99, though for the very last design of all, plate 100 (not included in the exhibition) Blake returns to his own mythological figures, Los, Enitharmon and 'the spectre of Urthona' (Los in spiritual form), united after the completion of their labours in the creation of the book *Jerusalem* itself (incidentally, Los holds both hammer and compasses, the latter, for all their use by Blake as a symbol of mathematical constriction (see Nos. 66–8 and 92), having played an essential part). The character of this chapter is typified by the address 'To the Christians' which answers the 'To the Deists' at the beginning of chapter 3; Blake supplies an apt comment on his own methods in the motto below the title,

> I give you the end of a golden string,
> Only wind it up into a ball:
> It will lead you in at Heavens gate,
> Built in Jerusalem's wall.

Plate 76, the last in the book in white-line engraving, shows Albion before the Crucified Christ. The two names 'Albion' and 'Jesus' were engraved below the figures but have been obscured in this copy. Albion is in the ecstatic pose of 'Glad Day' (see Nos.9–11), or, rather, of the drawing of the same figure seen from behind on the back of No.9 (fig.1 on p.31). Christ is shown Crucified on the Tree of the Knowledge of Good and Evil, and the sun is shown just beginning to rise on the left.

'The End of the Song' on plate 99 is marked by an even more magnificent design of the reunion of Jerusalem, standing for Man, and a God who unites the elements of Jesus and Jehovah. The text of *Jerusalem* culminates in a wonderful Apocalyptic vision, the concluding lines on this plate being,

> *All Human Forms identified, even Tree Metal Earth & Stone:*
> *All Human Forms identified, living, going forth & wearied*
> *Into the Planetary lives of Years Months Days & Hours reposing*
> *And then Awakening into his Bosom in the Life of Immortality.*
>
> *And I heard the Name of their Emanations; they are named Jerusalem.*

275 'Jerusalem', plate 51: Vala, Hyle and Skofeld

c.1804–5/c.1820
Line engraving printed in relief, finished in watercolour, sight
$6\frac{1}{8} \times 8\frac{3}{4}$ (15.5 × 22.2).
Signed 'W B inv & s[?]' as monogram and inscribed 'Vala', 'Hyle' and 'Skofeld' under the three figures.
Private collection, England

Although Blake did not make a regular practice of issuing separate designs from his illuminated books after the 'Small' and 'Large Book of Designs' of 1794–6 there are two separate copies of *Jerusalem* plate 51 which seem to have been so issued, this one and that from the Linnell collection now in the National Gallery of Victoria, Melbourne (a copy of the design only of plate 6 is in an American private collection; other separate plates from *Jerusalem* seem to be proofs, including the texts and often with proofs from *Europe* on the back, like Nos.69–71). The signature is a variant of Blake's usual monogram, a form that he seems to have abandoned after 1805, which suggests that the plate may have been engraved by then, but the Melbourne print is on paper watermarked 1820 and this copy may well have also been coloured, if not actually printed, about that time, when Blake was printing the complete copies of *Jerusalem*. On this version the letters above the 'W B' are obscure, but the Melbourne version confirms that they read 'inv & s' (for 'invenit et sculpsit', i.e. 'WBlake invented and engraved this').

This plate is one of only three of the full-page illustrations to *Jerusalem* that are oblong in format and therefore at right-angles to the text. One is the last plate of all, plate 100; the others act as dividers between chapters 1 and 2, and, in this case, 2 and 3, preceding the address 'To the Deists'. It shows the crowned Vala (the fallen Jerusalem, see p.127) crouched in despair with two of her acolytes: Hyle, a corruption of William Hayley (see p.78), whom Blake described as a 'corporeal friend but spiritual enemy', and Skofeld (also spelt Scofield, Schofield, Scofeld and Skofield elsewhere in *Jerusalem* and *Milton*), a corruption of John Scolfield, the soldier whose forcible ejection from Blake's garden had led to the poet's trial for sedition in 1804. A recently rediscovered drawing for the design, now in the Hamburg Kunsthalle, includes a further figure on the left (or on the right as one looks at the engraving, which is reversed). Hairy, crawling on all fours and looking out at the viewer, this figure has been identified as Hand, another of the sons of Albion.

274

275

276 *The Death Chamber: possible sketch for 'Jerusalem',*
    plate 25 c.1804–8(?)

Pencil, approx. $9\frac{7}{8} \times 12\frac{3}{8}$ (25 × 31.5).
Private collection, England

Although the main figure is identical to that in the watercolour of 'The
Blasphemer', *c.*1800 (No.164) the figures behind are completely different.
The main figure also appears, slightly altered, in plate 25 of *Jerusalem*
(No.264), though again the subsidiary figures are different; here a figure
prays before an altar while a sacrifice is being held. In style this drawing is
closer to other drawings for *Jerusalem* than to drawings for the Biblical
watercolours of *c.*1800–05, so it is possible that it is related to the book. On
the other hand, the existence of an elaboration of this composition in red
chalk (Fogg Museum) could mean that Blake was working on an
independent subject.

276

John Linnell, John Varley and the Visionary Heads, c.1819–25

In June 1818 one of George Cumberland's sons introduced the young painter John Linnell (1792–1882) to Blake; Linnell wanted help in engraving his portrait of Mr Upton, a Baptist preacher. By September Linnell had introduced Blake to John Varley (1778–1842). Further introductions followed, in 1824 to Samuel Palmer (1805–81), in 1825 to George Richmond (1809–96) and in 1826 to Edward Calvert (1799–1883). The patronage of Thomas Butts seems to have slackened off in Blake's later years and the introduction to Linnell was providential in that Linnell commissioned a succession of works, giving Blake regular payments up to his death in 1827; the second set of Job watercolours and the engravings have already been discussed (see Nos.197, 199–204).

The first important result of the meeting with Linnell was in fact probably the series of Visionary Heads done for John Varley. Varley is best known as a landscape painter in watercolour and as a teacher. He was also deeply interested in astrology, comforting himself for the various disasters that befell him, such as his house burning down twice and being tossed by a bull no fewer than three times, by the fact that this had been foretold in his stars. As Linnell wrote, Varley 'readily devoured all the marvellous in Blake's most extravagant utterances'. He was therefore delighted to meet an artist who could actually see visions, but there seems to have been at least some element of leg-pull in the Visionary Heads. These purported to be visions of historical and other figures that Blake saw late at night, usually at John Varley's. Again Linnell reports that 'it was Varley who excited Blake to see or fancy the portraits of historical personages. . . . Varley beleived [sic] in the reality of Blake's visions

more than even Blake himself–that is in a more literal & positive sense that did not admit of the explanations by which Blake reconciled his assertions with known truth'. Linnell's drawing of Blake and Varley talking seems to demonstrate their relationship exactly (see No.280).

Varley was also interested in the influence of the stars on character and physical appearance, and wrote a projected four-part *Treatise on Zodiacal Physiognomy*, of which only the first part was published in 1828, with engravings by Linnell. Blake's drawings formed a basis of some of the illustrations and are sometimes inscribed with the zodiacal sign of the 'sitter'. They therefore had a practical purpose and there are a number of tracings, counterproofs and copies, apparently by Varley and Linnell rather than by Blake himself, done in preparation for the engraved illustrations. Varley even had Linnell do him painted copies of two of the heads. These were done in October 1819, which is also the month of the earliest dated drawings of Visionary Heads by Blake himself (see No.285; a drawing of Richard Coeur de Lion is dated fifteen days earlier, on 14 October). Most of the drawings seem to have been done in 1819 or 1820, though one example is dated 1825.

Because of their anecdotal value (see particularly Nos.282 and 283) these drawings, hardly typical of the real nature of Blake's visionary art, became the most written about of his works over the next twenty-five years or so, often in highly exaggerated terms. Blake was often therefore dismissed as mad or all but so, until the revival of interest in his poetry and designs in the middle of the nineteenth century brought a more balanced assessment.

---

277 *Portrait Drawing of John Linnell* 1825

Pencil, approx. $6\frac{1}{2} \times 4\frac{3}{4}$ (16.5 × 12) on paper $14\frac{1}{16} \times 9\frac{3}{8}$ (35.7 × 23.8).
Inscr. by John Linnell, 'at Hampstead Drawn by Mr Blake from the life 1825. Intended as the Portrait of J. Linnell'.
Watermarked 'JWHATMAN 1825' (?).
National Gallery of Art, Washington (Rosenwald Collection)

277

John Linnell (1792–1882), the most important patron of Blake's later years and an important artist in his own right. At first he painted both landscapes and small portraits, but after 1850 he was sufficiently financially secure to abandon portraiture. Unfortunately the fresh naturalism of his early landscapes gave way to woolly stereotypes.

278 *Portrait Drawing of John Varley* c.1820–5

Pencil on paper, $11\frac{1}{2} \times 7\frac{13}{16}$ (29.2 × 19.8).
Inscr. by John Varley, 'Portrait of J. Varley by W^{m}Blake.' and 'J. Varley born augst. 17.1778 18.$\overset{pm}{56}$ + [Sagittarius] ascending'.
National Portrait Gallery, London

John Varley (1778–1842), the instigator of Blake's Visionary Heads, was a landscape painter, mainly in watercolour, and teacher. He had taught

278

279

Fig. 19 William Blake, *The Spirit of God
Moved upon the Face of the Waters*, c. 1820
(Abbot Hall Art Gallery, Kendal)

John Linnell 1805–6 and it was presumably through him that he met Blake in the late summer of 1818. He was fascinated by astrology, as is reflected in the inscription on the drawing. His brother Cornelius Varley (1781–1873) was also an important watercolourist and in addition a scientist, inventing the Graphic Telescope, a form of *camera obscura* with which one could copy the outlines of things seen through a lens; this may indeed have been used in making some of the replicas that exist of the Visionary Heads.

279 *Caricature of John Varley as an Elephant* c.1820–5

Pencil, approx. $4\frac{1}{2} \times 3\frac{1}{4}$ (11.5 × 8) on paper $7 \times 4\frac{3}{4}$ (18 × 12).
Inscr. probably by John Varley, 'William Blake'.
Abbot Hall Art Gallery, Kendal

The identification of the subject is due to Kenny Meadows, who gave the drawing to William Bell Scott c.1838. It alludes to Varley's well-documented size.

On the other side of this drawing is a wash drawing of the sea with a rainbow, probably the first day of Creation: 'And the Spirit of God moved upon the face of the waters' (Genesis 1 : 2; see fig.19).

JOHN LINNELL (1792–1882)
280 *Blake in Conversation with John Varley* 1821

Pencil, $4\frac{7}{16} \times 6\frac{15}{16}$ (11.3 × 17.6).
Signed 'J. L. Sept 1821' and inscr. 'Cirencester Place' and, under the figures, 'Mr Blake' and 'Mr Varley'.
Watermarked 'LMOTT [18]20'.
Syndics of the Fitzwilliam Museum, Cambridge

The drawing epitomises Varley's enthusiasm and Blake's passive scepticism, exemplified by the whole question of the Visionary Heads. As John Linnell wrote in his manuscript autobiography, 'I have a sketch of the two men as they were seen one night in my parlour near midnight, Blake sitting in the most attentive attitude listening to Varley who is holding forth vehemently with his hand raised. The two attitudes are highly characteristic of the men for Blake by the side of Varley appeard decidedly the most sane of the two.' Linnell lived in Cirencester Place, in what is now Westbourne Green, London, before moving to Hampstead in 1824.

JOHN LINNELL
281 *Portrait of William Blake* 1820

Pencil, $7\frac{15}{16} \times 6\frac{1}{8}$ (20.1 × 15.5).
Signed 'J.L. fect' and inscr. 'Portrait of Wm Blake. 1820'.
Syndics of the Fitzwilliam Museum, Cambridge

A drawing of Blake looking down, apparently concentrating on some activity. The strong effects of lighting suggest that it was drawn in the evening by lamp-light. The Fitzwilliam Museum owns a number of other drawings of Blake by Linnell and also by John Flaxman and George Richmond.

282 *The Head of the Ghost of a Flea* c.1819

Pencil on paper, $6 \times 7\frac{7}{16}$ (15.3 × 17.9).
Inscr. by John Varley, 'Original [this is now practically invisible] W. Blake'.
Tate Gallery, London

Page 98 from the Blake-Varley Sketchbook, first used by John Varley for landscape drawings but then taken up by Blake for recording the visionary appearances he saw when visiting Varley in the evening; one of the drawings is dated 29 October 1819 (see No.285). This page was removed from the sketchbook early on and belonged to John Linnell.

280

In his *Treatise on Zodiacal Physiognomy* Varley described Blake doing this actual drawing. 'I felt convinced by his mode of proceeding, that he had a real image before him, for he left off, and began on another part of the paper, to make a separate drawing of the mouth of the Flea, which the spirit having opened, he was prevented from proceeding with the first sketch, till he had closed it.' Sure enough, there is a separate drawing of the mouth of the flea open. 'During the time occupied in completing the drawing, the Flea told him that all fleas were inhabited by the souls of such men, as were by nature blood-thirsty to excess'.

John Linnell engraved two separate complete heads of the flea, with mouth closed and open, for Varley's *Treatise*, and is also said to have made a copy in colour. Blake's drawing may have been unconsciously influenced by a plate in Robert Hooke's *Micrographia, or some Physiological Descriptions of Minute Bodies made by Magnifying Glasses*, 1665.

283 *The Ghost of a Flea* c.1819–20

> Tempera heightened with gold on panel, $8\frac{7}{16} \times 6\frac{3}{8}$ (21.4 × 16.2).
> Signed 'WBlake Fresco'.
> *Tate Gallery, London*

281

Presumably developed from the drawing formerly in the Blake-Varley Sketchbook and recently with Martin Breslauer, though John Varley, who owned this painting, described it to Allan Cunningham in terms which suggested that it was the result of yet another visitation:

> I'll tell you all about it, sir [reports Cunningham], . . . I called upon him one evening and found Blake more than usually excited. He told me he had seen a wonderful thing – the ghost of a flea!
> 'And did you make a drawing of him?' I inquired.
> 'No indeed' said he, 'I wish I had, but I shall, if he appears again!'
> He looked earnestly into a corner of the room, and then said,
> 'here he is – reach me my things – I shall keep an eye on him. There he comes! his eager tongue whisking out of his mouth, a cup in his hand to hold blood, and covered with a scaly skin of gold and green;' as he described him so he drew him.

The story, whether it applied to the drawing or to the painting, obviously lost nothing in the telling. According to J. T. Smith, 'Blake said of the flea, that were that lively little fellow the size of an elephant, he was quite sure, from the calculations he had made of his wonderful strength, that he could bound from Dover to Calais in one leap'.

284 *The Man who Taught Blake Painting in His Dreams*

> c.1819
>
> Pencil on paper, $11\frac{7}{8} \times 9\frac{5}{8}$ (30 × 24.5).
> *Private collection, England*

282

The subject of this drawing, which was identified by William Rossetti as Lais (the Greek courtesan), has been made clear by two versions in the Tate Gallery. The first of these, which seems to be a counterproof of this drawing, is inscribed by John Linnell, 'Imagination of A Man who Mr. Blake has rec'd instruct[ion] in Painting &c from'. The second, which is an elaborated and tidied up version, probably by Linnell, is inscribed by him with two titles, one much the same as that just quoted, the other reading 'The Portrait of a Man who instructed M.r Blake in Painting &c. in his Dreams'. The drawing is thus a portrait of Blake's inspiration, in fact as it were a self-portrait of his own imaginative, visionary self.

This drawing, unlike the two versions in the Tate which belonged to John Linnell, remained with John Varley. The replicas (figs.20 and 21), with their try-outs for titles, were probably made with the intention of producing an engraving of the subject, probably for one of the unpublished parts of Varley's *Treatise on Zodiacal Physiognomy*.

285

283

285 *The Empress Maud in Bed* 1819

Pencil on paper, approx. 8 × 6⅛ (20.5 × 15.5).
Private collection, England

Page 25 from the Blake-Varley Sketchbook. This page remained part of the book until it was dismembered in 1968 and subsequently sold and dispersed in 1971. Previously the sketchbook had passed from Varley to his brother-in-law the painter William Mulready, after whose sale it was acquired by H. Buxton Forman, who gave it to William Bell Scott. Scott left it at Penkill Castle, the home of his friend Miss Alice Boyd, where it was rediscovered by David Clayton Stamm in 1967. On the facing page 24, now in the Tate Gallery, there is a plan of the bedroom, octagonal in shape, and a detailed drawing of the Gothic vault with a hanging lamp. On this facing page Varley has written, presumably following Blake's account as he drew 'The Empress Maud in Bed', 'The Empress Maud said rose water was in the vessel under the table octr.29 friday. 11 PM. 1819. & said there were closets which contained all the conveniences for the bedchamber.'

The Empress in question is presumably Maud, more usually known as Matilda (1102–67), the daughter of Henry I of England, who married the Emperor Henry V in 1114. After the Emperor's death in 1126 she returned to England and disputed her father's succession with her cousin Stephen. Her son eventually became King as Henry II.

This drawing is typical of a rather surprising side to Blake's work that only became apparent with the rediscovery of the Blake-Varley Sketchbook, a playfulness that not only involves teasing John Varley but also a light-hearted approach to the Gothic in a way that recalls less Westminster Abbey than Strawberry Hill.

284

Fig.20 John Linnell (?), after William Blake
*The Man who Taught Blake Painting
in his Dreams, c.*1820
(Tate Gallery)

Fig.21 John Linnell (?), after William Blake
*The Man who Taught Blake Painting
in his Dreams, c.*1820
(Tate Gallery)

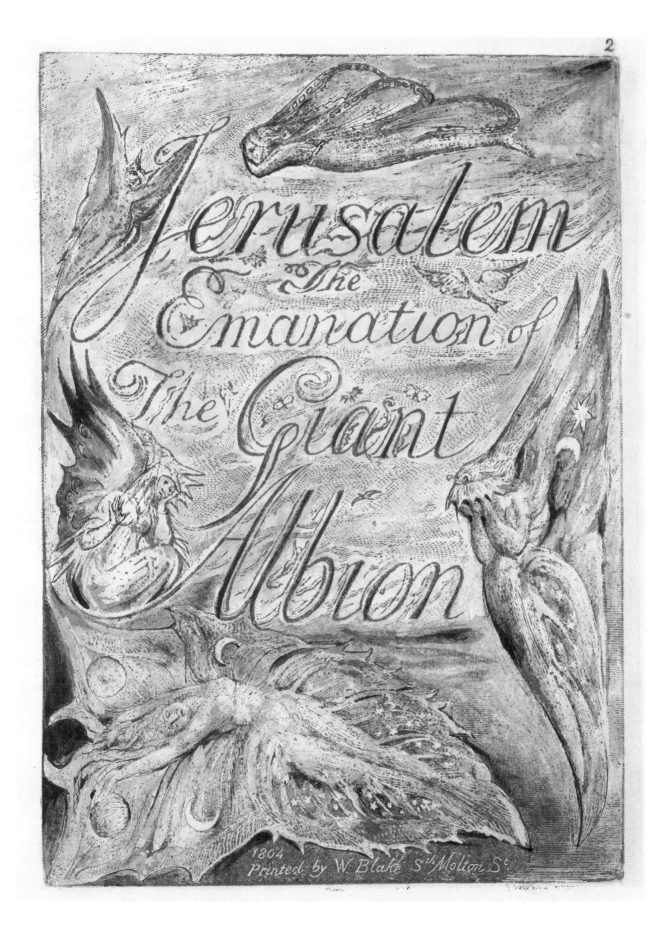

259 *Jerusalem: title-page, c.1804–5/c.1818–20* (entry on p.127)

307 *The Arlington Court Picture*, 1821 (entry on p.142)

286 *A Vision: The Inspiration of the Poet* c.1820(?)

Sepia wash over pencil, approx. $6\frac{3}{4} \times 7$ (17×18) on paper $9\frac{9}{16} \times 8\frac{1}{4}$ (24.3×21).

Inscr. by Frederick Tatham, 'William Blake–I suppose it to be a Vision Indeed I remember a conversation with Mrs. Blake about it. Frederick Tatham'.

David C. Preston

An angel stands by a seated, writing figure. The scene is lit by a lamp hanging from the ceiling of a small, pedimented, shrine-like chamber, itself set into a vast, bare rectangular room. The title was suggested by W. Graham Robertson who formerly owned the drawing and who wrote on a label on the back, 'A Vision. Probably representing the Poet, in the innermost shrine of the Imagination, writing from angelic dictation.'

Although different in character from the usual Visionary Heads, this drawing probably dates from about the same time. The paper appears to be watermarked 'RUSE & TURNER', and in the only other cases when Blake used this paper the watermark also included the date '1815'.

Illustrations to Thornton's Virgil, 1820-21

Just as Blake's illustrations to *The Grave*, seen through the distorting glass of another engraver, were the best known of Blake's works in his lifetime and the Visionary Heads were the most talked about in the years immediately following his death, so Blake's tiny woodcut illustrations to Virgil, again untypical of his art as a whole, were the most influential on other artists. They were the result of another of John Linnell's introductions, in this case to his doctor, Robert John Thornton, in September 1818. Thornton was also a writer, mainly on medicine and botany, though he also published a *New Translation of the Lord's Prayer* in 1827 which Blake vehemently condemned: 'I look upon this as a Most Malignant & Artful attack upon the Kingdom of Jesus By the Classical Learned, thro the Instrumentality of Dr Thornton.' However, illustrations to Virgil were obviously a much more congenial task than many that Blake had had to endure (at one point, in 1815, Blake was reduced to illustrating Wedgwood-ware for the firm's pattern books). Thornton had edited a school edition of *The Pastorals of Virgil*, first published in 1812, and by September 1820 Blake was working on some of the illustrations to the enlarged third edition which was published the following year. As well as a number of engravings after antique busts and coins he produced twenty-one designs illustrating Ambrose Philips' 'Imitation of Eclogue I'. These were to be printed from woodcuts, a rare medium for Blake, three or four to a page with the exception of the larger frontispiece. However, Thornton was dissatisfied with Blake's woodcuts and four of the designs were recut by a hack engraver before a chance conversation

with Lawrence, James Ward, Linnell and other artists caused him to stay his hand, but three of the four reworked designs were published. Moreover, Thornton published a disclaimer with the somewhat double-edged remark that Blake's woodcuts 'display less of art than genius, and are much admired by some eminent painters'. As a final indignity, Blake's blocks were slightly too large and had to be cut down. One of Blake's drawings was not used.

The impact of these exquisite designs is best expressed in the words of Samuel Palmer: 'I sat down with Mr. Blake's Thornton's *Virgil* woodcuts before me, thinking to give their merits my feeble testimony. I happened first to think of their sentiment. They are visions of little dells, and nooks, and corners of Paradise; models of the exquisitest pitch of intense poetry. I thought of their light and shade, and looking upon them I found no word to describe it. Intense depth, solemnity, and vivid brilliancy only coldly and partially describe them. There is in all such a mystic and dreamy glimmer as penetrates and kindles the innermost soul, and gives complete and unreserved delight, unlike the gaudy daylight of this world. They are like all that wonderful artist's works the drawing aside of the fleshy curtain, and the glimpse which all the most holy, studious saints and sages have enjoyed, that rest which remaineth to the people of God'. The designs had an overwhelming impact on Palmer's visionary works of the Shoreham period and also on the early engravings of Edward Calvert.

287

Illustrations to Thornton's 'Pastorals of Virgil' 1821

Seventeen wood engravings, approx. $1\frac{3}{8} \times 3$ (3.5 × 7.5) except No.287 which is $2\frac{7}{16} \times 3\frac{5}{16}$ (6.2 × 8.4).
Tate Gallery, London

288

These are recent pulls from Blake's original woodblocks, formerly in the Linnell collection and now in the British Museum. For four of the designs printed off one of the original uncut blocks see No.304.

As Thornton says in his introduction to Philips' 'Imitation of Virgil's First Eclogue', 'THENOT is the *happy*, and COLINET the unhappy *shepherd*'. Thenot also speaks with the experience of age, and chides Colinet for being so mournful 'when all things smile around', to which Colinet replies that it is his lot, unlike the lark and linnet, to mourn (Nos.287 and 288). Blake illustrates literally Thenot's comparison of his body bowing down 'as trees beneath their fruit in autumn bend' (No.289). When Colinet says that it will take all day to tell his woes and that Thenot's flocks will be neglected, Thenot replies that Lightfoot can guard them while 'I 'tween whiles, across the plain will glance mine eyes' (No.290).

289

Colinet begins his recital of griefs by comparing his plight with 'yonder naked tree, which bears the thunder-scar too plain, I see' (No.291). Thenot agrees that he was born in a 'hapless hour of time . . . when blightning mildews spoil the rising corn, or blasting winds o'er blossom'd hedge-rows pass, to kill the promis'd fruits . . .' (No.292); not even a good shepherd can preserve his flock against fox or wolf (No.293).

Colinet then regrets that he 'left, Sabrina fair, thy silvery flood', a reference to the naiad of the River Severn (No.294), and that he followed a 'fond desire strange lands and swains to know' (No.295, where he is shown passing a milestone marked 'LXII miles to London'). Thenot points the moral, 'A rolling stone is ever bare of moss', a chance for Blake to show some unfortunate wight rolling an unnatural path in front of an imposing classically-designed house (No.296). Colinet's tracks had taken him to Cambridge, where Blake shows King's College Chapel rising above the trees on the left (No.297).

290

Worse still, no 'pinching cold' was as bad as the 'blasting storms of calumny', or 'Untoward lads' making 'mock of all the ditties I endite' (No.298). However, Menalcas, 'Lord of these fair fertile plains . . . seems to like my simple strain', and Blake shows one of the 'yearly wakes and feasts' held for him by the shepherds (No.299).

291

As consolation Thenot concludes by inviting Colinet to 'fold thy flock with mine' (No.300) and share 'New milk, and clouted cream, mild cheese and curd, with some remaining fruit of last year's hoard' (No.301), and bids him 'now behold the sun's departing ray, o'er yonder hill, the sign of ebbing day; with songs the jovial hinds return from plow [No.302]; and unyok'd heifers, loitering homeward, low' (No.303).

It is interesting to note that although Blake's preliminary drawings such as Nos.305–6 define the forms in black lines and wash, when faced with the new medium of printing from wood Blake attacked the block as if it were a metal plate: form is defined by the fine, engraved lines, the surface of the block then being inked as in white-line engraving, the result being that the forms are defined by white lines rather than black.

292

304 *Illustrations to Thornton's Virgil: Four Uncut Designs*

1821

Thenot remonstrates with Colinet
Thenot under a Fruit Tree
Thenot remonstrates with Colinet, Lightfoot in the distance
Colinet departs in Sorrow, a Thunder-Scarred Tree on the Right.

Wood engraving, four designs in one, $6 \times 3\frac{3}{8}$ (15.2 × 8.6).
Trustees of the British Museum, London

An impression of the second, third, fourth and fifth designs before the original single woodblock was cut up and trimmed; c.f. Nos.288–91. Similar proofs exist of nos.6–9. Accompanying the proof of nos.6–9 in the Fitzwilliam Museum is a note by A. H. Palmer stating that the proof 'is one of two which were taken by Blake himself at Fountain Court at his own

293

294

299

295

300

296

301

297

302

298

303

press in my father's presence'. The British Museum proofs came from the Linnell collection but were presumably done at much the same time in Blake's first-floor rooms at 3 Fountain Court, off the Strand, where he lived from 1821 until his death. No. 304 is framed together with an impression from the uncut block bearing designs nos. 6–9.

The trimming of the blocks cramped Blake's compositions, but note on the other hand the greater definition obtained in the recent pulls, Nos. 287–303, taken on an old-fashioned hand-press but with infinite pains.

305 *Sketch for Thornton's Virgil, plate 2:'Thenot remonstrates with Colinet'* 1820–21

Pencil, pen and grey wash, irregular, $1\frac{9}{16} \times 3\frac{9}{16}$ (4 × 9).
Private collection, England

The drawing for No. 288. Formerly mounted in a book with nineteen other drawings for the Virgil woodcuts; the set was sold from the Linnell collection in 1918 and broken up and dispersed in America in 1924. There is no record of a sketch for the frontispiece, No. 287. However, there is an extra drawing, not engraved; the design, which came fourth in the album but is now untraced, shows Colinet and Thenot standing together conversing, with their sheep behind.

306 *Sketch for Thornton's Virgil, plate 6:'Blasted Tree and Blighted Crops'* 1820–21

Pencil, pen and grey wash, irregular, $1\frac{5}{8} \times 3\frac{3}{4}$ (4.1 × 9.6).
Private collection, England

The drawing for No. 292. See No. 305.

304

305

306

Late Tempera Paintings and other works, 1821–27

A number of Blake's later works have been included in earlier sections of this catalogue, and the general development of his later years has already been noted (see p. 112). One important late development however was a radical change in the technique of Blake's so-called tempera paintings. Whereas 'The Ghost of a Flea' of *c.*1819–20 (No.283) shows the same heavy texture as the works shown in Blake's 1809 exhibition, other late temperas have a much thinner paint film akin to watercolour, over a gesso ground laid on paper or panel; these have survived in much better condition. A possible exception is the so-called 'Black Madonna' in the Yale Center of British Art (Paul Mellon Collection), apparently dated 1825 though the signature and date may have been damaged and incorrectly repainted; this shows the characteristics of the earlier works and serves to set off the luminosity that Blake could now achieve. In other works Blake seems to have used watercolour or some form of tempera directly onto the panel or muslin support (Nos.308–10).

307

308
&
309

307 *The Arlington Court Picture* 1821

Pen, watercolour and gouache over a gesso ground on paper, $15\frac{3}{4} \times 19\frac{1}{2}$ (40 × 49.5).
Signed 'WBlake inventor 1821'.
National Trust, Arlington Court, Devon

This picture was discovered on top of a cupboard when Arlington Court was handed over to the National Trust. It had been framed by John Linnell's father James, was backed with a page from *The Times* of 11 January 1820, and had presumably been acquired by the then head of the Chichester family, Colonel John Palmer Chichester, of whom there are no recorded contacts with Blake or his circle.

Equally mysterious is the subject of the picture, usually called 'The Sea of Time and Place' (a quotation from *Vala or the Four Zoas*), 'The Circle of Life' or, more simply, as above. The most specific identification of the subject so far, though this is not universally accepted, is that it shows the incident of the 'Cave of the Nymphs' from the *Odyssey*, perhaps by way of the Neo-Platonist interpretation of Porphyry as published in a translation by Thomas Taylor in 1788. The kneeling figure in red would be Odysseus, the pointing figure next to him Athena, and the woman in the water the 'white goddess' Leucothea, who helped Odysseus to land on the island of Phaeacia after the break-up of his raft. Athena would seem to be showing Odysseus various aspects of Greek religious myth, which Blake had come totally to reject by this time.

Whatever the subject, this picture is one of the most exquisitely finished of Blake's works. In the filling of the surface with various incidents and figures it continues the tendency of such a work as 'The Judgment of Paris' of ten years earlier (No.215), showing Blake's anti-naturalism at its extreme and stressing the apparently dogmatic nature of the subject; one finds parallels, though hardly sources, in the mannerism of mid fourteenth and mid sixteenth-century didactic painting in Italy.

The medium of this picture, here analysed as basically watercolour and gouache or body colour over a gesso ground, seems common to several of Blake's late so-called 'temperas', which term has been retained elsewhere in this catalogue. There is a pencil sketch in the Pierpont Morgan Library.

308 *Winter* c.1821
309 *Evening* c.1821

Tempera on panel, $35\frac{1}{2} \times 11\frac{11}{16}$ (90.2 × 29.7) and $36\frac{7}{16} \times 11\frac{11}{16}$ (91.8 × 29.7) respectively.
Vaughan Johnson Trust

These two panels were painted for the Rev. John Johnson for the sides of a fireplace in his rectory at Yaxham, Norfolk; across the top was a frieze of 'Olney Bridge', now destroyed. They illustrate two passages from *The Task* by Johnson's cousin William Cowper (Book IV, lines 120–9 and 243–60 respectively).

Despite the associations of both Johnson and Cowper with William Hayley and Blake's years at Felpham, 1800–03 (see p.78; Blake painted a miniature portrait of Johnson in 1802) these pictures are stylistically and technically typical of Blake's late years and were probably painted following the rebuilding of Yaxham Rectory in 1820–1. In these pictures the 'tempera', probably a form of body-colour, seems to have been painted directly on to the wood. Either the fireplace was never set up or it was soon demolished, for there is a shopping list with the names of various wines on the back of No.309, dated 'March 6 1834'.

310

310 *The Characters in Spenser's 'Faerie Queene'* c.1825
Pen and watercolour on muslin, varnished and mounted on panel,
18 × 53½ (45.7 × 135.8).
Signed 'W B' (?).

H. M. Treasury and the National Trust, Petworth House, Sussex

This picture was still in Blake's possession at his death and was sold by Mrs Blake to Lord Egremont in 1827 for eighty guineas. It was probably intended as a pendant to 'The Canterbury Pilgrims' (see No.210), which had been sold to Thomas Butts. Despite the different medium and support it is more or less the same size and the procession of figures balances that in the other picture, moving in the opposite direction. In style and technique however this picture is typical of Blake's late work, and it is possible that it was a projected engraving, rather than the actual picture, that Blake intended as a pendant to the other composition, which he had engraved in 1810.

Typically Blake adds his own gloss to Spenser's text, introducing scenes in the sky to show that the figures are moving from Babylon on the right towards the New Jerusalem on the left. A typically Urizenic God of This World floats over the procession in the middle. The procession itself consists of Spenser's figures in the order of their appearance in *The Faerie Queene*, headed by Una and the Redcrosse Knight from Book 1, 'Holinesse'. Then follow the Palmer and Sir Guyon from Book 2, 'Temperance'. In the centre of the picture Britomart represents Books 3 and 4, 'Chastity' and 'Friendship'. Book 5, 'Justice', is represented by Sir Artegall and Talus the Iron Man (the subject of a large painting by John Hamilton Mortimer of 1778, now in the Tate Gallery), together with Prince Arthur. Finally comes Sir Calydore from Book 6, 'Courtesy'. Behind the procession can be seen various settings associated with episodes in the poem, such as the Cave of Despair on the extreme left.

311 *Count Ugolino and his Sons in Prison* c.1826
Pen, tempera and gold on panel, sight 12⅞ × 16¹⁵⁄₁₆ (32.7 × 43).
Signed 'W.BLAKE fec!'.
Private collection, England

311

Similar in size, technique and the form of signature, incised in the paint rather than written on top of it, to Nos. 312 and 313. The three works are presumably those referred to in Blake's letter to John Linnell of 25 April 1827: 'As to Ugolino, &c, I never supposed I should sell them; my wife alone is answerable for their having Existed in any finish'd state. I am too much attach'd to Dante to think much of anything else'. This is indeed based on one of the illustrations to Dante's *Divine Comedy* of 1824–7, a drawing left in pencil, untouched by watercolour, now in the British Museum.

The subject comes from the *Inferno* 33:43–75. Ugolino was imprisoned and starved to death by his political rival in Pisa, Archbishop Ruggieri, together with his two sons Gaddo and Ugoccione, and his two grandsons Anselmuccio and Nino il Brigata. Blake had used the subject many years earlier for plate 12 of the *Gates of Paradise*, first issued in 1793 and again in a revised form some twenty-five years later, where it illustrates the typically Blakean text, 'Does thy God O Priest take such vengeance as this?'.

The early history of this panel is not known but by 1876 it belonged to J. W. White and later to William Bell Scott.

312

312 *The Body of Abel Found by Adam and Eve* c.1826

Pen and tempera, in places over gold, on mahogany, 12¹³⁄₁₆ × 17¹⁄₁₆ (32.5 × 43.3).
Signed 'fresco W.BLAKE' (damaged, a further word, such as 'fecit' [see No.313], is missing below).
Tate Gallery, London

Like Nos.311 and 313 this is Blake's final version of a composition on which he had worked at intervals over many years, in this case a watercolour shown in his exhibition of 1809–10 as 'The body of Abel found by Adam and Eve; Cain, who was about to bury it, fleeing from the face of his Parents', and subsequently in John Linnell's collection (now in the Fogg Museum, Harvard University). This panel seems to have belonged to Thomas Butts; if so it would refute the general notion that Butts stopped collecting Blake's works in his last years.

Meanwhile Blake had again treated the subject, which is not in the Bible, in the two-page dramatic piece he produced in 1822 as probably his last work in illuminated printing, *The Ghost of Abel*. This work, addressed to 'Lord Byron in the Wilderness', opens, very much like the painting, in 'A rocky Country. Eve fainted over the dead body of Abel which lays near a Grave. Adam kneels by her'. In addition, however, 'Jehovah stands above' and overrules the plea for vengeance of the Ghost of Abel, who is seconded by Satan. Blake has moved on from his earlier negative assessment of Jehovah, who now, like Christ, upholds the 'Covenant of the Forgiveness of Sins'.

313

313 *Satan Smiting Job with Sore Boils* c.1826

Pen and tempera on mahogany, 12⅞ × 17 (32.6 × 43.2).
Signed 'W.BLAKE fecit'.
Tate Gallery, London

Like Nos.311 and 312 this is Blake's last word on a much treated subject, in this case from his various series of illustrations to the Book of Job (see No.193). Unlike the earlier versions, Satan is shown winged, and the clouds framing the setting sun are more schematic. In the engraving, plate 6, the marginal decorations and texts add further subtleties of meaning, but here the effect is more monumental and dramatic.

This picture belonged to George Richmond and subsequently to Frederick Locker and Sir Charles Wentworth Dilke, Bart. Like No.312, it has been specially cleaned for this exhibition.

314 *Epitome of James Hervey's 'Meditations among the Tombs', c.*1820–5 (entry on p.145)

333 *Beatrice on the Car, Matilda and Dante*, 1824–7 (entry on p.152)

314 *Epitome of James Hervey's 'Meditations among the Tombs'* c.1820–5

Pen and watercolour, $16\frac{15}{16} \times 11\frac{1}{2}$ (43.1 × 29.2).
Signed 'W Blake inv & [?] . . .' with traces of at least two further characters and the possibility that more were lost when the bottom of the watercolour was trimmed; for further inscriptions see below.
Tate Gallery, London

James Hervey was a Calvinist and a popular devotional writer. His *Meditations among the Tombs*, first published in 1746, consists largely of reflections on mortality and the Resurrection, and particularly on the pathos of separation caused by early death. The ecclesiastical setting and the identifications of the various resurrected figures in this watercolour are largely based on Hervey's text, but the central vision of a spiral of Biblical figures and the introduction of Hervey himself between two angels in the foreground is Blake's own.

Each figure is identified by an inscription. 'Hervey', between an 'Angel of Providence' and a 'Guardian Angel', stands before an altar which bears the Eucharistic bread and wine. Above he sees a sequence of incidents from the Old Testament arranged on a spiral staircase. At the top of this vision appears God the Father with a scroll; then 'Adam', 'Eve' and the 'Serpent'; 'Cain' and 'Abel' as children; 'Enoch'; 'Noah' with his Ark; the 'Mother of Leah & Rachel' and the 'Mother of Rebecca'; 'Abraham believed God', with Isaac; 'Aaron'; 'David'; and 'Solomon'. The sequence culminates in the Transfiguration, 'Jesus' with 'Moses' and 'Elias', directly over the altar.

Above God the Father is the source of the fire that fills much of the upper part of the picture, with the inscription 'God out of Christ is a Consuming Fire', a variant of Hebrews 12:29, quoted by Calvinists to prove the existence of Hell. Christ is therefore shown as intercessor, but God the Father dispenses both 'MERCY' and 'WRATH', a more positive role than Blake previously allowed him.

On the left of the picture a number of figures rise towards Mercy assisted by 'Ministering Angels'. Starting at the bottom, where there is a font labelled 'Baptism', they are 'Old Age', 'Babe', 'Wife', 'Husband', 'Infancy', 'Where is your Father' and 'These died for Love'.

On the right two 'Angels of Death', two 'Protecting Angels' and a group of 'Recording Angels' escort the resurrected 'Virgin', 'Widow', 'Father', 'Mother', 'The Lost Child', 'Sophronia Died in Childbed', 'Orphan', 'She died on the Wedding Day' and 'orphans'.

Stylistically this watercolour is considerably later than Blake's surviving depictions of the Last Judgment of 1806 and 1808 (see Nos.211 and 213) and in its smooth finish and dark but glowing colours it resembles such works as the later versions of 'The Wise and Foolish Virgins', done in the 1820s (see No.173).

From the Butts and George Thomas Saul collections. There is a drawing possibly for this composition in the Rosenwald Collection.

315 *The Laocoön as Jehovah with Satan and Adam* c.1820

315

Line engraving, $10\frac{3}{8} \times 8\frac{1}{2}$ (26.3 × 21.6); platemark $10\frac{15}{16} \times 9\frac{1}{16}$ (27.8 × 23).
Inscr. 'Drawn & Engraved by William Blake'; for the remaining inscriptions see below.
Mrs Charles J. Rosenbloom

Laocoön was the Trojan prince and priest who warned the Trojans against admitting the wooden horse and was killed with his two sons by serpents sent by Apollo or Athena. The incident is the subject of the famous Antique sculpture, carved in Rhodes about 25 B.C. and discovered in Rome in 1506. Admired and imitated by artists from Michelangelo onwards, it is now in the Vatican Museum. Blake engraved it as one of the seven plates to illustrate an article by John Flaxman on sculpture for Abraham Rees' *The*

Cyclopaedia: or, Universal Dictionary of Arts, Sciences, and Literature, published in 1820 though Blake's plate is dated 1 October 1815. Blake's visit to the cast room at the Royal Academy Schools, then in Somerset House, is the subject of the famous anecdote of how Fuseli came in and said, 'Why Mr Blake, you a student, you ought to teach us'. Blake apparently did two drawings after the Laocoön; one in pencil is in an American private collection, while the other, in pen and ink, is now untraced.

Blake made certain alterations to the sculpture as he would have known it from the cast at the Academy, in particular bending the right arm of the younger son (an anticipation of later, more correct restoration of the damaged original) and accentuating Laocoön's suffering by showing him with more contracted stomach muscles. In this he followed the great German Neo-Classical theorist Winckelmann (whose *Reflections on the Painting and Sculpture of the Greeks,* translated by Fuseli and published in 1765, he owned) in making the body as expressive as the face.

However, in this extraordinary engraving he went much further in reinterpreting the subject, using it for a final statement of his views on the art of Antiquity. In this he followed his theory, already expounded in his *Descriptive Catalogue* of 1809, that Greek and Roman sculptures were mere echoes of Old Testament originals (see No.206). This is made clear by the main title below the group: 'יה [Jehovah] & his two Sons Satan & Adam as they were copied from the Cherubim of Solomons Temple by three Rhodians & applied to Natural Fact or History of Ilium [Troy]', and by the comment on the fallen state of the Classical world, 'Art Degraded, Imagination Denied, War Governed the Nations'. Above the head of Laocoön is 'The Angel of the Divine Presence' (Jehovah; see No.159), 'Angel of Jehovah' in Hebrew, and 'Serpent-holder' in Greek. The two serpents are labelled 'Good' and 'Evil' and Blake comments, 'Good & Evil are Riches & Poverty, a Tree of Misery propagating Generation & Death'. Following this proposition, which implies that the terms good and evil are only relevant in the fallen world, it would seem to be Adam who is entwined by the serpent 'Evil'. Below the serpent labelled 'Good' Blake has inscribed 'Lilith' in Hebrew; the head of this son, presumably Satan, is framed with the words 'Satans Wife The Goddess Nature is War & Misery & Heroism a Miser'. In addition, 'Adam is only The Natural Man & not the Soul or Imagination'.

The remaining inscriptions are aphorisms on the nature of art. Only a selection can be given here: 'Science is the Tree of Death; Art is the Tree of Life; God is Jesus'; 'The whole Business of Man Is The Arts & All Things Common'; 'Christianity is Art & not Money; Money is its Curse'; 'Where any view of Money exists Art cannot be carried on, but War only'; 'Israel delivered from Egypt is Art delivered from Nature & Imitation'; 'No Secresy [sic] in Art'; 'The outward Ceremony is Antichrist'.

Only two copies of this print are known, that from the Linnell Collection now in an English private collection, and this example, the early history of which is not known but which was in the George C. Smith sale in New York in 1938. This copy bears a faint counterproof of another copy of the print, laid face down on this example while the ink was still wet, but otherwise seems to be identical to the Linnell copy.

316

316 *Free Version of the Laocoön* c.1825

Pencil, pen and watercolour, sight $21\frac{1}{8} \times 17\frac{1}{8}$ (53.7 × 43.5).
Inscr., probably by Frederick Tatham, 'The Laocoon'.
Private collection, England

This magnificent drawing is a free depiction of the subject of Laocoön and his two sons, not directly based on the Antique sculpture, and was probably done after the engraving, No.315. As in the engraving, Blake probably sees the three figures as Jehovah with Satan and Adam. Stylistically the drawing is close to the Dante watercolours of 1824–7 (see Nos.319–39).

317 *Christian with the Shield of Faith, from John Bunyan's 'The Pilgrim's Progress'* 1824–7

Pencil, pen and watercolour, approx. 7⅛ × 4⅞ (18 × 12.5) on paper 9¹¹⁄₁₆ × 7⁷⁄₁₆ (24.6 × 18.9).
Inscr. by Blake(?) '20', and, not by Blake, 'William Blake'.
Watermarked 'J WHATMAN 182[4]' (the last digit is missing owing to the trimming of the paper but can be reconstructed from others of the series).
National Gallery of Art, Washington (Rosenwald Collection)

317

This is from a series of illustrations to John Bunyan's *The Pilgrim's Progress*, apparently left unfinished at Blake's death; some are on paper water-marked with the date '1824'. The rest of the series, which comprises twenty-nine watercolours in all, is in the Frick Museum, New York. Some appear to have been completed by another hand, Mrs Blake's according to William Rossetti. However, this example, unlike the others, was inserted into a scrapbook assembled by Mrs Charles Aders, almost certainly in 1827, either before or just after Blake's death, and has escaped reworking.

The number '20' inscribed in the top right corner is similar to numbers on others of the series and seems to place this watercolour in the correct sequence as an illustration to *The Pilgrim's Progress*. Equipped from the Armoury of the Pilgrim's House, Christian sets forth accompanied by Discretion, Piety, Charity and Prudence. Behind can be seen the stately palace called Beautiful.

318 *Sketch, probably for Bunyan's Dream* c.1824–7(?)

Pencil, approx. 6¼ × 5 (16 × 12.7) on paper 8¹³⁄₁₆ × 7¹⁄₁₆ (22.3 × 17.9).
Inscr. by Frederick Tatham 'sketched by William Blake vouched by Fredk Tatham'.
Watermarked 'M & J LAY 1816'.
Mrs Edna M. Maggs

318

This is probably an alternative idea for the first of *The Pilgrim's Progress* watercolours (Frick Museum, New York): a figure representing inspiration floats overhead and reaches down to touch the head of the seated poet; however, the figure of the woman moving away on the left is difficult to explain. In the watercolour Bunyan lies asleep, while above him are sketched incidents from the dream that inspired *The Pilgrim's Progress*. On the other hand the drawing could be related to one of Blake's later series of illustrations to Milton, being on the same paper as those to *L'Allegro* and *Il Penseroso* (see Nos.239–50) and *Paradise Regained* (Fitzwilliam Museum).

The drawing is typical of Blake's later drawing style, in which a multitude of lightly sketched lines gradually picks out the main forms. Although this is a far cry from Blake's insistence on clear outlines it parallels the delicate accumulation of tiny brush strokes of the later finished watercolours which in the final result achieve the clarity of form on which Blake insisted.

The drawing, which remained in Blake's possession and passed to Frederick Tatham, later belonged to W. Graham Robertson.

Illustrations to Dante, 1824-7

Blake left a number of projects unfinished at his death in 1827, including an illuminated manuscript of the Book of Genesis, some drawings illustrating the Book of Enoch (an apocryphal Ethiopian text) and a series of watercolours illustrating Bunyan's *The Pilgrim's Progress* (see No. 317). By far the most important of these unfinished enterprises was the set of illustrations to Dante's *Divine Comedy* of which 102 drawings exist, in various stages of completion in watercolour, together with a number of preliminary drawings. Like the second Job series these were commissioned by Linnell and after the success of the Job engravings it was planned to engrave the Dante series also, though only seven plates were actually etched and even these were not fully completed at Blake's death.

Palmer gives an account of Blake at work on the series: 'on Saturday, 9th October, 1824, Mr. Linnell called and went with me to Mr. Blake. We found him lame in bed, of a scalded foot (or leg). There, not inactive, though sixty-seven years old, but hard-working on a bed covered with books sat he up like one of the Antique patriarchs or a dying Michael Angelo. Thus and there was he making in the leaves of a great book (folio) the sublimest design from his (not superior) Dante. He said he began them with fear and trembling. I said "Oh! I have enough of fear and trembling." "Then," said he, "you'll do." He

designed them (100 I think) during a fortnight's illness in bed!' Crabb Robinson, visiting Blake the following year on 17 December 1825, found Blake still at work however, using H. F. Cary's translation, but Blake also owned an edition in the original Italian. The translation of the inscription over Hell Gate (see No. 319) seems to be Blake's own and presumably he had learnt at least some Italian to help him with his task.

Even more than in the case of the illustrations to the Book of Job Blake's designs are not mere illustrations to the text but also act as a commentary upon it. Blake objected strongly to Dante's orthodox views on salvation. As Blake told Crabb Robinson on 10 December 1825, '*Dante* saw devils where I see none – I see only good.' On one of the drawings for the series (design 7; Fogg Museum) Blake wrote, 'Everything in Dante's Comedia shews That for Tyrannical Purposes he has made This World the Foundation of All, & the Goddess Nature is his Inspirer & not the Holy Ghost'. On another of the drawings (design 101; British Museum) he condemned Dante's idea of Hell as 'originally Formed by the devil Himself', adding, 'Whatever Book is for Vengeance for Sin & whatever Book is Against Forgiveness of Sin is not of the Father but of Satan the Accuser & Father of Hell'. For Blake's condemnation of Dante's idea of the role of the Church (represented by Beatrice) see Nos. 334, 335 and 339.

319

319 *The Inscription over Hell-Gate* 1824-7

Illustrations to Dante no. 4.
Chalk, pencil, pen and watercolour, $20\frac{3}{4} \times 14\frac{3}{4}$ (52.7×37.4).
Signed 'WB' and inscribed 'HELL Canto 3' and 'Lasciate ogni speranze voi che inentrate [? – the last word is obscure] Leave every hope you who in enter' over the arch.
Tate Gallery, London

Inferno 3: 1–21. Blake seems to have quoted Dante's text from memory; in the original it reads, 'lasciate ogni speranza voi ch'entrate'. The literal translation is presumably Blake's own.

The graceful relationship of the two figures of Dante and Virgil is typical of the seemingly inexhaustible variations on their interrelated poses throughout the series. Dante is clothed in red, Virgil in blue, colours which Blake associated with two of his four Zoas, Luvah and Los, who represent the feelings and the imagination respectively. Throughout the series it is Dante who reacts in astonishment and sympathy, Virgil who explains and calms him.

The impressionistic treatment of the flaming landscape of Hell with the tiny despairing figures in the distance, and of the foliage flanking the archway, is typical of the relaxation of Blake's late style, though the two main figures retain his much insisted upon clarity of form. Even in the completely finished watercolours of the series such as Nos. 322 and 334 the freedom and subtlety of Blake's application of colour are remarkable.

320 *The Vestibule of Hell and the Souls Mustering to Cross the Acheron* 1824–7

Illustrations to Dante no.5.
Pen and watercolour over pencil, $20\frac{3}{4} \times 14\frac{9}{16}$ (52.8 × 37).
Signed 'WB' and inscr. 'HELL Canto 3'.
Watermarked 'WELGAR 1796'.
National Gallery of Victoria, Melbourne

320

Inferno 3:22–71. The Acheron, an actual river in northern Greece which runs underground in several places, was in Antique literature the chief river of Hades; Dante adopted it as the river encircling his Hell, across which Charon, the Greek god of the dead, ferries the souls of the dead. Although Dante describes the figures of the damned as naked Blake has clothed many of them, often with emblems of worldly rank and power; the leading woman on the left recalls the Whore of Babylon (see No. 190). The damned are being attacked by wasps and hornets, and their blood and tears attract worms.

There is a pencil sketch in the British Museum.

321 *The Circle of the Lustful: Francesca da Rimini ('The Whirlwind of Lovers')* 1824–7

Illustrations to Dante no.10.
Pen and watercolour over pencil with some scratching out, $14\frac{7}{16} \times 20\frac{9}{16}$ (36.8 × 52.2).
Inscr. 'HELL Canto 5'.
City Museums and Art Gallery, Birmingham

321

Inferno 5:25–45, 127–42. Francesca da Rimini and her lover Paolo are seen in the separate flame above the prostrate Dante, who has fainted with pity. Other carnal sinners are swept up in the main whirlwind. Blake shows them reunited in love, as are Francesca and Paolo in the sun above Virgil, having found salvation in the reenactment of their first kiss, an embrace echoing that on plate 28 of *Jerusalem*, No.266. This is a typical 'correction' of Dante, whose orthodox condemnation of sin, particularly when that sin arose from unnatural restraint, was abhorrent to Blake.

There are a number of drawings related to this composition, though in some cases the relationship is very tenuous. This was one of the watercolours to be engraved by Blake; the print bears the title 'The Whirlwind of Lovers from Dantes Inferno Canto v' in mirror-writing.

322 *Capaneus the Blasphemer* 1824–7

Illustrations to Dante no.27.
Pen and watercolour, $14\frac{11}{16} \times 20\frac{3}{4}$ (37.3 × 52.7).
Signed 'WB' and inscr. 'HELL Canto 14'.
National Gallery of Victoria, Melbourne

322

Inferno 14:46–72. Capaneus, one of the seven kings who besieged Ancient Thebes, defied Zeus and was killed by a thunderbolt. Dante describes him as retaining his pride and disdain for the Gods even under torment.

This watercolour is typical of the high degree of finish of the completed watercolours of the series. The figure derives from an Antique figure of the Nile in the Vatican.

323 *Geryon Conveying Dante and Virgil Downwards towards Malebolge* 1824–7

Illustrations to Dante no.31.
Pen and watercolour over pencil or chalk, $14\frac{5}{8} \times 20\frac{3}{4}$ (37.1 × 52.7).
Inscr. 'HELL Canto 17'.
National Gallery of Victoria, Melbourne

323

seducers fleeing from devils, the subject of Blake's next illustration.

On the back is a slight chalk sketch, possibly of Farinata degli Ulberti, who figures in Canto 10.

324 *The Devils Under the Bridge* 1824–7

Illustrations to Dante no. 34.
Pen and watercolour over pencil, $14\frac{11}{16} \times 20\frac{3}{4}$ (37.2 × 52.7).
Inscr. 'HELL Canto 18'.
National Gallery of Victoria, Melbourne

Inferno 21:46–57. Despite Blake's inscription this drawing shows the punishment of the Lucchese magistrate for barratry (a form of fraud) which occurs in Canto 21, though the seducers pursued by devils of Canto 18 do appear in the background. The rock bridges of Malebolge described by Dante are shown by Blake as made up from petrified human bodies, a most expressive symbol of Fallen Man at his furthest remove from divine energy.

There is a possible sketch for this composition on the back of no. 22 from the series, 'The Minotaur' in the Fogg Museum.

325 *The Simoniac Pope* 1824–7

Illustrations to Dante no. 35.
Pen and watercolour, $20\frac{3}{4} \times 14\frac{1}{2}$ (52.7 × 36.8).
Signed 'WB' and inscr. 'HELL Canto 19'.
Watermarked 'WELGAR 1796'.
Tate Gallery, London

Inferno 19:31–126. Virgil clasps Dante to sweep him away from the wrath of Pope Nicholas III, punished for simony (the selling of ecclesiastical preferment) by being suspended head downwards in a well of fire until replaced by another Pope guilty of the same sin.

326 *The Baffled Devils Fighting* 1827

Illustrations to Dante no. 42.
Line engraving, $9\frac{9}{16} \times 13\frac{3}{16}$ (24.2 × 33.5).
Tate Gallery, London

Inferno 22:133–40. The two devils Alichino and Calcabrina, foiled by the escape of their prey Ciampolo the barrator, fall to fighting each other. Their fellow devils watch from the shore while Dante and Virgil retire in the distance.

324

325

326

327

This is Blake's engraving after the watercolour in the City Museums and Art Gallery, Birmingham. It was the last engraving he worked on and was left unfinished at his death. The figures on the shore show the vigour of his first strokes, which were usually tidied up in the finishing stages. This copy of the engraving, like No.327, was sold from the Linnell Collection in 1918 and was probably from the set of prints made by John Linnell jun. in 1892.

327 The Six-Footed Serpent Attacking Agnolo Brunelleschi 1826–7

Illustrations to Dante no.51.
Line engraving, $9\frac{5}{8} \times 13\frac{3}{8}$ (24.5 × 34).
Tate Gallery, London

Inferno 25:49–78. Set in the Circle of the Thieves, in which the condemned constantly change from human form to that of serpents and back again as they attack each other. In this extraordinary image Blake shows Cianfa de' Donati attacking Agnolo Brunelleschi and their two bodies merging into one. The next drawing, in the Fogg Museum, shows the next stage in the process, with Agnolo Brunelleschi sprouting scales, fins and a tail, his face hideously transformed.

This is Blake's engraving after the watercolour in the National Gallery of Victoria. There is a drawing for the watercolour in the Fondazione Horne, Florence, and a drawing apparently done between the watercolour and the engraving in the Huntington Library, San Marino.

328 Antaeus Setting Down Dante and Virgil in the Last Circle of Hell 1824–7

Illustrations to Dante no.63.
Pen and watercolour, $20\frac{3}{4} \times 14\frac{3}{4}$ (52.6 × 37.4).
Inscr. 'HELL Canto 31'.
National Gallery of Victoria, Melbourne

Inferno 31:112–43. The Circle of the Giants, who made war against the Gods. Antaeus is left unfettered because he held aloof from the war. He is best known for his defeat at the hands of Hercules, who learned that his strength depended upon contact with the ground and overcame him by lifting him up.

Here Blake stresses the size of the gentle giant by stressing the awkwardness of his pose. Flaxman, for instance, had minimised the disparity in scale in his illustration of the same scene by showing Antaeus kneeling.

328

329 The Souls of Those who only Repented at the Point of Death 1824–7

Illustrations to Dante no.75.
Pen and watercolour over pencil and black chalk, $14\frac{5}{8} \times 20\frac{13}{16}$ (37.2 × 52.8).
Inscr. 'P-g Canto 5 & 6'.
National Gallery of Victoria, Melbourne

Purgatorio 5:37–136, and 6:1–48. The souls of those slain violently but who saw the light at the last minute. Blake illustrates Dante's simile of the souls wheeling about like flaming vapours. It should, from the text, be Virgil who turned to look up towards the summit on which Beatrice awaits Dante, but the figure is in fact clothed in red, Dante's colour throughout the series.

On the back is a very faint sketch, perhaps for 'The Devil carrying the Lucchese Magistrate', no.37 of the series, also in the National Gallery of Victoria.

329

330

330 *The Lawn with the Kings and the Angels* 1824–7

Illustrations to Dante no.76.
Pen and watercolour over pencil, $14\frac{11}{16} \times 20\frac{13}{16}$ (37 3 × 52 8)
Inscr. 'P-g Canto 7 & 8'.
Watermarked 'WELGAR 1796'.
National Gallery of Victoria, Melbourne

Purgatorio 7:64–90, and 8:1–39, 94–108. Dante and Virgil are led by the latter's fellow-Mantuan, the poet Sordello (*c.*1200–69), to the Valley of Negligent Rulers; the rulers are guarded by two angels against the serpent who tries to invade their Eden-like garden. Blake shows the rulers in a grove of trees, symbolising error, which prevents them from seeing the angels, who are however visible to the three poets who represent the imagination.

331

331 *Dante at the Moment of Entering the Fire* 1824–7

Illustrations to Dante no.85.
Pen and watercolour over black chalk, $20\frac{13}{16} \times 14\frac{9}{16}$ (52.8 × 36.9).
Inscr. 'P-g Canto 27'.
National Gallery of Victoria, Melbourne

Purgatorio 27:19–48. Virgil has just entered the flames that guard the seventh Circle of Purgatory; the angel of that Circle hovers above him. Dante recoils in fear. The Roman poet Statius, who accompanies them, is on the extreme right. Blake adds the four female figures hovering in the flames, possibly his 'Daughters of Beulah' or Imagination; normally three in number, to represent the three-fold vision of Beulah (a sort of Purgatory in Blake's system), they are here shown as four, corresponding to the four-fold vision of Eden, the next stage in the poets' journey.

The sequence of six designs starting with this one is vital in Blake's reinterpretation of Dante's attitude to salvation and the Church.

332 *Dante and Statius Sleeping, Virgil Watching* 1824–7

Illustrations to Dante no.86.
Pen and watercolour over pencil, $20\frac{1}{2} \times 14\frac{1}{4}$ (52 × 36.8).
Inscr. 'P-g Canto 27' and in the moon above, 'dante['s dream –?]' and 'Leah and Rachel [?]'.
Ashmolean Museum, Oxford

Purgatorio 27:70–108. The poets rest after passing through the flames. Dante dreams of Leah and Rachel, the Old Testament types of the active and the contemplative life (Genesis 29–30), the one making a garland, the other regarding herself in a mirror, as in the text. Blake however shows them within the moon, a reminder that the poets are still in danger of relapsing into Beulah and of staying in Purgatory. The languid, static figures of the poets are contrasted with the active flame-like figures of the previous watercolour, with both symbolic and beautiful effect.

332

333 *Beatrice on the Car, Matilda and Dante* 1824–7

Illustrations to Dante no.87.
Pen and watercolour over pencil, $14\frac{7}{16} \times 20\frac{1}{2}$ (36.7 × 52).
Inscr. 'P-g –Canto 29'
Trustees of the British Museum, London

Purgatorio 29:13–150. Dante, having said farewell to Virgil, looks across the river Lethe towards the Garden of Eden, the Earthly Paradise; Virgil and Statius are seen between the trees on the right. From the opposite bank Dante is greeted by Matilda (probably the Grancontessa Matilda of Tuscany, a supporter of Pope Gregory VII, and of the Church against the Holy Roman Emperor) and told to look at the approaching procession. Dante describes the procession with many allusions to the Bible, particularly the Book of Revelation: the seven-branched candle-stick, the four-

and-twenty elders, and the chariot drawn by the griffin. On the chariot is Beatrice, the subject of the next illustration, No. 334.

334 *Beatrice Addressing Dante from the Car* 1824–7

Illustrations to Dante no. 88
Pen and watercolour, $14\frac{5}{8} \times 20\frac{3}{4}$ (37.2×52.7).
Inscr. 'P-g Canto 29 & 30'.
Watermarked 'WELGAR 1796'.
Tate Gallery, London

Purgatorio 29:92–129, and 30:31–3, 64–81. Dante's first meeting with Beatrice in the Earthly Paradise. Beatrice reproves Dante for his backslidings. For Dante the griffin and Beatrice symbolised Christ and the Church, and the three girls in the foreground Faith (in white), Hope (in green) and Charity (in red). The heads emerging from the peacock-like eyed-wings on the chariot are those of the four Evangelists.

However, this watercolour has been shown to be one of the key works in which Blake expresses his opposition to Dante's ideas. Many of Dante's details are subtly altered. Beatrice's olive wreath has been turned into a gold crown, Faith points towards a book, and the wheel of the chariot has become a vortex, the gateway between eternity and the created world (*Milton*, plate 17). It is difficult to avoid the conclusion that this exquisite, glowing watercolour shows the poet Dante submitting himself to the mystery of the Church, the Female Will, Blake's Vala in her fallen state as Rahab or the Whore of Babylon, an interpretation confirmed by the next illustration, No. 335.

335 *The Harlot and the Giant* 1824–7

Illustrations to Dante no. 89.
Pen and watercolour over pencil and black chalk, $14\frac{5}{8} \times 20\frac{13}{16}$ (37.2×52.8).
Inscr. 'P-g Canto 32'.
National Gallery of Victoria, Melbourne

Purgatorio 32:85–7, 142–53. In Dante's text Beatrice shows the poet the ills that occur when the relationship between Church and Empire is disturbed, as in Dante's own time: her chariot is transformed into a vision of the Church as Whore of Babylon, alternately embraced and chastised by a giant representing the kings of France; their relationship represents the 'Babylonian Captivity' of the Papacy at Avignon. But, though Blake follows Dante in showing Beatrice as a distinct figure, kneeling on the ground at the right with her attendants, he shows the Whore with her serpentine coils as a parody of Beatrice and her car in the previous illustration. Moreover, he places Beatrice at the foot of the tree of the knowledge of good and evil, distorting Dante's introduction of the tree as a symbol of justice and obedience in the ideal Empire, and reduces her seven attendants to three, the three Daughters of Beulah or Memory, the perverted art of the Fallen World. Blake implies that perversion of the Church is not just a temporary condition, but one implicit all along.

336 *Dante Adoring Christ* 1824–7

Illustrations to Dante no.90.
Pen and watercolour over pencil or black chalk, $20\frac{3}{4} \times 14\frac{5}{8}$
(52.7×37.2).
Inscr. '97'.
Watermarked 'WELGAR 1796'.
National Gallery of Victoria, Melbourne

Paradiso 14:91–108. The relative paucity of illustrations to this Book as opposed to the *Inferno* and *Purgatorio* (ten as opposed to seventy-two and twenty respectively) may be due to Blake having died before he had time to begin all his projected designs; the full extent of Blake's scheme is not therefore certain. However, this design, in which Dante kneels adoringly before the vision of Christ, makes a strong contrast to the previous run of watercolours in which he stands stiffly and submissively before Beatrice. Beatrice, although still accompanying Dante in the text, is nowhere to be seen in Blake's design.

On the back is a rough sketch perhaps for *Paradiso* 23. The large number '97' (there is a similar '96' on the back) is connected with a complex system of cross-indexing indicated by Blake on the backs of most of the drawings but not yet fully explained.

337 *Dante and Beatrice in the Constellation of Gemini and the Sphere of Flame* 1824–7

Illustrations to Dante no.93.
Pen, pencil, black chalk and watercolour, $13\frac{15}{16} \times 20\frac{1}{16}$ (35.5×51).
Inscr. 'Paradiso Canto 24'.
Ashmolean Museum, Oxford

Paradiso 24:10–18. Dante and Beatrice, standing in the constellation of Gemini under which Dante was born, are surrounded by the spirits of the redeemed. The twin spheres within which the two figures stand represent the twin stars of Gemini. Here the relationship of Dante and Beatrice is a much more positive one, and Blake seems to have used the text, with its lack of specific detail, to show the ideal harmony of Man and his Female Emanation.

338 *St. Peter, St. James, Dante and Beatrice with St. John the Evangelist also* 1824–7

Illustrations to Dante no.96.
Pen and watercolour over pencil, $14\frac{3}{8} \times 20\frac{1}{2}$ (36.5×52).
Inscr. 'Canto 25.' and 'Paradise Canto . . . [?]'.
Trustees of the British Museum, London

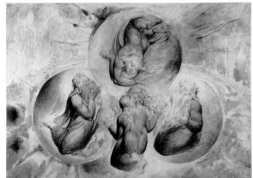

Paradiso 25:97–121. In the three designs culminating in this one (the other two are in the National Gallery of Victoria) Blake illustrates the successive appearances of St. Peter, St. James and St. John. St. Peter, who questions Dante on Faith, is represented by Blake's type for Urizen; St. James, who questions Dante on Hope, as Luvah; and St. John, who questions Dante on Love, as Los or the Poetic Genius. Together they represent Reason, Feeling and the Imagination. The overlapping of the three globes in which they are shown, embracing Dante and Beatrice whose echoing gestures reflect their harmony, is a marvellously vivid image of the reunion of Man's various elements that is the requisite of true salvation. Behind, on each side, Blake originally drew four angels, rather as in the famous Job illustration, 'When the Morning Stars sang together' (see Nos.195 and 201), but he later overpainted them in watercolour and replaced them with eight stars, probably to represent Dante's eight Heavens, the region of fixed stars, in which this scene occurs.

339 *The Queen of Heaven in Glory* 1824–7

Illustrations to Dante no.99.
Pen and watercolour over pencil and black chalk, $14\frac{5}{8} \times 20\frac{3}{4}$
(37.1×52.8).
For the inscriptions identifying details of the composition see below.
Watermarked 'WELGAR 1796'.
National Gallery of Victoria, Melbourne

339

Paradiso 30:97–126; 31:1–21, 115–42, and 32:1–9. Whereas Dante concludes his *Divine Comedy* with a vision of the Church Triumphant, presided over by the Virgin Mary, Blake, in the last of his illustrations (the designs conventionally numbered 100–02 are in fact illustrations to the *Inferno* to which no specific references can be attached), sums the series up with another condemnation of Dante's idea that salvation can be achieved through the Church, for Blake the embodiment of the Female Will in its fallen state.

This is made clear by Blake's inscriptions. 'Mary' holds a 'Sceptr[e]' and 'Looking [Glass]'. The head of the sceptre is shaped like a lily, a traditional symbol of the Virgin Birth, but here, transformed into a sceptre, it represents the worldly power of the Church Triumphant. The mirror can only reflect the material world. On the right a figure labelled 'Dominion' holds a 'Bible', 'chaind round', and this is balanced on the left by another figure labelled illegibly (? 'Laws', 'Thrones', 'Teams', 'Trains' or even 'Frame') who holds what is perhaps the Old Testament 'corded round'. Unlike these two closed books, those labelled 'Homer' and 'Aristotle' are left open. On the seventh Dante illustration (Fogg Museum) Blake shows Homer as the representative of 'the Poetry of the Heathen, Stolen & Perverted from the Bible . . .', while in his annotations of *c.*1820 to George Berkeley's *Siris*, 1744, he wrote that Aristotle and Plato 'considerd God as abstracted or distinct from the Imaginative World', as opposed to Jesus, Abraham and David who 'considerd God as a Man in the Spiritual or Imaginative Vision'.

Beatrice appears below Mary and is surrounded by other figures, most if not all apparently female. The whole group is clustered on an enormous flower, symbolising the vegetable world. Above are the 'Sun', so labelled, the moon and various planets and stars, material heavenly bodies.

Chronology

The information on which this is based can be largely found in Blake's letters and G. E. Bentley Jr's *Blake Records*; see Bibliography, p.162. Information dependent on hearsay is identified by the name of the source being given in brackets, e.g. Malkin, Gilchrist.

1757
28 November. Born at his parents' home, 28 Broad Street (now 74 Broadwick Street), Golden Square, Soho, London, the son of a hosier; baptised in St. James's Church, Piccadilly, 11 December.

1767
4 August. Probable birthdate of favourite brother Robert (see No.36).

1767–8
Entered Henry Pars' drawing school in the Strand at the age of ten (Malkin).

1769
Blake's father may have joined the Baptist Church, Grafton Street. Blake himself, his parents and his brother Robert were all to be buried in Bunhill Fields, the dissenters' burial ground.

1769–70
At age of twelve began writing the poems included in *Poetical Sketches* (published 1783) which contained writings of up to his twentieth year, 1777–8.

1772
Bound as apprentice for seven years to James Basire (1730–1802), the engraver, of 31 Great Queen Street, Lincoln's Inn Fields, and probably went to live in his home.

1773
Probable date of first known engraving, that after Michelangelo entitled on a later state 'Joseph and Arimathea among the Rocks of Albion' and then dated '1773' (see No.15).

1774
First securely datable drawings attributed to Blake, those of 'The Body of Edward I in his Coffin' (No.6).

1775
Dated drawings of monuments in Westminster Abbey attributed to Blake, including No.3.

1779
8 October. Admitted to the Royal Academy Schools as an engraver (though engraving was not apparently taught at this time). Though entitled to use the drawing facilities for six years he probably dropped out after a few months. Fellow students included his friends John Flaxman (1756–1826) and Thomas Stothard (1755–1834) (see No.8).

1780
May. First exhibit at the Royal Academy, 'Death of Earl Goodwin' (? British Museum; see No.17), sending in from 28 Broad Street. George Cumberland, in *The Morning Chronicle and London Advertiser* for 27 May, mentioned the work, 'in which, though there is nothing to be said of the colouring, may be discovered a good design, and much character'.

6 June. Borne along by the mob that liberated Newgate Prison in the Gordon Riots (Gilchrist).

About this time, on a sketching trip by boat up the Medway, with Stothard and another friend arrested as French spies but released on assurances from members of the Royal Academy (Stothard's daughter-in-law, in an account of *c*.1850).

Began doing commercial engraving for the radical publisher, Joseph Johnson.

1781–2
Fell in love, in his twenty-fourth year, with Polly Wood but was refused (Tatham).

1782
2 April. Robert Blake, presumably William's youngest and favourite brother, admitted to the Royal Academy Schools as an engraver (see No.36).

18 August. Married Catherine Butcher (or Boucher, born 25 April 1762), and moved to 23 Green Street, Leicester Fields (now Irving Street).

1783
Flaxman and the Rev. A. S. Matthew, husband of the blue-stocking Mrs Harriet Matthew, financed the publication of Blake's *Poetical Sketches*. Flaxman also secured Blake a commission for a drawing from John Hawkins, 'a Cornish Gentleman', on about 18 June.

1784
First met J. T. Smith at Harriet Matthew's.

26 April. Flaxman wrote to William Hayley that he was sending him a copy of Blake's *Poetical Sketches* and reported that John Hawkins had not only commissioned several drawings from Blake but 'is so convinced of his uncommon talents that he is now endeavouring to raise a subscription to send him to finish his studies in Rome'; this never happened. Flaxman also reported that 'M.ʳ Romney thinks his [Blake's] historical drawings rank with those of M.ʳ Angelo.'

May. Two works at the Royal Academy, 'A Breach in a City, the Morning after a Battle' and 'War unchained by an Angel, Fire, Pestilence, and Famine following' (see Nos.20 and 22), sent in from 23 Green Street.

4 July. Blake's father James buried, probably leaving him a small sum of money, enough to enable him to set up a print shop with James Parker (1750–1805, a fellow apprentice under Basire) at 27 Broad Street, next door to his birthplace, now occupied by his eldest brother James. Blake and Parker published two prints on 17 December, the only documented works of this partnership.

Autumn. Probable date of satirical manuscript *An Island in the Moon*, based on the literary circle of Harriet Matthew.

1785
May. Four works at the Royal Academy, three of the story of Joseph (Nos.28–30) and 'The Bard, from Gray' (untraced; see No.207).

By Christmas had moved to 28 Poland Street, Soho, leaving the Parkers at 27 Broad Street.

1787
February. Death of favourite brother Robert, buried 11 February.

1787–8
First got to know Henry Fuseli (1741–1825).

1788
'W Blakes Original Stereotype was 1788' (inscription on *The Ghost of Abel*, 1822). This reference to Blake's personal form of relief etching probably refers to *There is No Natural Religion* and *All Religions are One*.

From about this time associated with the radical circle of Joseph Johnson, William Godwin, Mary Wollstonecraft, Joseph Priestley and Thomas Paine.

1789
13 April. Among those signing a declaration that they believed in the doctrines of Emanuel Swedenborg at the first session of the New Church, but unlike Flaxman never actually joined the New Church and attacked Swedenborg in *The Marriage of Heaven and Hell*, 1790–93.

Tiriel usually dated to this year (see Nos.40–41). *Songs of Innocence* and *The Book of Thel* (see Nos.42–9).

1790
Autumn. Moved to 13 Hercules Buildings, Lambeth. Began *The Marriage of Heaven and Hell*.

1791
The French Revolution, to be published by Johnson as an ordinary book, got no further than page-proofs. His illustrations to Mary Wollstonecraft's *Original Stories from Real Life* published by Johnson (see Nos.50–53). Began engravings for John Gabriel Stedman's *Narrative, of a Five Year's Expedition, against the Revolted Negroes of Surinam*, completed 1793 but not published by Johnson until 1796.

1792
c. 7 September. Death of Blake's mother Catherine.

c. 12 September. Blake said to have warned Tom Paine to escape from England (Tatham and Gilchrist) but this is probably highly exaggerated; however, it reflects his continuing contacts with the radicals, now under pressure from Pitt's government as it reacted against events in France.

1793
The Marriage of Heaven and Hell (begun 1790), *Visions of the Daughters of Albion, America* (see Nos.59–62) and *For Children: The Gates of Paradise* (first version).

1794
Songs of Experience, Europe and *The [First] Book of Urizen* (see Nos.54–8, 63–83).

1795
The Song of Los, The Book of Ahania and *The Book of Los*.

Commissioned by Richard Edwards to illustrate Young's *Night Thoughts*, published 1797 (see Nos.104–24).

1796
Illustrated G. A. Bürger's *Leonora* (engraved by Perry). Publication of George Cumberland's *Thoughts on Outline* with eight plates engraved by Blake.

Probably began work on unfinished manuscript *Vala or the Four Zoas*, not abandoned until c.1807.

1797
Commissioned by John Flaxman to illustrate Gray's *Poems* for his wife Ann, commonly known as Nancy (see Nos.125–31).

1798
Annotated Bishop Richard Watson's *An Apology for The Bible in a Series of Letters addressed to Thomas Paine*. Also annotated Francis Bacon's *Essays* about this time.

1799
May. Exhibited small tempera painting of 'The Last Supper' at the Royal Academy.

August. First mention of the patronage of Thomas Butts (see p.75) and the would-be patronage of the Rev. Dr Trusler (see No.141).

7 October. Gift of a copy of *America* to C. H. Tatham, the father of Blake's later friend and *de facto* executor Frederick Tatham.

1800
May. Tempera of 'The Loaves and the Fishes' at the Royal Academy.

June. Publication of William Hayley's *Essay on Sculpture* with three engravings by Blake after Flaxman.

18 September. Moved to Felpham, near Chichester, under Hayley's patronage (see p.78). During his three years there he probably got to know the third Earl and Countess of Egremont at Petworth nearby.

5 October. Publication of Hayley's *Little Tom the Sailor* with engravings by Blake.

Annotations to Boyd's translation of Dante's *Inferno*, 1785, about this time.

1801
31 July. Flaxman passed on to Blake the Rev. J. Thomas' commission for illustrations to *Comus* and Shakespeare (see p.112 and No.254).

One engraving after Fuseli in Fuseli's *Lectures on Painting*.

1802

First series of *Ballads* by Hayley with illustrations by Blake (see Nos.146–8).

1803

First two volumes of Hayley's *Life of William Cowper*, with four plates engraved by Blake, one after his own design; volume III, with two further engravings by Blake after others, published 1804. Hayley's *Triumphs of Temper*, with six plates engraved by Blake after Maria Flaxman. Working on plates for Hayley's *Life of George Romney*, published 1809.

12 August. Blake ejected a soldier named John Scolfield from his garden, leading to a charge of sedition.

19 September. Returned to London, at first to his brother's house, 28 Broad Street, but by 26 October had settled at 17 South Molton Street.

1804

11 January. Acquitted on charge of sedition at Chichester.

Greatly impressed by the Truchsessian Gallery of Pictures, a speculative collection of Old Masters particularly notable for its 'Gothic' pictures by or after fifteenth-century Flemish and German artists, but also containing works attributed to the artists Blake particularly singled out for praise or blame in succeeding years.

Date on titlepages of *Milton*, not actually finished until 1808 or later, and *Jerusalem*, not finally completed until 1820 (see Nos.257–75).

1805

Second edition of Hayley's *Ballads* with illustrations by Blake (see Nos.146–8).

Commissioned by Robert Hartley Cromek to illustrate Blair's *Grave* (see Nos.152–8).

1806

Benjamin Heath Malkin's *A Father's Memoirs of his Child* published with frontispiece engraved by Cromek after Blake and with a biographical account of Blake in Malkin's introductory letter.

1807

May. Thomas Phillips' portrait of Blake (now in the National Portrait Gallery) exhibited at the Royal Academy.

1808

May. Two watercolours at the Royal Academy, 'Jacob's Dream' and 'Christ in the Sepulchre, guarded by Angels' (Nos.160 and 180).

The Grave published with Blake's designs engraved by Luigi Schiavonetti and a frontispiece after Phillips' portrait. Robert Hunt, in *The Examiner* for 7 August, attacked Blake's designs, as did the *Antijacobin Review* for November in a long article of some ten pages. However, *The Monthly Magazine* for 1 December said of the designs, 'there is considerable correctness and knowledge of form in the drawing of the various figures; the grouping is frequently pleasing, and the composition well arranged; some of them have even an air of ancient art, which would not have disgraced the Roman school. In the *ideal* part . . . there is a wildness of fancy and eccentricity, that leave the poet at a very considerable distance.'

Annotated Reynolds' *Discourses* about this time.

1809

May. Opening of Blake's exhibition of his own work, with his *Descriptive Catalogue*, at his brother's house, 28 Broad Street. Robert Hunt wrote a hostile review in *The Examiner* for 17 September. Though due to close on 29 September it was still open well into 1810 (see p.104 and Nos.16–17, 205–8 and 210).

1809–10

Seymour Kirkup (1788–1880) met Blake through Butts and, according to his account in 1865, was 'much with him from 1810 to 1816', when he settled in Italy.

1810

Blake's engraving after his painting of 'Chaucer's Canterbury Pilgrims' (No.210). Stothard's rival picture was the cause of the two friends falling out.

28 April. Henry Crabb Robinson visited Blake's exhibition, and took Charles Lamb there on 11 June.

1811

January. Henry Crabb Robinson's essay on 'William Blake, Künstler, Dichter, und Religiöser Schwärmer' ('Artist, Poet, and Religious Mystic') published in the first issue of *Vaterländisches Museum*, Hamburg.

July. The poet Robert Southey visited Blake.

1812

Blake exhibited four works, as a member, with the Associated Painters in Water Colour: 'The Canterbury Pilgrims', 'The Spiritual Form of Pitt', 'The Spiritual Form of Nelson', and 'Detached Specimens of an original illuminated Poem, entitled *Jerusalem, The Emanation of the Giant Albion*' (see Nos.210, 205–6 and 257–75).

1813

11 April. George Cumberland, on his Spring visit to London from his home in Bristol, visited Blake.

1814

3 June. Cumberland again visited Blake, 'still poor still Dirty' (but he described Stothard as 'still more dirty than Blake'). Flaxman and Fuseli remained his friends throughout these relatively undocumented years (Gilchrist).

1815

20 April. Cumberland's two sons, George and Sydney, visited Blake and found 'him & his wife drinking Tea, durtyer than ever . . .'. Blake showed them 'his large drawing in Water Colors of the last Judgement; he has been labouring at it till it is nearly as black as your Hat' (see p.104). 'His time is now intirely taken up with Etching & Engraving.'

Spring. Probable date of Blake's visit to the Royal Academy to copy the cast of the Laocoön for Rees's *Cyclopedia* (see No.315).

Summer and Autumn. Blake engraving outlines of Wedgwood-ware for their salesmen's pattern-books.

1816

Included in *A Bibliographical Dictionary of the Living Authors of Great Britain and Ireland*.

Probably got to know Charles Augustus Tulk, a friend of Flaxman and Coleridge, about this time.

1817

John Gibson, the young sculptor from Liverpool (1790–1866) called on Flaxman, Fuseli and, among others, Blake on his way to Rome.

The critic William Paulet Carey, writing about Benjamin West, praised Blake's illustrations to *The Grave*, described Blake as 'one of those highly gifted men, who owe the vantage ground of their fame, solely to their own powers,' regretted his lack of success, and reported that there had been some doubt as to whether he was still alive.

1818

20 January, or 20 June 1820. Blake at a dinner party given by Lady Caroline Lamb, also attended by Sir Thomas Lawrence (1769–1830), who later commissioned two watercolours by Blake (see Nos.172–3 and 253).

6 February. Coleridge, given a copy of *Songs of Innocence and Experience* by C. A. Tulk, wrote to H. F. Cary that Blake 'is a man of Genius–and I apprehend, a Swedenborgian [this was probably a bit of wishful thinking by Tulk, who was]–certainly, a mystic *emphatically*.' On 12 (?) February Coleridge wrote to Tulk, assessing the various *Songs* in five orders of excellence.

June (?). John Linnell (1792–1882) introduced to Blake by Cumberland's son George. On 12 September (if not earlier) Linnell introduced John Varley (1778–1842; see p.133) and John Constable (1776–1837) to Blake: on 19 September, Dr. Thornton. Linnell regularly visited art collections with Blake, and tried to interest other possible patrons in his work, as well as buying most of his output himself.

For the Sexes: The Gates of Paradise, a revised version of *For Children: The Gates of Paradise* of 1793, probably from about this time.

1819

14 October. First dated example of the Visionary Heads, drawn by Blake for Varley (see Nos.282–6).

1820

8 August. Letter in *The London Magazine* from Fuseli's pupil T. G. Wainewright (1794–1847), the painter, author and poisoner, advertising that 'my learned friend Dr. Tobias Ruddicombe, M.D. [Blake] is casting a tremendous piece of ordnance . . . "Jerusalem the Emanation of the Giant Albion".'

October (?). At a meal at the collector Charles Aders', Lawrence, James Ward, Linnell and others defend Blake's Virgil woodcuts against Thornton's plan to have them recut (see p.138).

The single plate of *On Homer's Poetry* and *On Virgil* probably etched about this time.

1821

Publication of Dr Thornton's *The Pastorals of Virgil* with Blake's woodcuts (Nos.287–303).

Blake moved to his last home on the first floor of 3 Fountain Court, off the Strand.

Sold his collection of prints to Colnaghi's at about this time.

1822

28 June. The Royal Academy Council resolved to pay Blake, 'an able Designer & Engraver laboring under great distress', twenty-five pounds.

The Ghost of Abel.

1823

1 August. Had his life-mask taken by James S. Deville (Fitzwilliam Museum), 'as representative of the imaginative faculty' (so Richmond told Mrs Gilchrist).

1824

6 March. Linnell moved to Hampstead, where Blake continued to visit him.

May. Visited the Royal Academy with Samuel Palmer (1805–1881), they having first met while Blake was working on the Job engravings. On 9 October Linnell took Palmer to see Blake while he was bedridden and working on the Dante drawings (see p.148).

12 June. Date of inscription on copy of Blake's *Descriptive Catalogue* given by Blake to Frederick Tatham (1805–1878), later his executor and biographer.

December (?). Blake's horoscope published in the periodical *Urania*, with a note on his works, particularly the Visionary Heads.

1825

George Richmond (1809–1896) first met Blake 'as a lad of sixteen' (Gilchrist) at C. H. Tatham's. Blake met other members of this circle of young artists and enthusiasts about this time: Edward Calvert (1799–1883), Francis Oliver Finch (1802–62), Palmer's cousin John Giles and Henry Walter.

Summer (?). Went with Palmer and Calvert to Palmer's grandfather's home at Shoreham, Kent.

10 December. Crabb Robinson's long account of Blake's conversation at a party at the Aders'. On 17 December Robinson visited Blake at home, finding him at work on the Dante illustrations 'of which I have nothing to say but that they evince a power of grouping & of throwing grace & interest over conceptions most monstrous & disgusting which I should not have anticipated'. On a further visit on 24 December Robinson read Blake 'Wordsworth's incomparable Ode [*Intimations of Immortality*] which he heartily enjoyed'. Either on this occasion or sometime in 1826 Robinson lent Blake a copy of Wordsworth's poems which Blake annotated.

1826

18 February. Blake gave Robinson his own manuscript copy of Wordsworth's *The Excursion*, again with his annotations. The next day Robinson sent Dorothy Wordsworth a summary of his conversations with Blake about Wordsworth, and reported that Coleridge had visited Blake, apparently taken by Tulk to see 'The Last Judgment' (James Spilling in *New Church Magazine*, 1887).

William Hazlitt, in *The Plain Speaker*, included Blake in a list of 'profound mystics' of his day together with Flaxman, de Loutherbourg, Cosway, Varley, etc.

1827

2 February. Robinson took the young German painter Jacob Götzenberger to see Blake; he 'seemed highly gratified' by the Dante illustrations.

12 August. Blake died at 3 Fountain Court. Obituaries appeared in *The Literary Gazette* for 18 August, *The Literary Chronicle* for 1 September, *The Monthly Magazine* for October, *The Gentleman's Magazine* for November, etc.

11 September. Catherine Blake went to live with Linnell at Cirencester Place (now Street) as his housekeeper.

1828

March or June. Catherine moved to 20 Lisson Grove, where she lived as Frederick Tatham's housekeeper.

J. T. Smith included a long section on Blake in the second volume of his *Nollekens and his Times*.

1830

Allan Cunningham's *Lives of the Most Eminent British Painters, Sculptors, and Architects* included a long section on Blake in the second volume, of which a revised edition appeared the same year. This was in part criticised in an anonymous article on 'The Inventions of William Blake, Painter and Poet' in the March issue of *The London University Magazine*, probably by C. A. Tulk.

1831

Catherine Blake retired to lodgings at 17 Charlton Street, Fitzroy Square, where she died on 18 October.

c.1832

Frederick Tatham's manuscript 'Life of Blake'.

1852

Henry Crabb Robinson's *Reminiscences*, a revised version of his diary, covering his meetings with Blake between 1810 and 1827.

1850s

John Linnell's manuscript autobiography, which breaks off c.1822; further worked on in 1863 and 1864.

1863

First edition of the *Life of William Blake, 'Pictor Ignotus'* by Alexander Gilchrist, who had died in 1861: D. G. Rossetti and his brother William helped Gilchrist's widow to see it through the press.

1892

A. H. Palmer's *The Life and Letters of Samuel Palmer*.

1893

A Memoir of Edward Calvert, Artist, by his third son, Samuel.

1926

The Richmond Papers, edited by A. M. W. Stirling from the papers of George Richmond and his son Sir William Blake Richmond.

Bibliography

To avoid cluttering up the entries, no acknowledgements or references to the literature are given in the catalogue; nor are full provenances or lists of exhibitions. For these the interested reader is referred to my forthcoming catalogue of Blake's paintings, drawings and separate colour prints, to be published by the Trianon Press for the William Blake Trust later this year. This does not include Blake's illuminated books as such, details of which are given *illuminated books* in Geoffrey Keynes and Edwin Wolf 2nd, *William Blake's Illuminated Books: A Census*, 1953, and G. E. Bentley, Jr, *Blake Books*, 1977. Reproductions of every plate from every book, with detailed interpretations of the illustrations, are given in David V. Erdman, *The Illuminated Blake*, 1974/5; the illuminated books are also fully reproduced in David Bindman, *Complete Graphic Works of William Blake*, 1978. Colour facsimiles of examples of every book have been published by the Trianon Press for the William Blake Trust, and certain books are also available in cheaper, sometimes paperback, reproductions.

Nor does my forthcoming catalogue include Blake's monochrome engrav- *engravings* ings, which are covered in the book by David Bindman already mentioned; specific categories are catalogued in detail in Geoffrey Keynes, *Engravings by William Blake: The Separate Plates*, 1956, and Roger R. Easson and Robert N. Essick, *William Blake: Book Illustrator: Volume 1, Plates Designed and Engraved by Blake*, 1972.

Several important Blake collections have been individually catalogued in *Blake collections* detail: W. G. Constable (ed.), *Museum of Fine Arts, Boston: Catalogue of Paintings and Drawings in Water Color*, 1949; C. H. Collins Baker and R. R. Wark, *Catalogue of William Blake's Drawings and Paintings in the Huntington Library*, 1957; Geoffrey Keynes, *Biblioteca Bibliographica*, 1964; David Bindman, *William Blake: Catalogue of the Collection in the Fitzwilliam Museum, Cambridge*, 1970; G. E. Bentley, Jr, *The Blake Collection of Mrs. Landon K. Thorne* (now in the Pierpont Morgan Library, New York), 1971; and Martin Butlin, *William Blake: A Complete Catalogue of Works in the Tate Gallery*, 1971. All these are more or less fully illustrated. Less detailed works on particular collections, also fully illustrated, are Helen D. Willard, *William Blake, Water-Color Drawings, Museum of Fine Arts, Boston*, 1957, and Martin Butlin, 'The Blake Collection of Mrs William T. Tonner' (now in the Philadelphia Museum), in *Bulletin, Philadelphia Museum of Art*, Vol.LXVII, no.307, July–September 1972, pp.5–31. The *Blake Newsletter* has published check-lists of the Blake collections of the British Museum, by Richard Morgan and G. E. Bentley, Jr (Vol.V, no.20, Spring 1972, pp.223–58), and of Lessing J. Rosenwald, by Ruth Fine Lehrer (Vol.IX, no.35, Winter 1975–6, pp.58–85); further such check-lists are to come.

The first full-scale biography of William Blake was Alexander Gilchrist, *Life* *biographies* *of William Blake*, 1863; there are later editions of 1880 and 1907, and, with notes by Ruthven Todd, 1942 and 1945. This book has never really been replaced, though a more up-to-date, 'standard' biography is supplied by Mona Wilson, *The Life of William Blake*, 1927, especially in the 1971 edition edited by Geoffrey Keynes. For the facts of Blake's life, day by day, year by year, and contemporary accounts of his life and work, see G. E. Bentley, Jr, *Blake Records*, 1969.

There are two standard texts for Blake's writings, Geoffrey Keynes, *The* *Blake's writings* *Complete Writings of William Blake*, 1957 and subsequent editions (with modernised punctuation), and David V. Erdman, *The Poetry and Prose of*

William Blake, 1965 and subsequent editions (Blake's verbatim text, but with only a selection of his letters).

monographs   The whole approach of this exhibition and its catalogue is deeply indebted to that of two art historians and their books: Anthony Blunt, *The Art of William Blake*, 1959, and David Bindman, *Blake as an Artist*, 1977. The selection and catalogue entries by David Bindman for the exhibition *William Blake 1757–1827*, organised for the Hamburger Kunsthalle in 1975, have been of great help. The need for a well-balanced, well-illustrated survey of Blake's work in the visual arts, a glaring want for many years, has also been answered by Morton D. Paley, *William Blake*, 1978. Blake and the art of his time have *Blake and his times* been treated in Ruthven Todd, *Tracks in the Snow*, 1946, Robert Rosenblum, *Transformations in Late Eighteenth Century Art*, 1967 and subsequent editions, and Geoffrey Grigson, 'Painters of the Abyss', in *The Architectural Review*, Vol.cviii, 1950, pp.215–20 (see also his *Samuel Palmer: The Visionary Years*, 1947).

philosophy and politics   Literary historians and critics have also, of course, made an invaluable contribution to Blake studies. Two general works stand out: S. Foster Damon, *William Blake, his Philosophy and Symbols*, 1924, and Northrop Frye, *Fearful Symmetry, a Study of William Blake*, 1947. More specifically devoted to Blake's political and social attitudes is David V. Erdman, *Blake: Prophet against Empire*, 1954 and, revised, 1969 and 1977.

individual works   Many of the most valuable interpretations of Blake's art are those devoted to specific works or series of works, starting with Joseph Wicksteed, *Blake's Vision of the Book of Job*, 1910 and, revised and enlarged, 1924. This has been brilliantly supplemented by Bo Lindberg, *William Blake's Illustrations to the Book of Job*, 1973. Other books in this category are Albert S. Roe, *Blake's Illustrations to the Divine Comedy*, 1953; G. E. Bentley, Jr, *William Blake: Tiriel*, 1967; Irene Tayler, *Blake's Illustrations to the Poems of Gray*, 1971; and Geoffrey Keynes, *William Blake's Laocoön, A Last Testament, with Related Works*, 1976. A detailed analysis by John E. Grant, Edward J. Rose and Michael J. Tolley of *William Blake's Designs for Edward Young's Night Thoughts*, edited by David V. Erdman and fully illustrated, is forthcoming. Other books devoted to specific works, again fully illustrated but more purely factual, less interpretative, are G. E. Bentley, Jr, *William Blake: Vala or the Four Zoas*, 1963, William Wells and Elizabeth Johnston, *William Blake's 'Heads of the Poets'*, 1969, and David V. Erdman, *The Notebook of William Blake*, 1973 and, revised, 1977. Geoffrey Keynes has edited anthologies of Blake's drawings, with brief commentaries, in 1927, 1956 and 1970, of his engravings in 1950, of his illustrations to the Bible in 1957 and of portraits of Blake and Mrs Blake in 1977.

periodicals and essays   There are two periodicals devoted to Blake, *Blake Newsletter*, 1967–77, when it became *Blake, An Illustrated Quarterly*, and *Blake Studies*, 1968 onwards. Important collections of essays are Arthur H. Rosenfeld (ed.), *William Blake: Essays for S. Foster Damon*, 1969; David V. Erdman and John E. Grant (ed.), *Blake's Visionary Forms Dramatic*, 1970; Stuart Curran and Joseph Anthony Wittreich, Jr (ed.), *Blake's Sublime Allegory: Essays on the Four Zoas, Milton and Jerusalem*, 1973; Morton D. Paley and Michael Phillips (ed.), *William Blake: Essays in Honour of Sir Geoffrey Keynes*, 1973 (this includes a check-list of all Keynes' publications on Blake up to 1973); and the special Blake issues of *Studies in Romanticism*, Spring 1977, and *Colby Library Quarterly*, June 1977. Particularly useful is Robert N. Essick (ed.), *The Visionary Hand, Essays for the Study of William Blake's Art and Aesthetics*, 1973, an anthology of previously published articles, and Geoffrey Keynes, *Blake Studies*, 1949, second enlarged edition 1971, a collection of his own articles.

The above paragraphs give only a small fraction of the vast number of publications on William Blake and are necessarily highly selective. For a complete list up to 1974, with brief descriptive notes, see G. E. Bentley, Jr, *Blake Books*, 1977. Frequent check-lists in *Blake Newsletter* and its successor chart the continuing flood.

Lenders

Compiler's Acknowledgements

First, may I add my own personal thanks for the magnificent generosity of the lenders listed above, and to the staffs of the various institutions who have supervised the loans and made them available. In particular I would like to thank the following, both for their helpfulness in discussing possible loans and for the information they have given me about their own works and those in other collections: Sir Geoffrey Agnew, Evelyn Joll and William Plomer of Thos. Agnew & Sons, Ltd; Jacob Bean of the Metropolitan Museum, New York; David Bindman; The Lord Cunliffe; Ruth Fine of the Lessing J. Rosenwald Collection; John Gere, Frances Carey and Timothy Clifford of the British Museum; George Goyder; The Hon. Patrick Lindsay; Duncan Robinson and David Scrase of the Fitzwilliam Museum; Charles Ryskamp, Director of the Pierpont Morgan Library; Brian Rushton of the Brooklyn Museum; Eleanor Sayre of the Boston Museum; and Andrew Wilton of the Yale Center for British Art (Paul Mellon Collection).

I am also grateful to all my friends in the Blake world who have discussed his work with me and fed me with information over the years; many feature as the authors of publications listed in the Bibliography (pp.162–3) but others, whose contribution may have been just as vital, do not. Sir Geoffrey Keynes, Chairman of the William Blake Trust, and Arnold Fawcus have spurred me on, as well as giving me invaluable help and advice.

Finally, I owe a special debt to my colleagues at the Tate Gallery, both for their direct assistance but perhaps even more for their tolerance and hard work in taking on my normal responsibilities during what has been a particularly active and busy period. Ruth Rattenbury, who is responsible for the organisation and the installation of the exhibition, Judy Egerton, Caroline Odgers and Ron Parkinson have given me particular help over the exhibition and catalogue.

Martin Butlin
November 1977